PAUL DOHERTY is the internationally renowned author of many histories and historical novels. He studied history at Liverpool and Oxford Universities, and gained a Doctorate at Oxford. He is now the headmaster of a London school and lives near Epping Forest.

Alexander the Great
The Death of a God

What – or Who – Really Killed the Young Conqueror
of the Known World?

PAUL DOHERTY

ROBINSON
London

Constable & Robinson Ltd
3 The Lanchesters
162 Fulham Palace Road
London W6 9ER
www.constablerobinson.com

First published in the UK by Constable,
an imprint of Constable & Robinson Ltd 2004

This paperback edition published by Robinson,
an imprint of Constable & Robinson Ltd 2005

A copy of the British Library Cataloguing in
Publication Data is available from the British Library

ISBN 1-84529-156-5 (pbk)
ISBN 1-84119-877-3 (hbk)

Printed and bound in the EU

1 3 5 7 9 10 8 6 4 2

To Mei-Ching Phua and her brother Bob of
Malaysia and East Molesley
with warmest regards and kind wishes!

Contents

Foreword

It seems that I have been studying Alexander the Great all my life. It began at the Palladium in Middlesbrough when, owl-eyed, I watched Richard Burton in the role of the Great Conqueror. Sitting in a dark cinema, and being taken back to Hollywood's version of history I was fascinated, as we all are. It has been a long journey from such an idealized view. My study of Classical Greek and the Greek koine only whetted my appetite for more knowledge about Alexander, as did the writings of Plutarch, Arrian and the rest.

Alexander the Great has meant different things to different people at different times. In the nineteenth century he was the European Ideal and the stories of his generosity were always emphasized. I was weaned on these until I came across the history of Alexander's life by Quintus Curtius and my doubts began. I remembered a certain passage in his history (Ch. 8, Bk 7), when twenty Scythian ambassadors met Alexander. True, their speeches may be embellished but I distinctly remember one section when the leading envoy accuses Alexander of making war on the human race and then goes on to argue how they had not harmed Alexander, so why should he harm them? Why should he come to punish plunderers in their country when he had plundered every nation on earth?

I began to look at Alexander's conquest and his character from a different perspective. No one can doubt Alexander's incredible courage, his genius for battle, his restless energy and the charismatic nature of his leadership. However, through the sources, I decided to concentrate on Alexander's death and his final days – after all, he did die young, suddenly and most mysteriously. Was his death the outcome of choosing glory and a short life? Or did that glory, and the darkness behind it, deliberately shorten his brilliant career? After sifting the evidence regarding Alexander's death, I here propose a new solution based on that evidence.

I would like to thank all who helped me, particularly those outstanding colleagues at the London Library. I am also very grateful to Mrs Angela Francescotti for her hours of typing to finish this manuscript.

Dr Paul Doherty
April 2004

Chronology

Philip marries Attalus' niece Cleopatra

Olympias and ALEXANDER go into exile

337   *Spring*. Hellenic League convened at Corinth
ALEXANDER recalled to Pella
Autumn. League at Corinth ratifies Greek campaign against Persia

336   *Spring*. Parmenio and Attalus sent to Asia Minor for preliminary military operations
June. Darius III Codomanus accedes to the Persian throne
Cleopatra bears Philip a son, Caranus
Alexander of Epirus marries Olympias' daughter Cleopatra
Philip murdered
ALEXANDER succeeds to throne of Macedonia
Late summer. ALEXANDER calls a meeting of the League of Corinth; confirmed as Captain General

335   *Early spring*. ALEXANDER goes north to deal with Thrace and Illyria
Revolt of Thebes, destruction of that city

334   *March–April*. ALEXANDER and his army cross into Asia Minor
May. Battle of the Granicus
General reorganization of Greek cities in Asia Minor
Miletus besieged and captured
Autumn. Reduction of Halicarnassus

333   ALEXANDER's column moves north to Celaenae in Phrygia and Gordium
Early spring. Memnon of Rhodes dies
Mustering of Persian forces in Babylon
Episode of the Gordian Knot
Darius moves westward from Babylon
September. ALEXANDER reaches Tarsus; becomes ill
Darius crosses Euphrates
September–October. Battle of Issus
ALEXANDER advances southward through Phoenicia

332   *January*. Byblos and Sidon submit
       29 July. Fall of Tyre
       September–October.Gaza captured
       ALEXANDER crowned as Pharaoh at Memphis

331   *Early spring*. Alexander visits Oracle of Ammon at Siwah
       April. Alexandria founded
       ALEXANDER returns to Tyre
       Darius moves his main army from Babylon
       18 September–October. Battle of Gaugamela
       Macedonians advance on Babylon which falls in *mid-October*
       Revolt of Aegis who is defeated at Megalopolis by Antipater
       Early December. ALEXANDER occupies Susa unopposed

330   *January*. ALEXANDER reaches and sacks Persepolis
       May. burning of temples etc. in Persepolis
       Early June. ALEXANDER sets out for Ecbatana
       Darius retreats towards Bactria
       Parmenio left behind at Ecbatana with Harpalus as treasurer
       Pursuit of Darius renewed
       Darius found murdered near Hecatompylus
       Bessus establishes himself as 'King of Kings' in Bactria
       Late August. march to Lake Seistan
       The 'conspiracy of Philotas'

329   *March–April*. ALEXANDER crosses the Hindu Kush
       April–May. ALEXANDER advances into Bactria; Bessus retreats across the
       Oxus
       June. ALEXANDER reaches and crosses the Oxus
       Bessus surrenders
       ALEXANDER advances to Samarkand
       Revolt of Spitamenes

329/8 ALEXANDER takes up winter quarters at Zariaspa
       Bessus executed

328   Campaign against Spitamenes
Autumn. Black Cleitus murdered

328/7   Spitamenes defeated and killed

327   *Spring:* Soghdian Rock captured
ALEXANDER marries Roxane
30,000 Persian 'Successors' recruited
The 'Pages' Conspiracy' and Callisthenes' death
Early summer. ALEXANDER re-crosses Hindu Kush; begins invasion of India

327/6   ALEXANDER reaches Nysa; the 'Dionysius episode'

326   Advance to Taxila
Battle of Hydaspes (Jhelum) against Rajah Porus
Death of Bucephalus
July. mutiny at the Hyphasis (Beas) River
Return to the Jhelum
Early November. ALEXANDER's fleet and army move downriver

326/5   Campaign against the Brahmin cities; ALEXANDER seriously wounded

325   *September.* ALEXANDER's march through the Gedrosian (Makran) Desert
Harpalus defects from Asia Minor to Greece
The Great Purge begins

324   *January.* Nearchus and the fleet sent on to Susa
The episode of Cyrus' tomb
ALEXANDER returns to Persepolis
Spring. arrival of 30,000 trained Persian 'Successors'
The Susa mass-marriages
March. The Exiles' Decree and the Deification Decree
Craterus appointed to succeed Antipater as regent, and escort veterans home
ALEXANDER moves from Susa to Ecbatana

Death of Hephaestion

323   Harpalus assassinated in Crete

ALEXANDER campaigns against Cosseans; returns to Babylon

ALEXANDER explores the Euphrates canals; boat-trip through the marshes

Antipater's son, Cassander, arrives to negotiate with ALEXANDER

29/30 May. ALEXANDER falls ill after a party; dies *10/11 June*

323–322 Uneasy peace between the Successors

Ptolemy takes over Egypt

322–321 Breakdown of peace between ALEXANDER's commanders: Wars of Succession begin

Principal Characters

CLEITUS	'The Black' or 'Black Cleitus', Alexander's personal bodyguard and senior commander. Cleitus had also served under Philip
ANTIGONUS	The 'One-eyed'. Senior commander under both Philip and Alexander
CRATERUS	Alexander's lieutenant and leading commander
COENUS	Leading commander
POLYPERCHON	Leading commander

Other Members of the Macedonian Court

PAUSANIAS	Philip's assassin
MEDIUS OF LARISSA	Macedonian naval officer
CHARES OF MYTILENE	Royal Chamberlain
ARISTOTLE	Alexander's tutor
CALLISTHENES	Alexander's official historian
ARISTANDER OF TELEMESUS	Seer, necromancer
LEONIDAS	Alexander's tutor
LYSIMACHUS	Alexander's tutor
CALANUS	Indian holy man
ANAXARCHUS	Resident sophist at Alexander's court
CLEOMENES	Alexander's governor of Egypt
APOLLODORUS	Alexander's co-governor of Babylon
PEITHAGORAS	Seer
MELEAGER	Macedonian officer
PROTEAS	Nephew of Cleitus: a notorious toper
THAÏS	Athenian courtesan at Alexander's court
HERMOLAUS	Royal page

The House of Parmenio

PARMENIO	Leading general under Philip and Alexander
PHILOTAS NICANOR HECTOR	Sons of Parmenio and officers in Alexander's army

The House of Antipater

ANTIPATER	Veteran general under Philip: left as Regent of Macedon by Alexander
CASSANDER	Son of Antipater, a leading protagonist in the Wars of Succession.
IOLAUS	Son of Antipater, Alexander's cupbearer
NICANOR	Son of Antipater

Persians

XERXES
CYRUS ⎫ Persian rulers of the fifth century BC
DARIUS ⎭

ARTAXERXES OCHUS III	Contemporary of Philip
DARIUS CODOMANUS III	Alexander's rival
MEMNON OF RHODES	Greek mercenary general in the pay of Darius III
MAZAEUS	Persian satrap of Babylon
SISYGAMBIS	Persian queen mother
BATIS THE EUNUCH	Commander of Gaza
ROXANE	Persian princess, wife of Alexander
BARSINE	Alexander's alleged mistress
BAGOAS	Eunuch, friend of Darius III and later of Alexander

BESSUS ⎫ Persian satraps who resisted Alexander
SPITAMENES ⎭

Athenians

| DEMOSTHENES | Orator, fervent opponent of Macedon |
| ISOCRATES | Orator, ardent supporter of a Greek campaign against Persia |

Other Rulers

ADA OF CARIA	Queen of Halicarnassus and the surrounding territories
PIXADORUS	Ruler of Halicarnassus in Caria, Queen Ada's rival
HERMEIAS	Petty Greek despot
ALEXANDER OF EPIRUS	Olympias' half-brother, ruler of a small but strategically placed kingdom on Macedon's border; married Alexander's sister, Cleopatra

Prologue

Babylon May 323 BC

'θεου γαρ ἀισα θεος
ἐκρανε συμφοραν'

'A God caused this fate,
A God created this disaster'
Euripides, *Andromache*
(line 1203)

Had the thirty-three-year-old Alexander of Macedon believed in
ghosts, they would have surrounded him in the bathhouse of
Nebuchadnezzar's palace, set amidst the lush fields, gardens and
orchards, a veritable paradise, despite the boiling heat of the Babylon
summer. According to Plutarch, the signs of an impending tragedy,
the portent of some gathering unknown terror, of unreasoning dread,
had filled Alexander's mind since he had moved into Babylon earlier
that summer. The soothsayers and fortune-tellers who thronged his
court may have told him the story about how a Babylonian king,

Belshazzar, had been forced to confront his own nightmares, face his own death and ponder the dissolution of his own empire in that very same city. Whilst Belshazzar had been feasting, the Finger of God had appeared to inscribe in burning marks on the walls of his palace the ominous warning: *Mene, mene, tekel u-phärsin*, which meant God had measured Belshazzar's sovereignty, weighed it in the balance, and found it wanting, and so his kingdom was to be divided.[1]*

Alexander's fever, which had appeared the night before, whilst he had feasted and revelled, had not abated. He had offered oblation to the gods and shared the rich produce from that sacrifice with others of his council whilst honouring his admiral Nearchus the Cretan. Nearchus had recently survived the perils of an exploratory voyage along the northern rim of the Indian Ocean and was set to lead Alexander's fleet along the shoreline of the Arabian Peninsula. Alexander had left this feast only to be persuaded by an old drinking friend, Medius of Larissa, a Thessalian with an eye for a good time and a tongue used to flattery, to join a private drinking party with some of the king's old cronies. Alexander had then fallen ill, so common report later put it, but this had not stopped him attending a second party with Medius. However, the fever became so raging, Alexander decided to adjourn to the imperial bathhouse and lie by its great pool in the hope that it would cool him.[2] It is not known whether Alexander had his favourite book brought down, the *Iliad*, which, ever since he was a boy, he had kept beneath his pillow next to a dagger.[3] Alexander knew Homer's heroic descriptions almost by heart. The book was such a treasured possession that he kept it in a beautiful casket looted from the treasure of Darius Codomanus, the Persian King of Kings, whom Alexander had overthrown at the Battle of Gaugamela some eight years earlier (331 BC).[4]

Alexander saw himself as a Homeric warrior, a second Achilles – from whom he could claim descent through his witch-queen mother, Olympias of Epirus, a fiery Molossian. She could trace her ancestry through Neoptolemus, son of Achilles, and his wife Andromache, the widow of Hector, taken as Neoptolemus' prize after the fall of Troy.[5] Alexander, like all his contemporaries, regarded such genealogy as a

*Sources and references begin on p. 203.

self-evident truth. The *Iliad* was Alexander's inspiration, the struggle Homer recounted was Alexander's vision of war, and Achilles, described by Homer as 'that most terrifying of men', was his role model. Achilles had chosen a brief, glorious life over a long, boring one. (Only in the underworld, after his death at the hands of Paris, and faced with an eternity of boredom does Achilles question the decision he had made. Achilles realizes what it is like to be a 'king of all the dead' not in the *Iliad* but in its sequel, the *Odyssey* when Ulysses visits the underworld.)[6]

Shaking with fever, beside the pool, Alexander of Macedon must have reflected upon his own 'immortal longings' and recalled that warning from the *Iliad*: 'The day of your death draws close' and, perhaps, 'he must die in his own palace of a painful illness.'[7] Alexander, the new Achilles of the West, was, in fact, seriously ill, following the same feverish pattern of sickness as his friend Hephaestion, who had played Patroclus to Alexander's Achilles. Hephaestion had died a year earlier (324 BC) at Ecbatana in northern Persia despite all of Alexander's prayers and sacrifices (see Part Seven, pp. 147–86). Did Hephaestion, like Patroclus in the *Iliad*, come back to haunt the king? To remind him of those early days together in the Grove of Nymphs at Mieza, just to the south of Pella, the new capital of Macedon? That had been the time of preparation, when perhaps Alexander first felt those immortal longings, that *pothos* (πoθoς), that deep, unquenching desire to achieve one's end – to be like his hero Achilles – *aniketos* (ἀνικετος) – that is, invincible?

Part One

The God

'σμικρας ἀπ᾽ αρχης νεικος ἀνθρωποις μεγα γλωσσ ἐκποριςει
τουτο δ᾽οι σοφοι βροτων ἐξευλαβουνται μη φιλοις τευχειν'

'From petty reasons, the tongue provokes great quarrels for men.
Men who are prudent, take care not to argue with their kin.'
Euripides, *Andromache* (lines 642–4)

From the very start, the signs of the coming of a God had been
clear to see, at least to some. Philip of Macedon, the conqueror of
those sprawling lands wedged between Greece in the south and the
Balkans to the north, had taken a new wife. Philip had fought off
rivals to the throne of Macedon, organized his army and, looking
south, planned to extend his hegemony over all Greece which, by
357 BC, was a collection of powerful city-states. Philip's main
challenge was from Athens and Thebes, 'the twin eyes of Hellas'. A
century of war had not diminished the intense rivalry between these
two city-states, yet neither of them was strong enough to win
supremacy either over its rival or the other states such as Sparta.[1]
The Greeks dreamed glorious dreams, articulated by the orator
Isocrates of Athens, of a unity, a brotherhood of states which would

launch a great campaign across the Hellespont. The purpose of such a campaign was to liberate the Greek colonies, the cities of Asia Minor, such as Ephesus and Miletus, from Persian domination as well as to punish the self-proclaimed King of Kings, ruler of the Persian Empire which, under despotic princes such as Xerxes, had dared to invade Greece, despoil its cities and tried to impose tyrannical rule on freedom-loving Greeks.[2] Like most dreams, such aspirations were fanciful. The Greek city-states were riven by political infighting between democrats and oligarchs. If compromise and harmony were maintained within the cities, then the intense rivalries between the different states created an impasse which could not be broken. Sparta had defeated Athens and torn down the long walls of the Piraeus, Athens' harbour, to the sound of pipes. Then Sparta in turn had declined and Athens had recovered from the dark days of 404 BC. The Athenians had rebuilt their walls, and refurbished their fleet, harbours and arsenals whilst Spartan supremacy had been shattered by the Sacred Band, the crack corps of the Theban army, at Leuctra in 371 BC.[3]

So the city-states continued to dream their dreams, whilst to the north barbaric Macedon, with its rich natural resources of woods, meadows, cattle herds, fish-filled rivers, silver and gold mines, flexed its muscles. The Macedonian royal house had long kept itself occupied with its own savage tribal wars. These ended abruptly with the emergence of Philip in 360 BC, a warrior king *par excellence* in a warrior society. Philip's title of king was never actually used, his status was rather 'first amongst equals', a generalissimo, a successful war commander, who secured the allegiance of other Macedonian warlords. A thickset, barrel-chested, heavy-bearded man with an eye for the ladies and a taste for undiluted wine, Philip had early established himself as an ambitious war leader. His jovial manner, ready wit and wicked sense of humour masked a cruel, ruthless and wily strategic brain. Outwardly the bluff Macedonian aristocrat in his broad-brimmed hat and purple cloak, in truth, he was a born intriguer. He had developed a fighting force, cavalry and foot, which was second to none, drilled and trained like professional mercenaries. Philip had studied the use of siege artillery, strengthened his fleet, and sought out harbours. But Macedon's real military strength rested on the well-organized, superbly drilled phalanx of spearmen with their 15-foot-long *sarissas* or pikes, fighting en masse and delivering the hammer blow of battle alongside auxiliaries, light-armed javelin men, archers and slingers. These in turn were supported by fast-moving, well-organized cavalry units eager to exploit any break in the enemy wall.[4]

Philip, for all his warmongering, understood the importance of diplomacy over force, to get his own way. He often repeated the maxim 'With children you cheat with knuckle bones, but, with adults, oaths.'[5] He was always eager to sign a treaty to reach a compromise, agree to a pact, or form an alliance – which could later be kept or broken according to circumstances. Philip would prefer to spend money on bribes than spill the blood of his precious troops. The historian Diodorus Siculus records how Philip used to boast that 'it was far more through the use of gold than of weapons that he enlarged his kingdom'.[6] If peace treaties were a means to achieve his aims, marriage alliances confirmed them. It became a common joke in Greece that 'Philip of Macedon always married a new wife with each campaign he undertook'.[7]

In 357 BC, Philip took, as his third wife, Myrtale, a princess of the Molossian royal house which ruled Epirus, a small but strategic state to the south-west of Macedon with ports and harbours giving access to the Ionian Sea.

Myrtale, not yet eighteen, had been initiated into the Maenadic rites which originated in the worship of Dionysius, the God of Wine.[8] Myrtale was ambitious and hot-tempered, with a nasty attitude to any opposition. She later changed her name to Olympias after Macedon's outstanding triumphs at the Olympic games which took place between the date of her marriage to Philip and the birth of her beloved son Alexander in 356 BC.[9] Olympias moved into a society where intrigue and violence were regarded as an occupational hazard, into a culture despised by its sophisticated southern neighbours who scoffed at the rustic culture of Macedon, ridiculed its coarse language and laughed at a kingdom whose army purified itself by marching between the corpse of a dog, disembowelled and cut in half by a priest.[10]

On the other hand, Olympias became queen of a kingdom whose ruler was proving to be a brilliant general and military genius, a ruthless politician who, if he could not bribe or lie his way to success, would deploy his well-organized army to achieve his will.

In this tumultuous and upwardly mobile society Olympias emerges as an individual obsessed with her own status and that of her son. She also shared one common trait with her new husband – a devotion to Dionysius, the God of Wine. Yet Philip, despite his apparent boorishness, was something of a cultural snob. He had moved the capital of his kingdom from Aegae to the more accessible Pella built amidst the foothills of the mountains of Macedon.[11] He had created and developed a new city, a magnet for artists as well as for drinkers. Philip was a true Macedonian, a hard-drinking man. Ephippus of Olynthus, a gossip, describes the Macedonians as a people 'who never understood how to drink in moderation'. He pointed out how they drank so much, so fast, that they were often drunk before the first course was even served.[12] According to the snobbish Athenians, who regarded the Macdeonians as poor second cousins, temperance and moderation were regarded as characteristics of the civilized, gulpers were vulgar, and the lavish consumption of undiluted wine was a characteristic of the barbarian.[13] The Macedonians were firmly bracketed amongst the latter, Philip their king being regarded as the best example. Demosthenes, the great freedom-loving orator of Athens (or so he described himself), called Philip 'a sponge', whilst Theopompos of Chios described Philip as a 'lover of drink who slept with a golden wine goblet beneath his pillow'.[14] Drink defined Philip's court, and like attracts like: Philip and his officers worshipped at the altar of Dionysius, the God of Wine. The court at Pella, Theopompos sniffily wrote, 'was the haunt for all the most debauched and brazen-faced characters in Greece and abroad to assemble . . . nearly every man in the Greek or barbarian world, of a lecherous, loathsome, or ruffianly character flocked to Macedon.'[15] Nevertheless, they were also, as Demosthenes conceded, 'admirable soldiers, well trained in the science of war'.[16] Philip developed the reputation of a 'bon viveur', a jovial rogue, around whom countless stories teemed.

On one occasion, half-drunk, Philip presided at the trial of two robbers. He sentenced the first to flee from Macedon and the second to chase him.[17] On another occasion, after taking a certain city, Philip had the prisoners processed by him whilst he sprawled on a captured throne drinking copiously. One of the prisoners asked to speak to him in confidence. Philip beckoned the man forward who, as soon as he was close enough, whispered to Philip that he was exposing himself. The inebriated victor hastily readjusted his tunic and cloak, thanked the man and promptly released him.[18]

The hard-drinking culture of Macedon's court was a lasting influence on Alexander. Drink proved to be a catalyst for conflict, violence and tragedy in the Great Conqueror's life. One of Philip's infamous *comoi* (drinking parties) provoked the most serious confrontation between Philip and his heir whilst Alexander's own drunkenness played a role in some of the major crises in his reign and, ultimately, his end. Nevertheless, though the love of wine might turn Philip's court into a Bacchanalian revel and portray Philip as a jovial old rogue, it also served as a mask. Philip could be ruthless, especially in the dynastic infighting with would-be claimants for his crown. In Macedon blood might be thicker than water but, when it came to political survival, not so precious. In such struggles no mercy was asked and none was shown. Philip proved this in 348 BC when he took the city of Olynthus. He captured his two half-brothers, potential rivals, and promptly executed them.[19] Philip's court might be a shrine to Dionysius, where uncut wine flowed like water, yet there was a more complex purpose to it. Philip gathered a coterie of like-minded men, Macedonian and mercenary, around him, not only as Theopompos remarked 'for their love of drinking and vulgarity' but also because, with them, he could 'have discussion on the most vital matters'.[20] These 'vital matters' were Philip's burning ambition to unite all Greece under him, either by force of arms or by subtle diplomacy. He wanted to make himself Captain General of Greece and launch a war against the power of Persia. The God of Wine, in his black goatskin garb, certainly sat at Philip's table but so did the fiery-eyed Eynalius, the Macedonian God of War, whose name Philip and Alexander's troops invoked in their resounding war cry as they shattered a host of enemies from the Haemus (Blood River) near

Chaeronea in Greece to the muddy waters of the Jhelum in modern Pakistan.

Philip was no idle dreamer, nor was he a political visionary. The great pamphleteer of Pan-Hellenism, Isocrates of Athens, preached such a war in his 'Panegyricus', urging all Greece, either under Athens or Sparta, to unite and unleash all-out war across the Hellespont. The 'Panegyricus' was first published in 380 BC. By 346 BC, Isocrates, despairing of those he first approached, now turned to Philip of Macedon, urging him in his well-publicized letter, 'An Address to Philip', to assume the mantle of Pan-Hellenism.[21] Philip was flattered. At last he was being acknowledged, accepted by the great city of Athens as more than a Macedonian pirate and free-booter. Isocrates' fellow citizen, Demosthenes, knew Philip better, and reckoned that there would be a heavy price to pay. Demosthenes constantly warned about 'the Barbarian in the north', adding that Philip was not interested in freedom but domination.[22] At first, however, Philip could do very little. He faced trouble in Greece, whilst Persia was ruled by Artaxerxes III Ochus, a man of iron and blood who ruthlessly imposed his own regime, whatever the cost, even if it meant the wholesale execution of every relative irrespective of age and sex, so that no rival could emerge to challenge him.[23]

Such a heady atmosphere permeated Macedonian politics when Philip met the redoubtable Olympias, also known as Myrtale. He had been struck by her five years earlier, when they met during initiation into a mystery cult on the island of Samothrace.[24] Philip must have been there for wine and pleasure; Olympias took the matter much more seriously. On her marriage to Philip, she imported the sacred snake cult, linked to the rites of Dionysius, into Macedon.[25] She also brought burning ambition. It would be untrue to conclude that her and Philip's later troubles were the result of a passionate marriage which soured when Philip turned to other women. Olympias was made of sterner stuff. Philip's different marriage alliances were part of the normal social fabric and his womanizing was an integral part of his character. To see Olympias as the scorned woman, the stricken victim of the green-eyed goddess, would be mistaken. Plutarch relates a peculiar story about one of Philip's mistresses, the Thessalian,

Nicesipolis who joined his entourage in 354 BC, three years after his marriage to Olympias. Rumours reached Olympias about how this new mistress was bewitching Philip with her potions and spells. Olympias, intrigued, sent for Nicesipolis and found her quite delightful. She laughingly rejected the gossip about Nicesipolis being a witch, and told her, 'You are your own best magic, my dear.' They became firm friends and, after Nicesipolis' death, Olympias raised her friend's daughter, Thessalonice, as her own.[26]

In July 356 BC, Olympias gave birth to Alexander, followed a year later by Cleopatra. According to the evidence, these were her only children. Olympias doted on her son. Only when Alexander's status was threatened, his power compromised or his person belittled did Olympias become the Gorgon Medusa of legend. Of course, such passion must have been stifling. The historian Tarn claimed that Alexander never cared for any woman 'except his terrible mother'.[27] The adjective should be terrifying. The Athenian orator Hyperides claimed that Olympias was too much, even from a distance, as Athens found to its cost when the city decided to renovate the temple of Dodona in Olympias' native Epirus. The possessive trait which so dominated Olympias thrills through every word of the warning she sent to Athens: 'The land of Molossus is mine. It is not for you Athenians to lay a finger upon a stone of that temple.'[28] When Alexander left Macedon in 334 BC, never to return, Olympias was left as queen mother with old General Antipater as regent – a shrewd move. Antipater couldn't stand Olympias, who always responded in kind: their mutual antipathy was a fine balancing act to maintain the political equilibrium in Macedon. Olympias and Antipater would unite to ruthlessly crush any opposition and, that achieved, return to watching each other like two fighting dogs. Both pestered Alexander with letters yet there was never really a contest for his affection. Alexander might assert that his mother charged a terrifyingly high rent for the nine months he had spent in her womb but he still adored her. He told one friend how, 'One tear shed by his mother wiped out ten thousand of Antipater's letters.'[29] Alexander's immediate act after his first great victory over the Persians at the Granicus (334 BC) was to send the precious goods looted from the Persians as a gift to his beloved mother.[30] According to Quintus Curtius, Alexander confided to close friends how the greatest reward for his efforts and labours would be if his mother could be granted immortality on her departure from life.[31] The remark not only testifies to Alexander's love for Olympias but the perception of himself as the new Achilles whose mother was immortal. Alexander had no better protector, supporter or adherent than this formidable woman who, decades later, died as she pitted herself against Alexander's inveterate enemies.[32] Olympias was a born street fighter in every sense of the word. Her protection and exaltation of her son began even before his conception. She sowed an awesome seed which had its own bloody legacy. She firmly believed that Alexander's conception was planned and brought about by the direct intervention of the Gods. Little wonder that Alexander was so singular. He was constantly presented with a reality so different from other men: he had been divinely conceived; therefore he had a divine mission. Nor is it surprising that such a son should, in all things, strive to emulate and surpass his charismatic father Philip. He, in turn, cannot be blamed for listening to the gossip that his overbearing foreign queen had cuckolded him, and that her arrogant son was simply a cuckoo in the family nest.

According to Plutarch, Olympias shrouded Alexander's conception and birth in divine mystery. On the night before the consummation of her marriage she dreamed that a thunderbolt pierced her womb, a great fire was kindled and the flames shot out further than she could see.[33] Some time later, according to the same source, Philip had a dream that he was sealing up his new wife's womb with wax which bore the impression of a lion. A number of Philip's advisers were not impressed and sowed their own seeds of doubt in his mind. They claimed that all the dream proved was that Philip was suspicious of Olympias and should keep a watchful eye on her conduct. The seer Aristander of Telemesus, who later made his fortune as Alexander's official fortune-teller and was greatly patronized by Olympias, ridiculed such doubts. According to Aristander, Philip's dream showed that the king couldn't seal up something that was not empty: Olympias was pregnant with a male child who would demonstrate all the qualities of a lion.[34] When the royal physicians confirmed the pregnancy, Philip was suitably impressed but, according to Plutarch, the old cynic was still suspicious. He took to spying on his wife and was repelled to see a serpent sharing his wife's bed.[35] Understandably, Olympias' hobby of handling trained snakes made Philip not so eager to share her embraces. Plutarch adds that, because of this sacrilegious peeping, Philip was chastened by Ammon and lost the sight of the eye he had pressed against the keyhole, when it was actually pierced during the siege of Methone.[36] Some of these stories are undoubtedly legend but many are based on fact; they all shroud Olympias, her relations with Philip and the conception of Alexander in a mixture of spiritual aura and sexual intrigue.

Olympias may have glorified her son's origins; she also planted the seeds of suspicion in Philip's mind. He must have entertained doubts about her fidelity and wondered about the actual paternity of a son who later challenged him. Undoubtedly, the way in which Olympias spread such stories did not help matters. According to Plutarch, Olympias, at least publicly, always rejected such stories as pious fiction and groaned at how 'Alexander would never stop mixing her up with the Goddess Juno.'[37] Privately, of course, Olympias would have done her best to encourage the tales and so her campaign continued. According to one story related by Plutarch, Alexander's birth in the summer of 356 BC spread terror abroad. On the same night he was born, the temple of Artemis in Persian-held Ephesus was burnt to the ground. The real cause was a madman but the flatterer Hegesias claimed it was because the Goddess was absent attending Alexander's birth. The Magi, priests of the Persian God Ahura-Mazda, are recorded as having understood what had happened, and running about beating their faces and crying 'that day had brought forth the Great Scourge and destroyer of Asia'.[38]

Be that as it may, the early years of the 'Great Scourge' are fairly light in detail. His nurse Lanice was the sister of 'Black Cleitus', the king's bodyguard. His first tutor, Leonidas, a kinsman of Olympias, was an old soldier with tough ways. According to an account given by Alexander to Queen Ada of Caria, Leonidas used to keep his meals meagre, drill him hard and search his possessions for any luxuries or sweetmeats hidden by his mother.[39] Leonidas' strict regime was offset by Alexander's personal tutor, Lysimachus, who flattered the boy and indulged his fantasies about Achilles. Lysimachus called himself Phoenix (the name of Achilles' tutor); Philip became Peleus, Achilles' father, whilst Alexander was, of course, Achilles reincarnate.[40]

Over all these domestic arrangements brooded the menace of Olympias, ever watchful of her son. According to Plutarch, in 358 BC, the year before Philip married Olympias, he had married another princess, Philinna of Larissa, a Thessalian who gave birth to a son, Arridhaeus. According to Plutarch, 'as a boy Arridhaeus had shown a pleasant character and displayed promise', until Olympias fed the boy a drug which, according to our source, 'impaired the functions of his body and did irreparable damage to his brain'.[41] Olympias certainly viewed Arridhaeus as a threat. Some seventeen years later, six years after her own beloved son's death, she finally settled with this hapless victim: he was cruelly executed at her behest in 317 BC.[42]

To lessen Olympias' baleful influence as well as provide his son with an excellent education, Philip decided to hire the best educator in all Greece. The sophists of Athens regarded Philip as a boor and his court uncivilized but Philip continued the policy of his predecessors in trying to attract scholars and artists to his court, a move openly mocked by the intellectuals of the great city. 'Shall we, being Greeks,' Thrasymachus the orator shrilled, 'become slaves to a barbarian?'[43] Demosthenes was more dismissive, 'He, Philip, is not a Greek nor related to the Greeks.'[44]

Philip set his face like flint against such insults and managed to persuade one of the greatest philosophers, Aristotle, himself a Macedonian, and the son of a court physician, to take over Alexander's education. Aristotle was a brilliant scholar, a dandy and, at the time, a very disappointed man, because he had been overlooked for promotion in the famous schools of Athens. More important to Philip than even his classical education, Aristotle was definitively anti-Persian, holding views very similar to those of Isocrates regarding the superiority of Greek culture.[45] Philip set up an academy in the precincts of the Grove of Nymphs at Mieza, a famous beauty spot and tourist attraction as late as Plutarch's day[46] (137 AD). Other young men were included. Several of Alexander's life-long companions –

Hephaestion, Cassander, Ptolemy, and others – became fellow scholars.[47] For three years, from 343 BC to 340 BC, Alexander lived and studied in those idyllic surroundings amongst the foothills of the Bermium Mountains, the lush wine-growing area of modern Noussa. The spot was also called the Gardens of Midas because, according to legend, it was here that Midas captured Silenus, by a mixture of wine and sacred water, so as to learn the secret of life. Silenus had to be ransomed by Dionysius who gave Midas the ambiguous gift of turning everything he touched to gold.[48]

In 340/339 BC, Alexander's academic life was brought to an abrupt conclusion. At the age of sixteen, his father being absent, he was made regent and had to launch a defensive campaign against the tribes of Thrace who had risen in rebellion. By the time that campaign finished in 339 BC Alexander was seventeen, educated, with some experience in government and bloodied in war.[49] The child is the father of the man. Alexander, both physically and spiritually, emerges on to the political scene as a person in his own right with a character and disposition based not on idealist interpretation or romantic theory but empirical evidence which can be analysed and assessed. As Strabo the Geographer wrote, 'These things, whatever truth may be in them, have at least been scrutinized and believed amongst men.'[50]

Alexander was striking in appearance. He was below average height, we know, because after his great victory over the Persians, he occupied Darius' palace and sat on the Persian king's throne and his feet dangled even above the footstool – an embarrassment quickly avoided when a page hastily removed the footstool and replaced it with a table. Alexander was muscular and compact. His hair, parted down the middle and ringleted around the forehead and the nape of his neck to resemble a lion's mane, was reddish blond. He was fair-skinned with a high complexion and his eyes were odd, one being greyish-blue, the other brown.[51] According to the *Alexander Romance*, his teeth were sharply pointed 'like little pegs',[52] his nose rose straight to the forehead above full lips and a rounded chin. His forehead bulged slightly over his eyes, his voice was high-pitched but became harsh when excited; his walk was fast and nervous. The court sculptor, Lysippus, provides the best, though stylized representation. Alexander had a characteristic leftwards inclination of the neck with an upward cast to the eyes which gave him a rather dreamy, girlish look. This gesture was often imitated by the young men of the court and it is difficult to decide whether this characteristic pose was due to some physical defect in his neck and shoulders or simple affectation.[53]

After three years' study under Aristotle, Alexander was certainly well educated and his three years in the Groves at Mieza must have had a profound effect on him. Aristotle encouraged his love of Homer and actually autographed the prince's copy of the *Iliad*.[54] Later, when Alexander was campaigning in Persia, despite the different crises facing him, Alexander asked his treasurer Harpalus to send him something to read. Harpalus put together a package to please his master which included the writings of Aeschylus, Sophocles and, above all, Euripides.[55] On a number of important occasions, such as the events leading to his father's murder or Alexander's own mad drunken slaying of Black Cleitus, Alexander quoted lines from that great playwright.[56] The rather mysterious source known as Nicobule claims that Alexander could recite the entire corpus of Euripides' work, in which case Alexander would have known the line: 'You are insane, you who seek glory and conflict amongst the weapons of war. You think, in your ignorance, you will find a cure for human misery there.'[57] Alexander must have recited those lines, yet they were ones that he studiously ignored for most of his life.

There were other influences, particularly in politics, where Aristotle must have had his greatest influence helping Alexander to theorize and articulate his own autocratic tendencies. During Aristotle's stay in the Groves at Mieza, Aristotle's close friend and father-in-law, the petty despot Hermeias, was captured by Persian agents and taken back to Artaxerxes to be cruelly tortured about what he knew regarding the mind of Macedon. Hermeias refused to break and died bravely. Aristotle composed the 'Hymn to Virtue' in Hermeias' honour and unleashed all his vituperation against Persia on the welcoming and attentive mind of Alexander.[58] Aristotle argued that all barbarians were slaves by nature so it was right and fitting for Greeks to rule over barbarians. Alexander should be a leader to the Greeks, Aristotle advised, and a despot to the barbarian Persians. He should treat the former as friends and relatives but deal with the barbarians as beasts or even plants.[59] Aristotle was preaching nothing new. Similar sentiments can be found in the speeches of Demosthenes or the racist taunts of Isocrates' 'Address to Philip'. Aristotle, as exemplified in his *Politics* (Book Three), also ingeniously circumvented the usual Greek hatred of autocracy, one-man rule, arguing that, if the outstanding personal virtue (ἀρετη) of the leader is superior to that of all other citizens put together, then kingship is justifiable.[60] With Alexander, Aristotle was preaching to the converted. Three great notions emerged to dominate his royal student. First the idea of *aniketos*, of being invincible, a title the Delphic Oracle would later confer on Alexander. Secondly, *pothos*, a deep unquenchable desire to achieve his ends, however difficult. Finally, Alexander's own unshakeable perception of the supremacy and excellence of his own destiny.

In the turbulent, machismo politics of the Macedonian court such a competitive attitude had to find a focus and, undoubtedly helped by Olympias, Alexander regarded his father as the best measure by which to judge himself. From the very beginning, whatever love or admiration existed between father and son, their relationship was strongly influenced by an intense rivalry which constantly looked for an outlet. Even the famous incident involving the horse Bucephalus attests to this growing rivalry, although Alexander was no more than a boy of nine years at the time. Philip was doing business with a horse trader and singled out a beautiful black stallion with a white starburst on its forehead. The horse proved very unruly. Alexander, standing by, pointed out that they didn't know how to handle him. Philip, teasingly, asked Alexander to show them how. The young prince rose to the challenge. He grasped the halter and moved the horse so that it would no longer be frightened by its own shadow thrown by the sun. Once he had calmed the horse down, Alexander mounted it and, riding bareback, put the stallion through its paces, much to the admiration of his father and onlookers. Philip was delighted. He gave the horse as a gift to Alexander. A bond of friendship was formed between boy and horse, this would last for thirty years until Bucephalus died near the Jhelum River in Pakistan where Alexander erected a city there in its honour.[61]

Philip was undoubtedly proud of his son but according to Plutarch, made the rather bitter-sweet remark, 'Son, you are going to have to find another kingdom, Macedonia isn't going to be big enough for you.'[62] A similar anecdote refers to a year later, in 346 BC, when Philip was entertaining envoys at Pella. Alexander delighted his guests by playing skilfully on the lyre, and Philip, with an obvious twinge of jealousy, asked his son if he was not ashamed of playing so well? Sarcastically inferring that for a king it was sufficient to find time to hear others play and not do it himself.[63]

This taunting, and Alexander's eventual retaliation, surfaced three years later when Philip appointed Aristotle as Alexander's tutor Philip told his son to study hard and added, tongue in cheek, 'in order that you may not do a great many things of the sort I am sorry to have done'. The remark is heartwarming. Philip is conceding his many mistakes, urging his son to be better than he. It also illustrates how Philip understood his son's urge to compete, to excel, trying to soften it with a father's assurance that, if his son studied hard at school, he would be better than himself.[64]

Alexander's cold-hearted retort must have alarmed Philip and demonstrates the pervasive influence of Olympias. Alexander took his father to task 'because he was having children by other women besides his wife'. The remark illustrates how, at only thirteen, Alexander, egged on by his mother, was growing increasingly obsessed with the question of succession once Philip had joined the Gods. Philip's retort was just as telling: 'Prove yourself honourable and good so that you may obtain the kingdom not because of me but because of yourself.'[65] Philip had adroitly turned Alexander's question back on itself, appealing to his son's intensely competitive nature, yet the remark was ominous, even threatening. Philip was warning Alexander that he must not expect to inherit simply because he was Philip's son but by his own virtue. Alexander and his mother must have reflected on such a reply. The damage was done. Alexander could not regard the succession as a *fait accompli*.

The rivalry between Philip and Alexander grumbled on with the gap between father and son growing wider. No father likes to see his primacy in the affections of his son being replaced by another, yet this happened. The young prince must have been offended by his father's tart reply and later declared that he'd grown closer to Aristotle than his own father, 'because the one had given him life but the other had taught him how to live well'.[66] Such an insulting and mean-minded declaration was a direct snub to his father and betrays Alexander's growing obsession about outstripping Philip's achievements. Arrian talks of how Alexander's growing love of fame made his father's military successes a source of mourning rather than rejoicing, 'because', as Plutarch reported,

> every success gained by Macedonia inspired in Alexander the dread that another opportunity for glory had been wasted on his father. Alexander had no desire to inherit a kingdom which offered him riches and luxuries. His choice was a life of struggle, of war and of unrelenting ambition.[67]

Philip was also keen to point out that his son, whatever his ambition, had a great deal to learn. When Philip discovered that Alexander was trying to secure the allegiance of certain Macedonian courtiers by bribery, he gave his son a short sharp lesson in political theory. Philip, the consummate blackmailer and briber, wrote to his son, 'What on earth gave you the stupid idea that you would ever make faithful friends out of those whose affections you had to buy?'[68]

Alexander emerges on to the political scene as a ruthless, ambitious, self-centred prig. He was once asked if he would race in the Olympics and replied, 'that only if he had other kings as competitors'.[69] He saw himself as unique, the new Achilles in training: his conception and birth had been the work of the Gods and he had a destiny with which no man could interfere. He also saw his education as exclusive. Years later, during his pursuit of Darius, Alexander learnt that Aristotle was about to publish his *Metaphysics* which contained a great deal of the philosophy Aristotle had taught Alexander in the Groves at Mieza. The Great Conqueror was stunned by the prospect of what he regarded as pearls were now being cast before swine.

'How can I,' Alexander arrogantly wrote to his former tutor, 'surpass other men if those doctrines which I studied become common property?'[70]

By the time he was in his late teens, Alexander's all-consuming absorption with himself and his own ambitions made him ignore other pleasures. Even his ever-watchful mother became concerned. Olympias grew particularly anxious about her darling son's lack of interest in the opposite sex. She hired a Thessalian courtesan, Callixeina, and begged her son to have intercourse with her. Alexander rejected both the woman and the offer.[71] Sex, like sleep, was very low on Alexander's list of priorities: he once remarked that they only reminded him of his own mortality, a fact he liked to ignore.[72]

Of course, it could be argued that, in the savage politics of the Macedonian court, such self-preservation and enhancement were the order of the day. Alexander had the political sense to realize that no succession could be assured or peacefully carried through. If he was to survive, he had to be a soldier, a warrior, a general, and prove to the great warlords of Macedonia that he was equal, even superior, to his illustrious father. He seized every opportunity to achieve this. During his first campaign against the Maedi, a Thracian tribe (340/339 BC), Alexander not only defeated the insurgents but founded a colony or city in his name, imitating the custom of his father.[73] During the same period Alexander is also reported to have gone to the help of Philip against other tribes. More importantly, in the bitter fighting along those wooded valleys where ambush was common, Alexander actually saved his own father's life, although it cannot be established whether this is fact, or part of Alexander's self-propaganda.[74]

Alexander's emergence on the political military scene fortunately coincided with a notable shift in the balance of power in mainland Greece. Philip, more confident at home, now looked south, eager to exert his influence over Athens and Thebes. Demosthenes, as usual, put his finger on the root of the problem. He had watched Philip's military build-up, the development of his powerful war machine, and shrewdly commented, 'Athens is not at war with Philip but Philip is certainly at war with Athens.'[75] Philip's gradual extension of his power southwards, the seizure of certain cities, and the control of important trade routes forced matters to a head. In August 338 BC, Philip's Macedonian phalanx brought the combined forces of Thebes and

Athens to battle at Chaeronea on Blood River in Bœotia. Philip commanded the infantry on the Macedonian right; Alexander led the cavalry on the left. Philip displayed his usual skill, breaking the enemy line by feigning a fake retreat: the Sacred Band, Thebes' crack troops, were left exposed. It was a classic Macedonian tactic, to break the opposing line then despatch the cavalry, charging in a diamond formation, to split and rupture the enemy battlefront. According to all accounts Alexander hit the Sacred Band with a hammer-like charge, a brilliant deployment which finished off what his father's strategy had begun. Common report, or propaganda, claims that Alexander was the first to burst through the enemy line and, after a fierce struggle, the Sacred Band simply ceased to exist.[76]

Chaeronea was a turning point in Greek history and the fortunes of Macedon. Philip, though now master of Greece, showed great clemency to the defeated, even sending Alexander to Athens as part of an embassy to offer generous terms.[77] Philip wished to dominate but not conquer Greece; his eyes were already turning east. He formed the League of Corinth and exploited this loose federation of city-states to issue propaganda against the Persians. The prospect of a Greek army crossing the Hellespont was now back on the political agenda, especially as Artaxerxes III Ochus had been assassinated and the Persian court was slipping into chaos.[78] The time for invasion was right.

Chaeronea was also a turning point in Alexander's life. In his eyes Chaeronea was an epic victory – he had truly won for his father, yet Philip had snatched the credit and the fruits of that victory for himself. Alexander later claimed, 'The famous victory at Chaeronea had been his [i.e. Alexander's work] but the gaining of such a great battle had been taken away by the envy of his father.'[79] Such a whispering campaign, undoubtedly helped by Olympias, began shortly after the battle. It was even alleged that the people of Macedon now regarded 'Philip as their general but Alexander their King'. Philip claimed to be delighted by such comments; in truth he wasn't.[80] Alexander was now adult, a veteran warrior, a proven battle leader. He might be Philip's son, but he was now also a rival and becoming a very dangerous one. Macedonian history clearly proved that blood and kinship meant little in the furious dynastic struggles of that kingdom. Philip's half-brothers became his bitter rivals, so he killed them. Should the threat become too great, undoubtedly, Philip would consider the same fate for his son. The old king must have regretted his remarks about how the adolescent Alexander would have to struggle for his succession. After Chaeronea there was every danger that would happen. King and prince had their own parties. Alexander's retinue was closely watched; Philip may have had spies amongst them and, when the danger posed by Alexander proved too great, they also faced disgrace.

Of course, Philip had the upper hand: he was surrounded by his own council and supporters. They pointed out that Olympias was not a Macedonian; her son Alexander was half Epirote, a fact not lost on the xenophobic Macedonian commanders in Philip's entourage. They did not take too kindly to Olympias or her arrogant son. They would be quick to interpret Olympias and Alexander's ambitions as grandeur and turn their aspirations to divinity against them. If Olympias hinted that Alexander was divinely conceived, if Alexander believed that he was Philip's superior – and there was considerable evidence for both these statements – their enemies were only too quick to whisper back that Olympias was an adulteress and Alexander her bastard child, desperate to seize everything Philip had won.[81] In the dynastic struggles of Macedon, the charge of illegitimacy was often used.

But in 337 BC, something else occurred, the very spark which would ignite the heaped brushwood of hatred, anger and resentment at the court in Pella: Philip fell in love.

After Chaeronea, Philip entered a new world of self-assurance. He was hegemon of Greece whilst Persia was growing increasingly vulnerable. Philip decided to manifest his new-found supremacy in a number of ways. He ordered the construction of a *tholos* at Olympia, a circular temple building, based on the one at the sacred shrine at Delphi. The architect, Leochares, was hired to celebrate Philip's achievements in this glorious building which would house statues of Philip's family carved in gold and ivory.[82] At the same time Philip began to share his power with other groups besides his son. He particularly advanced the interest of two leading Macedonian generals, Parmenio and Attalus. These two veterans were already linked by marriage, Attalus being Parmenio's son-in-law. Philip strengthened his own alliance with them by marrying Attalus' niece, Cleopatra (Arrian's history calls her Eurydice).[83] Now Philip's marriages were a source of constant amusement to his contemporaries, but this was different. Philip was not only tying his fortunes to certain of the great houses of Macedon, he truly loved Cleopatra. More importantly, such an alliance, in the eyes of all court observers, marked a dramatic and decisive step by Philip to distance himself from his over-weaning third wife and ruthlessly ambitious son. Satyrus, the biographer, quoted by Athenaeus, shrewdly summed up the situation: 'Philip married Cleopatra with whom he had fallen in love. He brought her home to supplant Olympias and so threw the entire course of his life into confusion.'[84] Olympias viewed Cleopatra as a clear rival. Philip's new wife was at least twenty years younger than her husband, a full-blooded Macedonian capable of producing a second heir. Arrian's description of the situation is a fine example of his classic understatement, 'There was a lack of confidence between Alexander and Philip after Philip took Eurydice [Cleopatra] to wife and disgraced Olympias, the mother of Alexander.'[85]

Both Satyrus and Arrian talk of yet another new marriage, of Olympias being supplanted, indicating that this love-match with Cleopatra went hand-in-hand with Philip's divorce from Olympias: an outright attack upon her status and, by implication, on Alexander's. In a word Philip no longer trusted either Olympias or her son and viewed them as a threat.

This is not mere supposition. The wedding feast of Philip and Cleopatra provoked a crisis which exposed the deep festering relationship between king and prince. Alexander reluctantly attended the feasting, taking the place of honour opposite his father. The rest of the party lounged on couches around the hall, heads garlanded, bellies full of uncut wine and hearts full of malicious glee at the young prince's discomfiture. The violence erupted immediately. On being greeted ostentatiously by his father, Alexander declared, 'When my mother remarries I'll invite you to her wedding.' This was not only a jibe but a warning. Olympias came from Epirus, a small but very strategically placed kingdom on Macedon's borders. Plutarch takes up the story: 'Attalus stood up, and called upon all Macedonians to pray to the gods that a legitimate successor to the kingdom be born of Philip and Cleopatra.'

The taunt was so cruel and so clear, great emphasis being placed on the word legitimate, that there is very little doubt that Attalus' remark had been well prepared and reflected a common joke between Philip and his immediate entourage. Olympias' propaganda about the possible divine conception of her son was now being thrown back in her face and that of Alexander who responded according to form, as his tormentor thought he would. 'Villain,' Alexander shouted, springing to his feet. 'Are you calling me a bastard?' And he threw his own goblet in Attalus' face. Wedding feast or not, the groom still came armed. Philip drew his sword, lurched from his couch but the wine he'd drunk and his injured leg sent him sprawling to the floor.

'Look,' Alexander taunted, 'here is a man preparing to cross from Europe to Asia yet he can't even make it from one couch to another!'[86]

Later that night Alexander fled Macedon, taking his mother with him. She found refuge in the court of Epirus whilst her son sought sanctuary amongst the tough Illyrian tribes to the north.[87] Philip took no action during the winter 337/336 BC but simply watched and waited. He knew the danger was serious. He controlled Greece and was preparing an invasion across the Hellespont; he didn't relish the prospect of Alexander setting up some government in exile and interfering in the affairs of Macedon once the Persian expedition was launched. Due to the diplomacy of Demeratus of Corinth, who had bought Bucephalus for Philip to give to Alexander, a rather frosty accord was reached between father and son. Olympias would stay in Epirus but Alexander was allowed to return.[88]

Yet nothing had changed. Alexander had neither learnt anything nor forgotten anything. In 336 BC, Philip tried to arrange a marriage alliance between his mentally retarded son, Arridhaeus and the daughter of Pixadorus who ruled the strategic city-port of Halicarnassus in the province of Caria in Asia Minor. Alexander, highly sensitive, came to the astonishing conclusion that once again Philip was trying to circumvent him. He opened his own secret negotiations with Pixadorus through Thessalus, a travelling actor. Philip found out, Alexander being probably betrayed by someone in his own entourage. Philip was speechless with fury but decided not to take any serious punitive action. He did not wish to provoke a new crisis. Philip confronted Alexander with his supposed treachery, gave him a public dressing down and exiled many of Alexander's entourage.[89]

In the spring of 336 BC, the Persian expedition was launched. Generals Parmenio and Attalus took an advance guard across the Hellespont where, at first, they achieved outstanding success, capturing the strategic city of Ephesus.[90] Philip, however, decided to wait and settle matters at home. He was aware of Olympias still seething at the court of Epirus and decided to remove any danger from that quarter by proposing a marriage between its king, Olympias' half-brother (also called Alexander) and Philip's daughter Cleopatra. Philip also decided to mix business with pleasure. The marriage would take place at Macedon's old capital of Aegae where envoys from all the Greek city-states, with the exception of Sparta, would offer Philip gold crowns. Philip had decided to revel in his glory. Greece was settled and subservient, Olympias exiled, Alexander isolated. Philip's new wife Cleopatra had given birth first to a healthy baby boy and, more recently, a daughter.[91] Philip's generals were now challenging the Persian might in Asia Minor; all Philip needed was the approval of the Gods for his next great achievement. He had already despatched envoys to the Oracle at Delphi. These had brought back the message, 'Wreathed is the bull, all is ready, the slayer is at hand.' Philip believed that the bull was the Persian Empire and he was the sacrificer. Events were to prove this interpretation disastrously wrong.[92]

The celebrations at Aegae, the banquets and meetings, were to reach their climax with a great procession into the old amphitheatre. Philip would be preceeded by twelve statues of the Olympians, his own following behind. He would then enter the amphitheatre escorted by the two Alexanders, his disgraced son and his future son-in-law. Philip would receive the approbation of the envoys of Greece, deliver a sterling speech and declare what was to happen next. Philip also decided to act the great democrat.[93] On the morning in question he dressed simply in tunic and robe with a wreath about his head, and to show that he was no dictator or tyrant, he had dispensed with his bodyguard. In many successful assassinations the guards are always withdrawn first. This happened at Aegae. Philip was unaware that one of his guards, Pausanias, had a serious grudge to settle with him. The historian Diodorus Siculus describes the lurid events which turned Pausanias into a regicide.

> There was a Macedonian, Pausanias, who came of a family from the district of Orestis. He was a bodyguard of King Philip and was much loved by him because of his beauty. When he saw that the king was becoming enamoured of another Pausanias [a man of the same name as himself], he addressed this second Pausanias with abusive language, accusing him of being a hermaphrodite, always ready to accept the loving advances of everyone. Unable to endure such an insult, the other Pausanias kept silent for the time, but, after confiding to Attalus [Philip's general], one of his friends, what he proposed to do, he brought about his own death voluntarily and in a spectacular fashion. For, a few days after this, as Philip was engaged in battle with Pleurias, king of the Illyrians, Pausanias stepped in front of Philip and, receiving on his body all the blows directed at the king, so met his death. The incident was widely discussed and Attalus, the same man at whom Alexander had flung his cup, and a member of the court circle and influential with the king, invited the first Pausanias to dinner. After he had plied him with unmixed wine till he was drunk, Attalus handed the unconscious Pausanias over to his muleteers to abuse in their drunken licentiousness. Pausanias eventually recovered from his drunken stupor and, fiercely resenting the abuse to his person, charged Attalus before the king with the outrage. Philip shared Pausanias' anger at the cruelty of the act but did not wish to punish Attalus at that time because of their relationship, and because Attalus's services were needed urgently. Attalus was the nephew [actually the uncle] of the Cleopatra whom the king had just married. As he was a warrior,

valiant in battle, he had also been selected as a general of the advance force being sent into Asia. For these reasons, the king tried to placate the righteous anger of Pausanias at his treatment, giving him costly presents and advancing him in honour among his bodyguards.

Philip had forgotten Pausanias, who was still numbered amongst his retinue. The king was more concerned with the dazzling show of wealth which, as Diodorus put it, 'was to strike awe into the beholder'. The twelve Olympian gods had preceeded the king, but any surprise by the spectators at the appearance of a thirteenth statue, that of Philip, was soon replaced by the dramatic events which unfolded just within the gates of the amphitheatre. Pausanias, a Celtic dagger concealed about his person, abruptly broke from the rest, rushed towards the king and thrust his dagger into the king's ribs, killing him instantly. The assassin then tried to flee back towards the city gates where horses were waiting for him to make his quick escape. Pausanias, however, tripped on a vine root. Three of his pursuers, Perdiccas, Leonnatus and Attalus (not Philip's general) caught up with him and stabbed him with their javelins. 'Such was the end of Philip,' Diodorus lamented, 'who had made himself the greatest of kings in Europe in his time, and because of the extent of his kingdom had made himself a throned companion of the twelve gods.'

Philip had abruptly discovered the true nature of his immortality, but now the king was dead, Alexander his son, and successor, immediately claimed the crown. The speed and relative smoothness of Alexander's succession begs the question: was Pausanias a lonely, bitter assassin, or was he simply the weapon wielded by others? And who were these others? Olympias? Alexander? Both? The primary sources present conflicting evidence. Arrian describes Philip's murder as the work of a lone, vengeful assassin but Arrian is biased. He wrote his history in the second century AD when the murder of a successful ruler, like Philip, by his own son, would be regarded as the worst example of parricide, a sacrilege, a true abomination. Arrian can be objective but his apotheosis of Alexander at the end of his work clearly illustrates his profound admiration for a brilliant general and successful politician.

Other sources are more guarded. In his *Politics* Aristotle, whilst discussing princes who had been assassinated for personal rather than political reasons, argues that Pausanias was the sole assassin. 'Philip,' he writes, 'was attacked by Pausanias because he permitted him to be insulted by Attalus and his friends.' The shrewd philosopher has no more to say but, there again, he was biased. Alexander had been his pupil, a student who declared that Aristotle was more of a father to him than Philip. Moreover, Aristotle was astute enough to realize that, if he had to choose between the living and the dead, the best solution was to compromise: Philip's death was the work of one man and no blame can be attached to Alexander. Aristotle's conclusion is quite significant because of the stories which circulated about Alexander's murder in Babylon sixteen years later in which Aristotle, the great philosopher and former royal mentor, was portrayed as being involved (see Part Four, p. 100).

Diodorus Siculus also depicts Pausanias as a lonely, brooding man thirsting for revenge, 'Not only on the one who had done him wrong but also on the other who refused to avenge him.' However, he does add the rather surprising statement, that Pausanias was encouraged to commit regicide by the sophist, Hermocrates. Pausanias had asked him how could one become famous? Hermocrates replied, 'By killing one who had accomplished the most because as long as he was remembered so would his killer be.'

Plutarch, however, spreads the net a little further and implicates Olympias. 'It was Olympias who was principally blamed for the murder, it was believed that she encouraged the young man and incited him to take revenge.' Justin, not so accurate a source, repeats the allegation:

> Pausanias was provoked to act by Olympias . . . she had felt no less resentment at her divorce and the preferment of Cleopatra than Pausanias had at the insults heaped upon him . . . it is certain Olympias had horses prepared for the escape of the assassin.

Justin then graphically describes how, after Philip's murder, Olympias hastened back to Macedon to pay ostentatious respect to the assassin's corpse nailed to a cross, rather than to that of her former husband.

The same night that she arrived, [Olympias] put a crown of gold on the head of Pausanias, as he was hanging on a cross: an act which no one but she would have dared to do, as long as the son of Philip was alive. A few days after, when the body of the assassin had been taken down, she burnt it upon the remains of her husband, and made him a tomb in the same place; she also provided that yearly sacrifices should be performed to his [Pausanias'] *manes* [spirit], possessing the people with a superstitious notion for the purpose . . . Last of all, she consecrated the dagger with which the king had been killed, to Apollo, under the name of Myrtale, which was Olympias's own name when a child. And all these things were done so publicly, that she seems to have been afraid lest it should not be evident enough that the deed was promoted by her.

Justin's allegation has a sting in its tail. If Olympias was frightened that the deed might not be ascribed to her, was she trying to protect someone, and who else but her beloved Alexander? The other authorities are not so conclusive about this. Though Plutarch blames Olympias, he adds, 'A certain amount of accusation attaches itself to Alexander also.' Plutarch adds a rather curious story, about how Pausanias approached Alexander for help. The prince listened carefully then quoted some lines from Euripides in which Medea threatened 'the father, bride and bridegroom all at once'. The verse refers to that part of the play where Creon of Thebes is highly anxious about what Medea might do to him, his daughter and new son-in-law after she had been rejected and shamed by her husband. This could have been an analogy between the characters of the play and Attalus, his niece Cleopatra and Philip, Medea, of course, being Olympias. All three, Attalus, Cleopatra and Philip, were dead within the year. Plutarch also adds, 'that there was deep hostility between Pausanias

and the house of Attalus'. Plutarch, undoubtedly an admirer of
Alexander, then tries to negate the effectiveness of what he said by
describing how the new king 'took care to hunt down and punish
those who were involved in the plot'. Justin, however, describes
Alexander as one who encouraged Pausanias in such 'an atrocious
deed'.

Naturally, the question of Alexander's involvement in his father's
murder has been the subject of heated discussion amongst historians.
I believe Alexander was, at the very best, a passive observer and at the
very worst, an active participant, perhaps, even, the organizer of the
assassination of his own father.

• The primary sources are, in the main, in favour of Alexander.
Arrian was a fervent admirer and was dependent for a great deal of his
information on the now lost history of Ptolemy, son of Lagus,
Alexander's companion, future general, and the founder of a new
dynasty in Egypt. After Alexander's death Ptolemy seized Alexander's
corpse for burial in Egypt thus proclaiming his friendship for his dead
master as well as symbolizing that he was Alexander's legitimate
successor in Egypt (see Part Eight, pp. 196 *et seq.*). Ptolemy would hardly
describe Alexander as a parricide. Moreover, at the time of Philip's
death, Ptolemy was a member of Alexander's entourage and, if the heir
apparent became suspect, so did those around him, his supporters and
adherents. Ptolemy, as shall be seen later, was to play a unique role in
Alexander's death; perhaps only then did he reveal his true feelings
about the death of Philip who was also rumoured to be his father.
Aristotle, too, was biased and would be fearful of casting any blame
upon Alexander's name or memory. Diodorus Siculus could also be
described as reserved: the lack of any real discussion or analysis of
Philip's murder in his work does give rise to speculation. The other
sources are not so defensive of Alexander. Plutarch certainly refers to
the suspicion that he was involved whilst Justin firms up the allegation.

• Plutarch's assertion that Alexander hunted down all those
involved in his father's death is not truly accurate. Alexander was
quick to blame others, including Demosthenes of Athens and even
Darius, king of Persia. It is true certain Macedonian nobles belonging

to a rival clan (the House of Aeropus) were executed and their ashes sprinkled over Philip's grave but, there again, the removal of these potential rivals was to protect Alexander more than avenge his father's death. The sources certainly do not produce any evidence to suggest that Pausanias was being managed by any other faction or group at the Macedonian court. Arrian simply mentions in passing the execution of possible rivals.

• The excavations of Philip's tomb at Vergine show that the king was given the lavish funeral of a hero whilst, later on, Alexander seriously considered the deification of Philip.[94] These were more of a sop than anything else. Philip dead could be honoured because Philip dead was no longer a problem. Historians who do not agree with my thesis will point out how, in 331 BC, when Alexander trekked his long and very dangerous journey through the sands of Libya to the Oracle of Ammon at Siwah, he did ask the Oracle if any of his father's assassins were still alive.[95] Alexander's 600-mile pilgrimage to a shrine whose Oracle ranked with Delphi was a mixture of fact and propaganda. Ammon was a hybrid God, possessing all the characteristics of the Greek Zeus and the Egyptian Amun-Ra. The reason for the pilgrimage, just after the fall of Egypt to Alexander's forces and before his final confrontation with Darius, was Alexander's *pothos* – his deep unquenching desire to establish his divine paternity, as well as complete a journey done by the God-Men, Hercules and Perseus. Alexander was not rejecting Philip but, like other great heroes, discovering his double paternity where his mortal father was subordinate to the work of the divine seed. This would be the context of Alexander's question about his father's murderers still being alive. Such a question seems quite remarkable when one considers Olympias, who certainly *was* involved in her husband's murder, was still hale and hearty and continuing to prove herself a thorough nuisance back in Macedon. Historians have seized on Alexander's question as proof not only of his own innocence but that he never actually knew the truth about who was involved. However, a more sinister explanation is possible. During his campaigns against the Persian Empire, Alexander's sense of his own divinity became greatly enhanced, encouraged by his outstanding successes. The influence of

Olympias on the young Alexander's mind was far reaching and, despite her protestations, she continued to wield this influence, even telling her son 'the truth' about his supposed paternity just before he left for Asia.[96] Alexander's achievements simply encouraged such ideas to grow. He must have wondered whether he *was* truly divinely conceived. One of the reasons for his pilgrimage to Siwah was to ask the Oracle about his relationship with Ammon, the same Hellenized Egyptian God Philip had been told to sacrifice to, when he had spied on his wife and asked the Delphic Oracle for advice. The question Alexander posed at Siwah can be viewed in four ways. First, are any of my father's murderers still alive? This could have been to test the veracity of the Oracle, the priest who claimed he could see through the shifts of time and predict the future as well as comment on the present and the past. Secondly, the question could be viewed as a form of confession in that Alexander, although not an active participant in the assassination of his father, was seeking some form of absolution for standing by and allowing it to happen. The third interpretation is that Alexander was involved in mental casuistry, trying to free himself of any guilt for his father's death. To put it succinctly: if Ammon was his father, then Alexander was not guilty of parricide, because Philip was not truly the person who begot him. The Oracle of Siwah was just as disingenuous in its reply. It berated Alexander on this very topic – his father was immortal – how could he die? According to the propaganda, Alexander then rephrased the question – had his father's murderers been brought to justice? The reply, equally ambiguous, was intended to please and exonerate Alexander: Philip's death had been fully avenged – whatever this meant. Finally, throughout his life, Alexander was dogged by his father's memory; in every crisis (Philotas, Black Cleitus, the 'Pages Conspiracy', and the mutiny at Opis) reference is made to how Alexander was deserting Philip's ways. Alexander was constantly compared to his father and he always reacted passionately. Such behaviour, on both sides, provokes the suspicion that many may have secretly laid Philip's murder at Alexander's door – a charge Alexander found very difficult to confront in public – so he dealt with it by issuing propaganda such as details of his visit to the great Oracle at Siwah.

• Alexander certainly had the personality to carry through such a disgraceful act. By 336 BC he was twenty years old, blooded in war with some training in government, priggish in behaviour, hot-tempered, resolutely dedicated to his own advancement and openly resentful against his father, not only because of Philip's offences against Olympias but, more importantly, against himself. By 336 BC, Alexander viewed Philip as a hindrance, an obstacle to his own ruthless ambition. He had voiced such sentiments throughout his adolescence. After Chaeronea, he truly believed that *he* was the victor and, according to the whisperers, already viewed himself as king. The Pixadorus affair showed that Alexander was prepared, despite previous warnings, to engage in negotiations in defiance of his father, as if *he* were the sovereign ruler. Alexander's resentment against Philip never died. Twelve years later, after he had won the most outstanding victories, destroyed the Persian Empire and reached the borders of India, his resentment against his father still festered. Arrian reports how, when Alexander addressed the Macedonian troops at Opis in 324 BC, he described Philip's achievements for both the kingdom and the army, but claimed that they paled in significance in comparison with his own: 'My father's achievements for you, great as they are in themselves, are actually small when compared to ours.' In Alexander's case, apparently, time did not heal. He was quite prepared to consider deification for his father but he wanted men to talk of him as they did of Homer's Achilles: 'He is better by far than his father.'[97] Even those primary sources which openly admire Alexander talk of his bounding ambition. Plutarch wrote that Alexander 'valued his good name more than he did his life and his crown . . . his passionate desire for fame gave him a pride and a splendour of vision far beyond his years.' Arrian remarks how Alexander was 'dominated' by a 'love of fame', whilst 'his thirst for praise was absolutely insatiable'.[98] In Alexander's character there is a pathology, an absolute obsession with his own ambitions, achievements and the way others regarded him. Accordingly, he would not take too kindly to his father's advice and criticism, let alone warnings and threats. Philip's actions after Chaeronea must have seriously disturbed the vaulting ambition of such a ruthless son. Philip realized far too late that Alexander was now a highly dangerous young man. Attalus' taunt at the wedding feast only reflected the thinking of Philip and his advisers. Alexander was a foreign upstart, possibly not the king's son and certainly not a full-bloodied Macedonian. Such an insult was tantamount to a declaration of war. Alexander was being threatened and Alexander never forgot. He must have become alienated from his own people, culture and customs and, with his boundless energy, searched for a new identity. He left Macedon and his beloved mother in 334 BC, never to return. Historians will argue that Alexander simply wanted to march to the rim of the world, but it was more than that. Alexander saw himself as an individual, unique in every aspect, totally different from those who prepared to live and even die for him. Alexander's most serious confrontations with his commanders such as Cleitus were over a son's attempts to break from the ways of his father Philip and the customs of Macedon (see Part Five, p. 117). One story, given in many of the sources, provides a powerful insight into Alexander's mind between Philip's death and his departure for Asia.

In 336 BC, Alexander called a meeting of the city states, members of the League of Corinth. After the talking was over Alexander decided to seek out the famous philosopher, the cynic, Diogenes of Sinope. Diogenes was a recluse; he'd never bothered to seek Alexander out as other philosophers and writers did to petition him for favour, so Alexander went searching for him. Diogenes was not impressed. Alexander found the philosopher sunbathing against a wall. Instead of jumping to his feet and kneeling, Diogenes simply shaded his eyes and stared up at Alexander. At last the young king asked if there was anything he could do for the philosopher?

'Yes,' Diogenes replied. 'You're blocking the sun. Would you please stand to one side?'

Afterwards, Alexander's retainers mocked the philosopher.

Alexander, however, retorted. 'You may say what you like but, if I wasn't Alexander, I would like to be Diogenes.'

The story is quite famous and could be dismissed as ponderous affectation, but it sums up one extreme of Alexander's character.[99] If he was not a king, bound up with his own eternal ambition he would be a recluse, cut off from everybody, needing nothing and being subservient to no one. Of course, Alexander lived at the other extreme, at the heart of power and eager for more. The taunts and insults of the likes of Attalus were probably part of Alexander's adolescence, provoked by his own pride and his mother's overweening ambition, yet Alexander was a pragmatist, names might not harm him, but sticks and stones certainly did. Philip's actions after Chaeronea were a direct threat. Philip had formed a new political alliance advancing the interest of Parmenio and Attalus. Philip had married a woman he loved, who, despite the confusion amongst the primary sources, certainly presented the king with a daughter and a baby son – Caranus – who might dash Alexander's hopes of the succession. Philip controlled Greece. He was on the verge of launching his crusade against Persia and yet Alexander was in disgrace. He would either be left under house arrest in Macedon, or, more likely, as he himself did with men he couldn't trust, be taken as some form of hostage against his mother, forced to trail in Philip's dust and bask in his father's reflected glory. Alexander's friends had been exiled, his mother driven from court and, thanks to Philip's negotiations, not even the small kingdom of Epirus could offer any help. Little wonder, after Philip's death, that Alexander and Olympias moved ruthlessly to crush all opposition and so restore the balance. The House of Aeropus, a leading clan of Macedon which had a claim to the throne, lost two of its sons in the immediate aftermath of Philip's assassination. The third, the Lyncestian, saved by his marriage to a daughter of General Antipater, became a virtual hostage in Alexander's camp.[100] Another possible claimant to the Macedonian throne, Amyntas, living in retirement, saw the writing on the wall and immediately fled to Persia. Publicly, Alexander could wash his hands of any involvement in the grisly end of Philip's new wife and children: Olympias took care of those. According to one source, she thrust both children face down into a charcoal fire and gave their mother the choice of poison or the halter. The poor woman chose the latter. Alexander was absent from court at the time. He later expressed his shock, but he was king, he was responsible. Olympias was not punished and, when Alexander left Macedon, she remained as queen mother with the senior general Antipater as regent.[101]

• Alexander was also a master strategist, a brilliant general on the battlefield, his timing, as well as his search for an enemy's weakness, were outstanding. Such skills played their part in the assassination crisis of 336 BC. Philip had left himself vulnerable: his closest allies, Parmenio and Attalus, were across the Hellespont, in no position to influence the Macedonian troops in their confirmation of Alexander as Philip's successor. The third remaining senior general, Antipater, remained in Macedon. He must have resented the promotion of his two colleagues. He certainly played a key role in helping Alexander during those frenzied days following Philip's assassination.

Antipater moved swiftly, exploiting his authority as a senior general to present Alexander to the troops to be hailed as king, Philip's legitimate successor. Antipater then closely cooperated with Alexander in the subsequent military and political manoeuvres.[102] Once Alexander was king he moved against Attalus. He opened secret negotiations with Parmenio in Asia, despatching a special envoy, Hecaetus, 'with orders to bring back Attalus alive, but, if not, to kill him as soon as possible'. Hecaetus was successful. Parmenio was separated from Attalus, undoubtedly bribed with offers of high command for both himself and his sons. When Alexander launched his invasion of Persia he had to depend, at least for a while, on the House of Parmenio, but Alexander never forgot. Within five years of the invasion, Parmenio and his three sons were dead. In 336 BC, however, Alexander was hunting different quarry. Attalus was removed. He made a futile attempt to ingratiate himself with the new king but he was shown no mercy and executed.[103]

• Finally, the actual details of Philip's murder do implicate Alexander. Evidence exists that the assassin Pausanias was no friend of Attalus, whilst he had approached Alexander for help, only to receive that cryptic quotation from Euripides. Moreover, on the morning of his death, Philip may have had no guards but, according to the sources, he did have two young warriors close by: Alexander his son, smouldering with resentment, and Alexander of Epirus, Olympias' half-brother. There is no record of any attempt by either of them to protect Philip or avenge themselves, whilst those who pursued and killed Pausanias were all Alexander's friends: Attalus (Attalus II), Leonnatus and Perdiccas. Philip's death exposes Alexander's ruthlessness, yet it is also ironic that many of the circumstances – and people – surrounding Philip's death were also present when Alexander died so mysteriously in Babylon some thirteen years later.

Despite the blood-letting and executions of his rivals, Alexander moved swiftly to harmonize relations with the Lords of Macedon. He assured them that he would continue Philip's policies, with one exception: all Macedonian citizens would be exempt from direct taxation.[104] Such a bribe ensured Alexander's swift and smooth succession within his own kingdom, though the situation beyond its borders was a different matter.

The news of Philip's death spread swiftly amongst the barbarians to the north, causing immediate unrest as the tribes moved to block vital roads and valley passes.[105] In Greece Thebes rose in revolt and expelled its Macedonian garrison from the Cadmea, its citadel. In Athens, Demosthenes, mourning the death of his daughter, was first to hear the news of Philip's death. Demosthenes put aside his mourning garb, donned his best robes, put a wreath on his head and proclaimed he'd had a dream that Athens would soon receive some very good news. Once Philip's death was officially proclaimed, the Athenians immediately voted a gold crown to the assassin.[106] Alexander and his council were aware of all these developments. They advised prudence but, according to Plutarch, 'Alexander rejected this advice, declaring he was going to move with extreme boldness.' Alexander would terrify his enemies into submission.[107]

During the late spring and early summer of 336 BC, Alexander launched a whirlwind campaign of breathtaking speed and brilliance. The Thessalians had seized the Vale of Tempe, a narrow river gorge commanding the routes into southern Greece: if Alexander wished to pass through he would have to negotiate with them. Alexander simply had his engineers cut steps on the seaward side of Mount Ossa and brought his troops up behind the enemy. The Thessalians immediately sued for terms. Alexander succeeded Philip as *archon* of their federation, enjoying the same status and power as his father, receiving revenue from the tribes and, more importantly, gaining the use of their superb cavalry. Alexander was then able to reach Corinth where he was accepted as *hegemon* of the Corinthian League. Thebes immediately submitted when Alexander threatened to march on the city, whilst Athens quickly disguised any glee at Philip's death or temptation to rebel against his successor.[108]

Alexander was determined to win the approval of all the powerful organizations throughout Greece be they councils or temples. After finishing his business in Corinth Alexander went to consult the Oracle of Apollo at Delphi about the future success of his campaign against Persia. He arrived during the wrong season when the Pythia, the priestess of Apollo, was forbidden to consider any request or issue a reply. She refused to enter the sacred cave and breathe in the fumes of the God. Alexander lost his temper, grabbed the priestess and tried to drag her off to the shrine, whereupon she exclaimed, 'You are invincible, my son.' Alexander released her. He had received the reply he wanted and left Delphi, determined that all Greece would accept the same.[109]

In the spring of 335 BC, Alexander had to face fresh revolts in Thrace, a rugged wild country to the north, where the tribesmen used the mountains and narrow passes to their best advantage. Once again, Alexander showed his genius of performing the unexpected: he succeeded in subduing wild tribes, such as the Triballians, and even launched a punitive campaign against the Getae across the Danube. The campaign was long and punishing. Alexander advanced so far north that rumours percolated back into Greece that Alexander had been killed and his army destroyed. Demosthenes, who considered Alexander a poltroon, urged his fellow citizens and those of Thebes to rebel. Alexander had to hurry back to face widespread revolt throughout Greece. He marched his troops some 300 miles in thirteen days. Athens submitted immediately. Thebes refused to accept that Alexander was still alive, so he despatched envoys to the city asking for their submission.[110] Urged on by recently returned exiles, the

Thebans declared Alexander to be 'the tyrant of Greece'. According to Diodorus, 'the insult stung Alexander.' He gave way to a fiery rage and vowed he would inflict the most extreme punishment on the Thebans and their city. He took up position outside the Electra Gate. The Thebans deployed their troops, but they were no match for Alexander's veterans who pushed them back against the walls. A gate was found open and the Macedonian army poured into the city. Some 6,000 Thebans were killed; at least another 30,000 taken prisoner.

Alexander called a meeting of the League of Corinth and asked what he should do with the captured city as Thebes had few friends amongst the League. It was decided that the city should be razed: not one stone should be left upon another, and 30,000 of its inhabitants sold into slavery. Alexander implemented the decree. Only sacred persons and places, priests, temples and shrines, along with the family home of the poet Pindar, were exempt. The Athenians, terrified at what had happened, begged for mercy and, surprisingly, received it. Plutarch maintains that 'Alexander's fury may have been sated with the blood of Thebes or perhaps he wished to offset his cruel and hideous treatment of the Thebans by performing an act of mercy.' Alexander had performed a hideous act, he had plucked out one of the eyes of Hellas and, later in his career, bitterly regretted his destruction of one of Greece's most ancient and sacred cities. According to Plutarch, Alexander believed that most of his mistakes during the next twelve years were 'caused by the anger of the god Dionysius who wished to avenge the total destruction of his favourite city'.[111]

Alexander had shown himself to be a totally ruthless master. He had wiped out one source of rebellion against his rule, leaving him free to turn east. Alexander and his army fell back on Pella, where he began his preparations in earnest to cross the Hellespont. By removing and executing Attalus, Alexander was left without one of the joint commanders of the Macedonian expeditionary force. This was the first of many setbacks he had to face before he crossed the Hellespont. And now Darius III, the new Persian king, who had hired the skilled Greek mercenary, General Memnon of Rhodes, compelled Parmenio to fall back. Parmenio was eventually recalled to become Alexander's second-in-command.[112]

In the spring of 334 BC, Alexander marched from Pella for the last time, following the same route that Xerxes, the great Persian king, had when he had invaded Greece. Alexander took with him an army of about 50,000 men. Its backbone comprised 15,000 foot brigaded into six phalanxes. These were Philip's veterans, armed with the *sarissa*, a 15-foot pike with a leaf-shaped blade. As the *sarissa* had to be held with both hands, only a small button-like shield hung round the neck to protect the left shoulder. The *sarissa* weighed about 15 lb (7 kg), and the phalanxes were assembled in lines some 16 ft (5 m) deep. In battle, the front line lowered their pikes, the other ranks closing up, pressing in to force a gap in the enemy line. The heads of the phalanx men were protected by the Bœotian rounded helmet with a pronounced rim at front and back. Each brigade had its own colour and insignia. Along with these Alexander had about 2,000 Companion Cavalry, superb horsemen who rode without stirrups, their helmets either being Bœotian or Phoenician, adorned with the colours of their particular unit which were also advertised on the *shabraque*, or saddle cloth, of their horses.

Mercenaries from Thessaly (cavalry), Thracian scouts (light horsemen), slingers from Rhodes, archers from Crete and infantry from the northern tribes formed the rest of the force. Alexander also took musicians, scientists and writers.[113] He even had his own official historian, Callisthenes, a relative of Aristotle. The army secretariat was under Eumenes of Cardia; Deiades was in charge of the siege equipment, significantly developed under Philip, whilst many of Alexander's staff officers were companions from the Groves of Mieza, men such as Attalus [II], Perdiccas and Leonnatus. These men were often classed as 'Friends', 'Companions' or 'bodyguards' of the king. They were trusted retainers being used by Alexander as guards or administrators: Ptolemy of Lagus was one of their number.

Once Alexander had completed the 300-mile march from Pella to the Hellespont, the main body of his army under Parmenio crossed from Sestos to Abydos. Alexander, however, still had his mind full of Achilles: he moved to the peninsula of Elaeum where Agamemnon allegedly sailed from Europe to attack Troy. He paid sacrifice at the tomb of Protesilaus, because, during the Trojan War, he was the first

Greek warrior to set foot on Asian soil. Only after this did Alexander embark for conquest. Alexander had his own navy, in the main rather untrustworthy captains who commanded ships loaned by the League of Corinth. Fortunately, they had little work to do in the crossing because it was not the sailing season and the Persian fleet had yet to assemble. Once aboard his flagship, Alexander sacrificed a bull to Poseidon and, as the enemy coastline emerged from the mist, he dressed in full battle armour. When the flagship came to beach, he jumped from the prow and, according to Diodorus, hurled his spear into the sand, declaring, 'He received Asia as a spear-won prize from the gods.' Alexander believed that he had beached his ship in the same harbour as the Greeks had when they had come to attack Troy. He immediately made sacrifice and marched off to Troy to visit the ruins. Like some modern tourist Alexander was taken round what was left of the old city, being shown all sorts of relics. Alexander took what he wanted for himself and, with his close friend Hephaestion, paid tribute at the alleged site of the graves of Achilles and Patroclus.[114]

Once he left Troy, however, Alexander swept like a wolf through the Persian Empire, launching all-out war against Darius III Codomanus, King of Kings, Lord of Persia, who ruled an empire which mingled Medes, Babylonians and Assyrians, and today would have covered modern Palestine, Syria, Israel, Egypt, Turkey, Iraq and Iran. Darius III was a ruler who also tried to exercise his power even over the wild tribes north of the Danube – the Scythians and the Getae. He had also made his influence felt far to the east, in what are now western Pakistan and the north-western provinces of India. Persia was an empire where the will of the king had force of law. The King of Kings answered only to Ahura-Mazda, source of all creation, the God of Fire, whose sacred flame burnt eternally in the opulent royal palace of the great Apadana in Persepolis, the Place of Audience, the Hall of Columns which was approached by its 111 steps. Greeks regarded the Persian Empire as their natural enemy. Previous invasions of Greece by the Persian emperors Xerxes, Cyrus and Darius were seen as a sacrilegious attempt to wrest liberty from freedom-loving Greeks: the Persians were tyrants who, with very little justification, despotically ruled the Greek settlements and cities of Asia

Minor, such as Ephesus and Miletus. Darius III's empire possessed vast resources in both material and manpower. It could field an army of cavalry and foot drawn from over 100 nationalities as well as hire the best mercenaries from all over Greece.

It is beyond the scope of this book to describe the eleven years Alexander spent ravaging the Persian Empire. In brief, he succeeded beyond all expectations, destroying Persian armies at the Granicus (334 BC), Issus (333 BC) and Gaugamela (331 BC). He took the so-called impregnable cities of Miletus, Halicarnassus (334 BC), Tyre and Gaza (332 BC). He destroyed the Persian military machine, seized Darius' treasure and annexed all his provinces, which he then distributed to his friends and allies. He burnt Persepolis, seized Darius' treasure house and family, and eventually hunted down the hapless King of Kings who died manacled and wounded by his own followers in an ox-drawn cart, his last minutes being witnessed by a common Macedonian soldier who was searching for water.

Alexander's victory against the King of Kings was complete but, brushing aside the protests of his Companions, Alexander continued further east into what is now western Pakistan, striking north into the Hindu Kush to confront the military might of Rajah Porus and his Indian troops (326 BC). Eventually, Alexander was obliged to retreat through the horrendous Gedrosian Desert (now known as the Makran) into western Persia (325 BC), as his army dwindled and his generals and troops rebelled. They had grown increasingly opposed to Alexander's idea of his own invincibility and refused to share his great desire to achieve whatever else was left to be achieved.

By 325 BC the cost to Alexander had been great: the Macedonian army had been on the march for eleven years, the king's mobile court was riven by intrigue, conspiracy and sudden death. The internecine political struggle between different factions had not been subordinated by the pursuit of some all-conquering vision. Alexander had clashed with the House of Parmenio, his father's senior general and utterly destroyed it. He had confronted the conservatives of his court led by the likes of Black Cleitus, Callisthenes, his official historian, as well as the adolescent insolence of some of the royal pages. Alexander had dealt ruthlessly with them all. By 325 BC, even the House of Antipater back in Macedon, guarding the homeland against possible insurgents, came under Alexander's hard scrutiny and was found wanting. One of Antipater's sons Iolaus was the king's cupbearer; another, Cassander, Antipater's son and envoy to Alexander. But such closeness, in Alexander's eyes, was no guarantee of loyalty: such men might have to be removed. This sentiment was not lost on others of Alexander's retinue, leading figures such as Generals Perdiccas, Seleucus, Ptolemy, Antigonus and the rest. Alexander had entered Babylon to plan and plot afresh but, by the end of May of 323 BC, the Conqueror of the World was reduced to a sweating invalid, wrapped in blankets beside the bathing pool of a former King of Kings whose life, wealth and empire Alexander had destroyed. The end to the Great Conqueror was also close at hand, but how had it been brought about?[115]

Part Two

Warnings at Babylon

'ὤμοι εγω, κακον
όιον όρω τοδε και
δεχομαι
χερι δωμασιτ᾽ ἀμοις᾽

'Alas me! What tragedy I see and accept in my own hands,
in my own house!'
Euripides, *Andromache* (lines 1173–4)

Shortly after his great victory at Gaugamela in 331 BC, Alexander
had advanced on Babylon. He was very wary of its Persian satrap,
Mazaeus, Darius' ruler of the city, who had also commanded the
Persian right flank at Gaugamela. Alexander moved forward in full
battle order, his troops ready for any conflict. However, he was to
be pleasantly surprised. The Roman historian Quintus Curtius
provides a graphic description of the city and the reception awaiting
him.

'As Alexander was advancing towards Babylon, Mazaeus, who had
fled thither after the battle, came with his adult offspring, and
tendered the surrender of himself and the city. His overture was

gratifying: the siege of a place so strong would have been a tedious operation. Mazaeus' rank was illustrious, and his bravery acknowledged. He had distinguished himself in the recent action: such an example might induce others to submit. Alexander, therefore, courteously received him with his children. He, nevertheless, leading his army in person, formed it into a square, and cautioned it to enter the city in order of battle. On the walls stood a great proportion of the Babylonians, eager to behold their new sovereign. The majority went out to meet him. Among these was Batophanes, governor of the citadel, and keeper of the royal treasure. Unwilling that Mazaeus should surpass him in attention, Batophanes had strewn the road with flowers and garlands, and had placed on each side silver altars piled with frankincense and other costly perfumes. Intended presents followed him: droves of cattle and horses; lions in cages, and female leopards. The procession was continued by Magi chanting hymns; and by the Chaldaeans (the Chaldaeans make known the motions of the planets, and the revolutions which measure time). Then advanced the musicians with lyric instruments, whose office it was to sing the renown of their monarch. The train was closed by the Babylonian cavalry; the high wrought accoutrements of the men and horses were extravagant rather than magnificent.

'Alexander directed the multitude of citizens to follow in the rear of his foot. In a carriage, surrounded by his guards, he entered the city, and then repaired to the palace. On the following day, he began to take an account of the heirloom-furniture, and of all the treasure of Darius . . .

'In this capital the Macedonian leader halted longer than anywhere: no place proved more destructive of military discipline. No contamination can surpass the manners of the city; no systematic corruption can offer more stimulations and allurements to debauchery. Here parents and husbands, so as they be paid for the atrocity, can endure their children and wives to prostitute themselves to their guests. Throughout Persia, the chiefs and nobles take pleasure in licentious revels. The Babylonians are grossly addicted to wine, and the consequences of drunkenness. At the beginning of their feasts, the women are decorously habited; after an interval, they throw off their upper garment, and gradually proceed in violating modesty; at length (to use words the least disgusting) they lay aside the last veil. Nor is this the infamous practice only of the courtèsans, but of the matrons and their daughters, who regard this vile harlotry as an act of complaisance.'[1]

Quintus Curtius adds that the Macedonian troops received such a rapturous reception in such a decadent atmosphere that, had an enemy attacked, they would have been most vulnerable. Nevertheless, Alexander returned here in 323 BC and was not disappointed. Diodorus Siciulus writes, 'as on the previous occasion, the citizens received the troops most hospitably and everyone turned their attention to relaxation and pleasure.' Diodorus then adds, 'since everything necessary was available in profusion'. The last line is most telling. Babylon was strategically placed; it had defensible walls overlooking the fertile fields. Above all Alexander needed, especially after his disastrous retreat from India, an administrative centre to rule his sprawling empire. During his recent India campaign Alexander had been joined by a holy man Calanus. Plutarch describes how Calanus was amazed at the Great Conqueror's constant marching and, to make his point, Calanus picked up a dry, shrunken ox hide. When he stepped on the edge, other parts of the ox hide would roll up but, when Calanus placed his full weight in the centre, the ox hide flattened out completely. Alexander took the point; if his empire was not to fragment he needed to establish his rule from the centre.[2] According to Strabo the Geographer, 'Alexander did not regard Susa (another imperial city) as the royal residence but rather Babylon which he intended to develop even further.' And again in the sixteenth chapter of that same work, Strabo adds, 'At all events Alexander preferred Babylon since he saw it surpassed other cities in every respect.'[3]

Babylon was the home of the gods, the dwelling place of Bel-Marduk, a city vividly described by Herodotus and its palaces by Philostratus, a sightseer during the reign of Nero some 350 years later, who depicted the beauties and elegance of the royal buildings at Babylon in his *Life of Apollonius of Tyna*.[4] Babylon stood between the two great glittering serpents: the Tigris and Euphrates rivers. It was surrounded by lush lands dominated by the blue-green swaying palm trees. Water from the two great rivers flowed everywhere, brought in by a complex system of irrigation canals to fertilize the mastic, acacia, date and palm trees as well as the thick beds of rushes and the countless species of wild flowers and herbs. The walls of Babylon built by Nebuchadnezzar, destroyed by Xerxes and restored by later rulers, dominated the surrounding countryside. Herodotus described how these enamelled and painted fire-brick walls were so thick that the passageways between them seemed like cavernous tunnels, sealed off by huge bronze doors and guarded by statues of dragons and bulls. Above the walls gleamed the copper domes of temples, palaces and the brooding towers of the ziggurats, the high mounds on which the Babylon temples were built. The streets ran straight, cutting past houses built three or four storeys high. The city was so arranged that each street was close to the city wall and, more importantly, to one of the many narrow bronze doors which gave access to water. Babylon's fortifications defined the city and protected it. Little wonder that Alexander chose it as a potential capital. He had laid siege to great cities and recognized the strength of walls on which four horse chariots could pass each other without hindrance; such fortifications would provide superb defence against any enemy. Babylon also enjoyed an imperial grandeur. Beyond the walls, leading into the city proper, rose the beautiful Ishtar Gate, encrusted with precious lapis-lazuli and guarded by lions and dragons painted in a variety of colours. Near this was the principal ziggurat – the temple mound which had once supported the pure gold statue of the God Bel-Marduk, until Xerxes seized it and melted it down for his own treasure. Alexander had vowed to restore this temple mound to all its former glory.

On returning to Babylon in 323 BC, Alexander would have followed the Sacred Way down to the palaces described by Apollonius of Tyna, where the apartment walls were decorated with gold, silver and precious carvings of rosettes and palmettes. These palaces owned their own paradises: the rich black soil supported fresh lawns, orchards, groves and gardens interspersed with luxurious pavilions, fountains and gold-edged pools of purity. The asphalt courtyards were sprinkled three times a day by slaves emptying sheepskins of water to keep the ground cool. This place of opulence was Alexander the Great's last resting place and yet, despite its beauty, haunted by warnings and omens.

Alexander's Indian campaign of 326 BC had provoked a serious mutiny. It had ended with the retreat through the scorching, snake-infested Gedrosian Desert where tens of thousands had died. This setback marked the beginning of the portents and omens about his death. As Alexander was superstitious and religious to the point of mania, he was deeply disturbed by these. He had a legion of seers, sorcerers and soothsayers led by Aristander of Telemesus who had held a similar position at the court of Alexander's parents.[5] Alexander's religious preparations before he launched his invasion across the Hellespont were breathtaking and exemplified his religious neuroses: he had held a nine-day festival at Dium, sacrifices on the Elaeum Peninsula, the sacrifice of a bull while crossing the straits, and on his arrival in Asia more oblations, as well as at Troy. Such activities reveal a highly superstitious man, an undoubted legacy of his redoubtable mother.[6]

Omens and portents dominated Alexander's campaigns. When he laid siege to the city of Tyre in 332 BC, Alexander dreamed that he was chasing an elusive satyr and that he eventually caught him. Plutarch reports how when Alexander's seers were presented with the details of this dream, they were completely mystified but then produced an ingenious solution. They pointed out how the first syllable of satyr, SA ($\sigma\alpha$) means 'yours' in Greek, whilst the second ($\tau\upsilon\rho\varsigma$) meant 'Tyre'.

'My lord,' they declared. 'The dream means Tyre will eventually be yours.' The city was stormed, fell and was completely razed. Tens of thousands were slaughtered and at least 2,000 of its defenders cruci-fied along the seashore, 'As a warning,' Curtius says, 'to other cities of the area.' Thirty thousand of its inhabitants were sold to slavery, though Alexander decreed that anyone who took refuge in a temple would be immune.[7] Alexander had begun the siege of Tyre by demanding its citizens allow him sacrifice to Hercules. They refused, so their city was annihilated. A short while later Alexander made the same request of the eunuch Batis, commander of Gaza, another Phoenician city. Alexander was refused so he laid siege. During the preparations to take the city, a bird dropped a stone on Alexander's head. When asked what this signified, Aristander, that guru among the legion of the king's prophets, replied that the city would be taken but at a great personal cost to the king. Aristander was proved correct. Quintus Curtius reports how during the siege Alexander was hit by a slingshot, hurled with such violence that it pierced both shoulder and body armour to inflict a serious shoulder injury. A short while later, when his sappers had breached part of the wall, Alexander received further wounds to his leg. He recovered to lead a storming party into the city. The entire garrison was put to the sword and the civilian population sold into slavery. (Batis was reserved for more special punishment, and Curtius provides the graphic details: holes were made through Batis' feet and ropes threaded through them. His body was then tied to Alexander's chariot and he was dragged at its tail in front of his destroyed city until dead.)[8] In the Great Conqueror's mind, religion and battle went hand-in-hand. Plutarch paints a grim scene of Alexander and his sorcerer Aristander sacrificing to the dark God Phobos, the God of Fear, before the Battle of Gaugamela: 'Alexander . . . spent the night in front of his tent in the company of his diviner Aristander with whom he performed certain mysterious sacred ceremonies and offered sacrifices to the God of Fear.'[9]

Nevertheless, if Alexander was prey to such superstition, he was the first to recognize it himself. More importantly, if superstition or the affairs of the Gods impeded his ambition, they would always take second place to that ambition. The treatment of Batis showed that Alexander's superstition did not encompass the dignity of human life. Nor, when he burnt Thebes, did Alexander pay attention to the city being sacred to Dionysius. Alexander was faced with a similar problem when dealing with the Gordian Knot in 333 BC, a year before his attack on Tyre and Gaza. The town of Gordium owned a legendary wagon dedicated to Zeus; allegedly, this once belonged to the mythical Midas and the wagon's yoke was bound to a pole by a large complex knot of thickened vine twig without any visible ends. It was virtually impossible to untie, but the prophecy declared that the man who loosened the knot would rule all Asia. Alexander was challenged by this. A number of versions exist about what he did next, but Alexander, frustrated, would not be bound by custom or religious practice. He studied the knot, realized that he couldn't undo it, so drew his sword, slashed the knot in two and so solved the problem.[10]

Indeed, Alexander, in a temper of ambition, became a different man. Quintus Curtius describes how, in India, Alexander was impatient to take a fortified town holding out against him. A soothsayer warned him either to abandon the siege or postpone it because of possible danger to Alexander's life.

'Look,' Alexander retorted heatedly, 'when you are busy about your mysteries inspecting the innards of some animal, you would be rather annoyed if someone interrupted you, wouldn't you?'

The soothsayer quickly agreed.

'Well,' Alexander replied, 'can you imagine that a mind like mine, concerned about more important matters than a sheep's entrails, can find nothing more annoying than a superstitious, interfering soothsayer. Now, get out of my way.'[11]

Alexander, therefore, veered between deep superstition and downright cynicism. The same happened when he faced an array of auguries at Babylon in 323 BC. Alexander couldn't decide what attitude to adopt, as if he knew that once he accepted omens, the floodgates would be opened: a fact not lost on anyone who knew Alexander's mind and wanted to darken the Great Conqueror's mood with a sense of impending disaster. Omens, of course, have another purpose: they are very useful, in hindsight, for explaining how actual events were the work of the Gods, or the web of fate, rather than human ingenuity.

The warnings about Alexander's death seemed to surface either during or after his disastrous Indian campaign. According to Plutarch, while his army was on the march, Alexander had become alarmed by reports that a sheep had given birth to a lamb with an image of a tiara on its head. On each side of this were growths like teats. 'Looking upon the prodigy with horror, Alexander consulted his Chaldaean magicians. After a great deal of discussion, the king informed his Companions that he was more troubled for their sake than for his own as he was afraid how, after his death, Fortune would throw the empire into the hands of some obscure weak man.' It was rather surprising for Alexander to be so thoughtful about what might happen after his death. This could be the first early sign that he was aware of a growing discontent amongst his commanders, so he responded with a veiled warning of his own about what might happen should he be removed. In the end, however, such warnings did not hinder those who plotted against Alexander's life.[12]

During the Indian campaign Alexander's entourage had been joined by the holy man Calanus, who then stayed with the Macedonians during their retreat from India. In 324 BC, a year before Alexander's own death, Calanus fell ill at Persis. He was seventy-three years of age and declared that he intended to cremate himself rather than be party to his gradual deterioration. Alexander protested, but Calanus was insistent, so Ptolemy was ordered to build a funeral pyre. Calanus peacefully approached this, made sacrifice and told the Macedonians to rejoice. According to Strabo, Calanus 'embraced the rest of the King's entourage but refused to take leave of his royal friend saying he would see him again in Babylon'. Apparently Alexander was deeply disturbed by this, he was 'robbed of serenity by superstitious fears and . . . offered daily sacrifice to propitiate the menacing gods'. A short while later Alexander's great friend, Hephaestion, died at Ecbatana of symptoms very similar to those Alexander himself suffered in his final illness. The king was stricken with grief and, according to Diodorus, ordered

all the peoples of Asia to quench what the Persians call the sacred fire until such time as the funeral shall be ended. This was the custom of the Persians when their kings died but many thought the order was an ill omen and that heaven was foretelling the King's own death.[13]

After Hephaestion died, Alexander ordered his friend's embalmed corpse to be taken before him by Perdiccas, a senior general, to Babylon for a lavish funeral. Alexander followed on behind. Even before he had entered the city, Alexander was warned how dangerous

Babylon would be for him. Plutarch reports 'that a host of crows fell to the ground'. Arrian reports 'how the Chaldaean magicians came out of the city to warn Alexander not to enter'. Alexander dismissed them saying, 'Prophets who guess correct are the best,' a line from Euripides which showed that Alexander, at the time, did not take such warnings too seriously. Diodorus Siculus, however, gives a more detailed story.[14]

Alexander prepared his army and marched towards Babylon in easy stages, interrupting the march frequently to rest the army. While he was still 300 furlongs from the city, the wise men called Chaldaeans, who have gained a great reputation in astrology and are accustomed to predict future events by a method based on age-long observations, chose from their number the eldest and most experienced. By the configuration of the stars they had learned of the coming death of the king in Babylon, and they instructed their representatives to report to the king the danger which threatened. They told their envoys also to warn the king that he must, under no circumstances, enter the city; that he might escape the danger if he restored the tomb of Bel-Marduk which had been demolished by the Persians, but he must abandon his planned route and pass the city by.

The leader of the Chaldaean envoys was not courageous enough to approach the king directly but secured a private audience with Nearchus, one of Alexander's Friends, and informed him of everything in detail, asking him to convey it to the king. After Alexander learned from Nearchus about the Chaldaeans' prophecy, he was anxious and grew more and more disturbed as he reflected upon the ability and high reputation of these people. After some delay, he sent most of his Friends into Babylon, but changed his own route so as to avoid the city, and set up his headquarters in a camp at a distance of 200 furlongs.

This act caused general astonishment and many of the Greeks came to see him, notably among them the philosophers, including Anaxarchus. When they discovered the cause for his action, they plied him with arguments drawn from philosophy and changed him to the degree that he came to despise all prophetic arts, and especially that held in so high regard by the Chaldaeans. It was as if the king had been wounded in his soul and then healed by the words of the philosophers, so that he now approached Babylon with his army.[15]

Alexander entered Babylon, enjoying its opulence, and became involved with the pressing affairs of empire. Nevertheless, the omens and the portents did not diminish. Arrian, quoting one of his sources Aristobulus, provides the following interesting story.

Apollodorus of Amphipolis, one of Alexander's Companions, commander of the force which Alexander left behind with Mazaeus, the satrap of Babylon, wrote to Peithagoras his brother, one of those seers who prophesy from the flesh of victims, to prophesy also concerning his own welfare. Peithagoras then wrote in answer to him asking who it was that he chiefly feared, that he wanted the help of prophecy. Apollodorus replied that it was the king himself and Hephaestion. Peithagoras then sacrificed first in the matter of Hephaestion; and as the lobe could not be seen on the liver of the victim, he reported this, and sealing his letter sent it to Apollodorus from Babylon to Ecbatana, assuring him that he had nothing to fear from Hephaestion, for in a short time he would be removed from his path. This letter, Aristobulus says, Apollodorus received on the day before Hephaestion died. Then Peithagoras sacrificed again in the matter of Alexander, and for Alexander also the liver of the victim showed no lobe. Peithagoras then sent a similar letter to Apollodorus about Alexander. Apollodorus did not keep his counsel, but told Alexander the news he had received, with the idea of showing a kindness to the king, by advising him to beware lest any danger should at this time come upon him. He states further that Alexander thanked Apollodorus and, when he reached Babylon, asked Peithagoras what particular warning caused him to write thus to his brother. He replied that he found the liver of the victim without a lobe. Then when Alexander enquired what this sign portended, Peithagoras replied: 'Something very serious.' However, Alexander was far from being incensed against Peithagoras, but rather had a higher opinion of him for speaking the truth outright. This, Aristobulus says, he learned at first hand from Peithagoras.[16]

If this wasn't bad enough, Alexander's detailed preparations for his new campaign were interrupted by more signs from heaven. Diodorus Siculus gives a graphic description of one of them.

Once, when the king was being massaged with oil and the royal robe and diadem were lying on a chair, one of the natives who was kept in chains was spontaneously freed from his fetters, escaped his guards' notice, and passed through the doors of the palace with no one hindering. He went to the royal chair, put on the royal dress and bound his head with the diadem, then seated himself upon the chair and remained quiet. As soon as the king learned of this, he was terrified at the odd event. He walked to the chair and, without showing his agitation, asked the man quietly who he was and what he meant by doing this. When he made no reply whatsoever, Alexander referred the portent to the seers for interpretation. He later put the man to death in accordance with their judgment, hoping that the trouble which was forecast by his act might light upon the man's own head. He picked up the clothing and sacrificed it to the gods to avert evil, yet he continued to be seriously troubled. He remembered the predictions of the Chaldaeans and was angry with the philosophers who had persuaded him to enter Babylon. He was impressed anew with the skill of the Chaldaeans and their insight, and generally railed at those who used specious reasoning to argue away the power of Fate.[17]

Arrian describes another instance.

Most of the tombs of the kings of Assyria are built in the lakes and in the marshlands. And as Alexander was sailing along the marshes, for he – as is said – was steering the trireme, a strong breeze blew off his sun-hat with a ribbon attached to it. The hat, being heavy, fell into the water, but the ribbon was carried off by the breeze and caught on a reed growing near a tomb of the ancient kings. This itself seemed an omen about his destiny. One of the sailors, however, swam off to fetch the ribbon. He removed it from the reed but could not carry it in his hands, since it would have become wet as he swam, so he tied it about his head and so brought it across. Most of the historians of Alexander say that he gave him a reward of a talent for his smartness, but bade them behead him, since the prophets so advised him not to leave alive that head which had worn the royal ribbon. Aristobulus, however, states that the sailor received the talent, but was flogged for fastening the ribbon about his head. Aristobulus also says that it was one of the Phoenician sailors who brought back to Alexander his ribbon; some say it was Seleucus (one of Alexander's leading generals) and that this prophesied the death of Alexander and great empire for Seleucus. For, at any rate, Seleucus was the greatest king of those who succeeded Alexander, and ruled over the greatest extent of territory, next to Alexander.[18]

Little wonder, Plutarch reported, how 'the anguish of Alexander's mind so increased that he almost despaired of heaven's help'. Matters were not helped when Alexander heard a story of how, in the royal menagerie, a donkey, possibly maddened by the heat, had broken free and kicked a magnificent lion to death. Plutarch reports,

Alexander gave himself up to superstition. His mind was so preyed upon by vain fears that he turned the least thing, which was anyway strange and out of the way, into a sign of a prodigy. His court swarmed with sacrificers, purifiers and seers, they could all be seen there exercising their different talents.[19]

Of course, portents and omens can be read retroactively into any great event whilst hindsight makes prophets of us all. However, just as significantly, omens and portents can be fashioned as psychological weapons to torment the mind of the victim. Alexander, despite all his superstition, would have appreciated the 'bon mot' of the Roman poet Claudian, 'I know the meaning of the wise Egyptian runes and the arts whereby the Chaldaeans impose their will upon the subject gods.'[20] Alexander was not above doing that himself. Curtius reports how when Alexander wanted to cross the Jaxartes River, he was privately warned by Aristander that the auguries were not good. Aristander then made the mistake of letting slip publicly what he had confided to the king. Alexander was, understandably, furious. Aristander left the tent only to come hastening back a short while later to report that he had sacrificed again and the auspices were the best he had ever seen.[21]

Omens and portents, as reported by most of the principal authorities, came thick and fast during the last few weeks of Alexander's life at Babylon. Now such phenomena are beloved by the chroniclers as much as they are by soothsayers. Even today, when a leading politician like Kennedy is assassinated, people look back and pluck at this and that as a definitive warning of what was going to happen. What is remarkable about the portents and omens at Babylon is how many of them seem to be associated with Alexander's leading commanders. According to Diodorus, the Chaldaean prophecies were brought to Alexander's attention by the admiral of his fleet and boyhood companion, Nearchus. Another commander, Apollodorus, was involved in making sacrifices which allegedly indicated that something terrible was about to happen. The story of the king's hat is bound up with Seleucus, another Companion of Alexander, who seized part of the empire after Alexander's death. Finally, the incident involving the stranger occupying the king's throne shows a remarkable laxity in those who were supposed to guard the king, Companions such as Ptolemy who, according to many sources, was given the direct responsibility for the king's safety, even to guarding his tent personally.[22] In my view these portents and omens were deliberately targeted at a king tired and exhausted after a campaign and still suffering the mental trauma of losing his bosom friend Hephaestion a year earlier, whilst another close friend and ally, General Craterus, was now marching back to Macedon with 10,000 veterans bound for retirement. By late summer 323 BC, Alexander was highly vulnerable, depressed, lacking the personal security of his two best friends. Indeed, the portents and omens were not so much a warning about the king's death, as the articulation of rumour and gossip that something even more hideous was about to happen.

Part Three

The Death of a God

'Οιμοι καθ' έλλαδ ώς κακως νομιζεται σταν τροπαια
πολεμιων στηση στρατος όυ των πονουντων τουργου
ήγουνται τοδε άλλό στρατηγος την δοκησιν άρυται'

'Oh how strange the customs are in Greece! When the troops
display trophies over an enemy, the people don't regard this as
the achievement of those who've done the deed. Instead, the
general receives the honour.'
Euripides, *Andromache* (lines 693–6, the verses Cleitus quoted
before he was killed)

Alexander fell suddenly ill on 29 May 323 BC. His condition grew
rapidly worse and he died on 10 June. To establish the true cause and
circumstances of his death, a careful analysis of the source material is
essential.

Quintus Curtius
'From a splendid entertainment which he had given to Nearchus and
the captains of the fleet, Alexander, retiring to rest, was met by
Medius of Larissa. This officer, prolonging at his own board a

separate feast to his friends, strenuously invited the king to honour the sitting. Alexander remained with the party of Medius the rest of the night, and all the following day, in the course of which he drank a cup to each of the twenty guests. The indisposition under which he was carried from the scene of excess incessantly increased in violence; and, on the sixth day, disease had nearly exhausted in him the powers of nature. Meanwhile, the anxious soldiers obtained admission to his presence. As they saw him, their tears flowing, they presented the appearance, not of an army of visitors to their king, but of mourners over his grave. Of the circle round his bed the grief was eminently full: as Alexander beheld them, "When I am gone, where," said he, "will you find a king worthy of such men?"

'It transcends belief, that in the sitting posture to which he had raised himself when the troops were admitted, he remained till the whole army, to the last man, had saluted him. The multitude dismissed, as discharged from the last debt of life, he threw back his weary frame.

'His friends having been bidden to approach close, for his voice began now to fail, his signet drawn from his finger he delivered to Perdiccas, accompanied with an injunction to convey his body to Hammon (Ammon of Siwah). To those enquiring, "To whom he devised the empire," he answered: "To the most worthy . . . I already foresee, in that debate, mighty funeral games prepared for me." Asked by Perdiccas, "When he willed that divine honours should be paid him," he replied, "When themselves were happy." These were the last words of the king: soon afterwards he expired.'[1]

Diodorus Siculus

'. . . he was then invited by Medius, the Thessalian, one of his Friends, to take part in a *comus*. There he drank a great deal of unmixed wine in memory of the death of Hercules and, finally, filling a great cup, downed it in one gulp. Instantly he cried aloud as if pierced by violent pain. Alexander was escorted by his Friends, who led him by the hand back to his apartments. His chamberlains put him to bed and tended him closely but the pain increased so the physicians were called. None was able to assist and Alexander continued in severe discomfort and acute suffering. At length, despairing of life, he took off his ring and entrusted it to Perdiccas. His Friends asked: "To whom do you leave the kingdom?" He replied: "To the strongest." These were his last words: that all of his principal Friends would stage a vast contest in honour of his funeral.'[2]

Arrian

'Alexander had offered the usual sacrifices to the Gods in thanksgiving for good fortune and partly as a result of the prophets' advice. He was feasting with his friends and drinking late into the night. He also shared the victims of sacrifice and wine with the army, distributing them to their units and cohorts. Some reports allege he desired to leave the carouse and retire to his bedroom. However, Medius, one of his most trusted Companions at that time, met him and invited him to come and take wine with himself as it would be a lively party.

'In fact, the Royal Diaries report it this way: that he drank and caroused with Medius. Afterwards he rose and bathed, went to sleep, and later dined with Medius. He again drank till late in the night and, leaving the carouse, bathed. After bathing he ate a little and slept just where he was [the bath house], the fever already taking hold. However, he was taken by a litter each day to his religious duties and sacrificed according to his usual routine. After attending to these sacrifices he lay down in the men's quarters till nightfall. In the meantime, he instructed the officers about the planned march and voyage. One was to prepare to march three days later, and the others, who would leave with him, to sail on the fourth day.

'Afterwards, he was carried on his litter to the river. They embarked on a boat and sailed across to the garden where he again bathed and rested. Next day again he bathed and offered the customary sacrifices. He then retired to his room, lay down and conversed with Medius. He bade his officers meet him next morning early. He then dined lightly; was carried back to his chamber where he remained in a high fever the whole night. The next day he bathed, and after this sacrificed. He then explained to Nearchus and the other officers all about the voyage, planned for three days' time and how it was to be managed. On the following day, he bathed again, and sacrificed. Afterwards, he summoned his officers and instructed them to ensure all was ready for the voyage. He bathed in the evening, and after bathing, became very ill. Next day he was again carried to the house near the bathing place. He sacrificed and, although very ill, he summoned his principal officers and again briefed them about the voyage. The following day, he was carried out to do sacrifice and still continued instructing his officers about the voyage. Next day also, being very ill, he still made the usual sacrifices. He ordered, however, the generals to wait in the court, and the commanders of thousands and half-thousands to wait before the doors. When the officers came in he recognized them, but could no longer speak. He remained in high fever the next two days and nights. All this is written in the Royal Diaries. His soldiers wanted to see him. Some hoped to see him alive. Others because there was a rumour that he'd already died and they suspected this was being concealed by the bodyguards. Most, however, moved by grief and a desire to see their king, softly pushed in to see Alexander. Apparently, he was already speechless when the army filed by, though he greeted each one, raising his head with difficulty and speaking to them with his eyes. According to the Royal Diaries, an all-night vigil was kept [in the temple of Serapis] by Pithon, Attalus, Demophon and Peucestas, with Cleomenes, Menidas and Seleucus. They asked the God whether Alexander should be brought into the temple for prayer and so be healed. An Oracle was delivered by that God, that Alexander should not be brought into the temple as it would be better for him if he stayed where he was. This was what the Companions announced. Shortly afterwards, Alexander breathed his last: this, after all, being the "better" thing. Apart from this, neither Ptolemaeus [Ptolemy] nor Aristobulus have reported anything else. Some, however, claim that his Companions asked him to whom he left his kingdom. Alexander replied, "to the best." Others claim that he added that he saw that there would be a great funeral contest over his death.'[3]

Plutarch

'One day, after he had given Nearchus a sumptuous treat, he went, according to custom, to refresh himself in the bath, in order to retire and rest. In the meantime, Medius came and invited him to take part in a comus, and he could not refuse him. There Alexander drank all that night and the next day, till at last he found a fever coming upon him. This fever did not, however, seize him as he was drinking the cup of Hercules, nor did he find a sudden pain in his back, as if it had been pierced with a spear. These are circumstances invented by writers, who thought the catastrophe of so noble a tragedy should be something exciting and extraordinary. Aristobulus tells us, that in the rage of his fever and the violence of his thirst, he took a draught of wine, which threw him into a frenzy, and that he died in the thirtieth of the month Daesius [June according to the Macedonian calendar].

'In his journals (the Royal Diaries) the account of his sickness is as follows: "On the eighteenth of the month Daesius, finding the fever upon him, Alexander lay in his bathroom. The next day, after he had bathed, he removed into his own chamber, and played many hours with Medius at dice. In the evening he bathed again, and after having sacrificed to the Gods, he ate his supper. In the night the fever returned. The twentieth, he also bathed, and after the customary sacrifice, sat in the bath-room, and diverted himself with hearing Nearchus tell the story of his voyage, and all that was most observable with respect to the ocean. The twenty-first was spent in the same manner. The fever increased, and he had a very bad night. The twenty-second, the fever was violent. He ordered his bed to be removed, and placed by the great bath. There he talked to his generals about the vacancies in his army, and desired they might be filled up with experienced officers. The twenty-fourth he was much worse. He chose, however, to be carried to assist at the sacrifice. He likewise gave orders that the principal officers of the army should wait within the court, and the others keep watch all night without. The twenty-fifth he was removed to his palace, on the other side of the river, where he slept a little, but the fever did not abate; and when his generals entered the room he was speechless. He continued so the following day. The Macedonians, by this time, thinking he was dead, came to the gates with great clamour, and threatened the great officers in such a manner that they were forced to admit them, and suffer them all to pass unarmed by the bedside. The twenty-seventh, Pithon and Seleucus were sent to the temple of Serapis, to enquire whether they should carry Alexander thither, and the deity ordered that they should not remove him. The twenty-eighth in the evening he died." These particulars are taken almost word for word from his diary.'[4]

Justin

'Returning, therefore, to Babylon, and allowing himself several days for rest, Alexander renewed, in his usual manner, the entertainments which had been for some time discontinued, resigning himself wholly to mirth, and joining in his cups the night to the day. As he was returning, on one occasion, from a banquet, Medius, a Thessalian, proposing to renew their revelling, invited him and his attendant to his house. Taking up a cup, he [Alexander] suddenly uttered a groan while he was drinking, as if he had been stabbed with a dagger, and being carried half dead from the table, he was excruciated with such torture that he called for a sword to put an end to it, and felt pain at the touch of his attendants as if he had wounds all over. His friends reported that the cause of his disease was excess in drinking. On the fourth day, Alexander, finding that death was inevitable, observed that "he perceived the approach of the fate of his family, for the most of his kin had died, under thirty years of age". He then pacified the soldiers, who were making a tumult, from suspecting that the king was the victim of a conspiracy, and after being carried to the highest part of the city, admitted them to his presence, and gave them his right hand to kiss. While they all wept, he not only did not shed a tear, but showed not the least token of sorrow; so that he even comforted some who grieved immoderately, and gave others messages to their parents; and his soul was as undaunted at meeting death, as it had formerly been at meeting an enemy. When the soldiers were gone, he asked his friends that stood about him, "whether they thought they should find a king like him?" All continuing silent, he said that, "he knew, and could foretell, and almost saw with his eyes, how much blood Macedonia would shed in the disputes which would follow his death, and with what slaughters, and what quantities of gore, they would perform his obsequies." At last he ordered his body to be buried in the temple of Jupiter Ammon. When his friends saw him dying, they asked him "whom he would appoint as the successor to this throne?" He replied, "The most worthy." Such was his nobleness of spirit, that though he left a son named Hercules, a brother called Arridhaeus, and his wife Roxane was with child, yet, forgetting his relations, he named only "the most worthy" as his successor; as though it were unlawful for any but a brave man to succeed a brave man, or for the power of so great an empire to be left to any but approved governors. But as if, by this reply, he had sounded the signal for battle among his friends, or had thrown the apple of discord amongst them, they all rose in emulation against each other, and tried to gain the favour of the army by secretly paying court to the common soldiers. On the sixth day from the commencement of his illness, being unable to speak, he took his ring from his finger, and gave it to Perdiccas: an act which soothed the growing dissension among his friends; he seemed intended to be so in Alexander's judgment.'[5]

The story of Alexander's death could be put down to alcoholic excess: indeed this is, according to Justin, what his Friends (the Companions) were publishing to his army. Such drinking bouts had been reported by another fragment of the Royal Diaries, not quoted by Arrian; this time it's the Roman writer Aelian referring to events which took place the previous year in the month of Daesius.

The things about Alexander that are not good. They say that on the fifth of the month Daesius, he drank at Eumenes'; then on the sixth he slept from the drinking; and as much of that day as he was fresh, rising up, he did business with the officers about the next day's journey, saying that it would begin early. On the seventh he was a guest at Perdiccas' and drank again, on the eighth he slept. On the fifteenth of the same month he also drank, and on the following day he did the things customary after drinking. On the twenty-fourth he dined at Bagoas'; the house of Bagoas [a Persian eunuch, friend of Alexander] was ten stades from the palace; then on the twenty-eighth he was at rest.

Accordingly one of two conclusions must be true, either that Alexander hurt himself badly by drinking so many days in the month or that those who wrote these things lie. So it is possible to keep in mind henceforth that the group for which Eumenes is a member . . . make such statements.[6]

The garrulous Athenaeus of Naucratis extensively quotes from another source: Ephippus of Olynthus' book, in which Ephippus describes the fatal incident at Medius' party in great detail, and actually mentions Proteas, a well-known toper. The report is as follows:

Proteas of Macedon, also, drank a very great deal, as Ephippus says in his work, *On the Funeral of Alexander and Hephaestion*, Proteas enjoyed a sturdy physique throughout his life, although he was completely devoted to the practice of drinking. Alexander, for example, once called for a six-quart cup and, after a drink, proposed the health of Proteas. He took the cup, and when he had sung the king's praises he drank, to the applause of everybody. A little while afterwards Proteas demanded the same cup, and again drinking, pledged the king. Alexander took it and pulled at it bravely, but could not hold out; on the contrary, he sank back on his cushion and let the cup drop from his hands. As a result, he fell ill and died, because, as Ephippus says, Dionysus was angry at him for besieging his native city, Thebes.[7]

The problem with all these sources, and this applies to the entire life and career of Alexander of Macedon, is that, in the main, they were written hundreds of years later by Roman historians who drew from other more contemporary sources which only exist in fragments. Arrian, a governor under the emperor Hadrian, lived in the second century AD: his main source is the history by Ptolemy, one of Alexander's leading generals and later founder of the Ptolemaic Dynasty in Egypt, who probably published his work shortly before his death in 282 BC. Arrian often quotes Ptolemy (or Ptolemaeus) as he does Aristobulus, an official in Alexander's camp who also wrote a history, which is no longer extant, except in Arrian's work. A third source for Arrian were the Ephemerides or Royal Diaries. A great deal of controversy has raged regarding these. In the nineteenth century, scholars believed these Royal Diaries were the fragments of a greater work. Modern historians believe that the Diaries cover only the last two years of Alexander's life. Indeed there is a growing consensus that the Diaries, as regards Alexander's death, may have been an edited version, part of a propaganda campaign to provide an official account of what actually happened in the events surrounding Alexander's death.[8]

Diodorus Siculus was a Sicilian who lived in the first century BC and wrote his scholarly *Universal History*. Diodorus sometimes gets his dates wrong whilst modern scholars bitterly contest what sources he used. Quintus Curtius lived in the first century and Justin in the third century AD. All these had access to source material about Alexander though they do not have the same status as Plutarch who lived in the first/second centuries AD, the same period as Arrian, a scholar and biographer who had access to historians who were contemporaries of Alexander but whose accounts are no longer extant.

Nevertheless, all these sources provide a coherent picture of Alexander's last few days. There are differences between Arrian and Plutarch but, in the main, their stories agree. It would seem that there was general feasting in the army; Alexander had singled out Nearchus of Crete, his admiral, for special honour. Nearchus had been sent to explore the northern rim of the Indian Ocean. Alexander had believed for a while that both his admiral and fleet were lost on their return from India and was overjoyed when they reappeared safe and sound. In Alexander's new plans to conquer Arabia and advance along the North African coast, he had singled out Nearchus.

Once the official feasting was over, Alexander was about to retire, but Medius of Larissa invited him to a private party. Medius was a Thessalian, an officer in the fleet, a close friend and drinking partner of Alexander. Plutarch describes him as 'a leader and skilled master of the chorus of flatterers who danced around Alexander and were banded together against all good men'.[9] According to Ephippus, Medius' *comus* was quite a drinking party. From another source, to be discussed later, it would seem that there were about twenty guests at this private drinking party, including Perdiccas, Meleager, Pithon, Leonnatus, Cassander, Peucestas, Ptolemy, Philip the Physician and Nearchus of Crete: all close Companions, friends and leading officers in Alexander's entourage. In Diodorus' account, this is the occasion when the king fell ill. Diodorus gives a graphic description of Alexander sickening very abruptly.

There is confusion about what happened next. According to Arrian and Plutarch, the king recovered sufficiently to dine with Medius again but the fever continued. Alexander slept in the bathroom and then was taken across the river to another palace where he bathed and rested. For the next few days, Alexander's activities were limited to bathing, sacrificing, eating light meals and consulting principal officers, such as Nearchus, about the coming campaign, especially the despatch of the fleet. Only towards the end did Alexander agree to meet senior officers, but he was in such a high fever, he'd lost the power of speech and died some time on 9/10 June.

The cause of Alexander's death has been fiercely debated. Leukaemia, or malaria contracted from the swamps of the Euphrates, helped and assisted by alcoholic poisoning have been proposed. Most historians do agree that alcohol played a major part in Alexander's death, as it had in his life. Was uncut wine, therefore, the true cause of the Great Conqueror's death?

Part Four

Alexander, the Drunken Libertine?

'ἀλλ᾽ ἐι σ᾽ ἀφειην μη φρονουσαν, ὡς θανοις᾽

'If I let you die when you are out of your mind, what then?'
Euripides, *Andromache* (line 845)

Alexander's father Philip had been a hard drinker, and Alexander
soon proved to be the same. Plutarch, at first persuaded by his source
Aristobulus, maintained that Alexander was no toper: he writes 'his
entertainments lasted many hours but they were lengthened more
by conversation than by drinking'. In his later work *Moralia*, Plutarch
changed his mind. Alexander drank copiously and this led to changes
in his personality: 'When he was drunk he would sometimes become
offensive, sneering and arrogant. He would then sleep often until
midday and sometimes for the whole of the following day.' Curtius
says the situation became worse as Alexander grew older, 'he spent
his days as well as his nights at protracted banquets.' Wine, according
to Curtius, fanned Alexander's two great vices: 'his pride and his
temper'. Even Arrian, who hero-worshipped Alexander, sadly
concedes that Alexander became addicted to 'a new and barbarous
way of drinking'. Justin shrugs it off, declaring that Alexander was

just like his father, 'a lover of wine'.[1] Now in the Groves of Mieza, Aristotle must have talked about the classical Greek symposium, so beloved of Plato, with its intelligent discussion and discreet behaviour, a sharp contrast to the Macedonian *comus*, which was nothing more than a drinking spree where the wine was not watered, boasts were made, toasts offered and accepted, friends long gone remembered, heroes hailed and virtues saluted. These were warrior parties bustling with all the energy of military men relaxing and often drinking until they were senseless. They were marvellous occasions for flatterers such as Medius of Larissa, and Alexander appeared to love them.

Nevertheless, despite his drinking, Alexander was no Caligula or Nero, no dissolute Roman emperor lounging with the likes of Petronius, drinking black Falernian and engaging in every type of obscenity. The purpose of the *comus* was hard drinking and blunt talk. On some occasions, women were present – like the *comus* at Persepolis – when the Athenian courtesan, Thaïs, persuaded Alexander into burning the palace.[2] Alexander and his Companions, those generals and brigade commanders such as Perdiccas, Leonnatus and Attalus, were tough and hardened. They experienced all the rigour and horror of ancient warfare: night marches, the freezing snows of the highlands, the searing heat of the desert, hideous thirst, ravenous hunger, danger from snakebite, wild animals, violent storm and turbulent rivers. In many ways, these warriors are reminiscent of hardened gangsters yet they cannot be faulted for their truly breathtaking courage and stamina.

In such a society, where machismo was so admired, the leader had to excel above all others, be it on the battlefield or on the drinking couch. Alexander proved his remarkable skill in both areas. His superb charge at the Battle of the Granicus in 334 when he rolled up the Persian left wing, engaging members of Darius' high command in hand-to-hand combat, is an exhilarating hymn to his bravery and extraordinary horsemanship. Plutarch gives us a vivid description of this glorious charge.

In the mean time, Darius's generals had assembled a great army, and taken post upon the banks of the Granicus; Alexander was under a necessity of fighting there, to open the gates of Asia. Many of his officers were apprehensive of the depth of the river; and the rough and uneven banks on the other side, and when Parmenio objected to his attempting a passage so late in the day, Alexander replied, 'The Hellespont would blush, if, after having passed it, he should be afraid of the Granicus.' Alexander threw himself into the stream with thirteen troops of horse: and as he advanced in the face of the enemy's arrows, in spite of the steep banks which were lined with cavalry well armed, and of the rapidity of the river, which often bore him down or covered him with its waves, his motions seemed rather the effect of madness than sound sense. He held on, however, till by great surprising efforts, he gained the opposite banks which the mud made extremely slippery and dangerous. When he was there, he was forced to stand an engagement with the enemy hand to hand, and with great confusion on his part, because they attacked him and his men as fast as they came over, so he had no time to form them. For the Persian troops charging with loud shouts, and with horse against horse, made good use of their spears; and, when those were broken, of their swords . . .[3]

Naturally, Alexander's detractors were eager to ignore the above and depict him as an Oriental despot, ever ready to dress the part. Athenaeus, quoting the sharp-tongued Ephippus, describes how

Alexander used to wear the sacred vestments even at his entertainments. Sometimes he would wear the purple robe, cloven sandals, and the horns of Ammon, as if he were the god; and sometimes he would imitate Artemis, whose dress he often wore while driving in his chariot; having on also a Persian robe, but displaying above his shoulders the bow and javelin of the goddess. Sometimes also he would appear in the guise of Hermes; at other times, and indeed almost every day, he would wear a purple cloak, and a tunic shot with white, and a cap which had a royal diadem attached to it. When he was in private with his friends he wore the sandals of Hermes. He also often wore a lion's skin, and carried a club, like Hercules . . . And Alexander used to have the floor sprinkled with exquisite perfumes and with fragrant wine; myrrh was burnt before him, and other kinds of incense; and all the bystanders kept silent, or spoke only words of good omen, out of fear . . .[4]

In fairness, such an account must be contrasted with the description of Alexander during the opening phase of his invasion of India. Envoys from the city of Nysa arrived in the king's camp to find the Great Conqueror dressed like some common soldier, still armoured and covered in dust from head to toe. The envoys were so astonished to see such a formidable warrior dressed so commonly that they prostrated themselves silently before him: understandably Alexander was flattered and received them most graciously.[5]

It is important to stress that Alexander's drinking, even in the mouth of detractors such as Ephippus of Olynthus, was not an excuse for any sexual depravity or licentiousness. The rather priggish behaviour of his youth is offset by the remark of Plutarch, 'that sex and sleep reminded Alexander of his own mortality'. Alexander's personal relationships, be it as a lover or a comrade, appeared sacred to him: his friendship with his life-long friend, Hephaestion, has been the subject of much speculation.

Hephaestion was Patroclus to Alexander's Achilles; they were undoubtedly very close. Alexander introduced Hephaestion to Sisygambis, Darius' mother captured after the Battle of Issus, as 'another Alexander'. Whether Alexander regarded Hephaestion as a lover or twin brother has never been decided. However, Hephaestion enjoyed such favour that when Olympias grew jealous of him and attacked the king's close friend in her letters to her son, Alexander showed these to Hephaestion and allowed him to write a stinging reply with the stark warning, 'Stop quarrelling with us, do not be angry or threatening. If you persist we shall be most annoyed. You must realize that Alexander means more to us than anything.' Diodorus does not tell us what Olympias' reaction to such a letter was, but her fury can only be imagined. Diodorus adds that Alexander loved Hephaestion amongst all his group. 'In his lifetime Alexander preferred Hephaestion to all others.'[6]

Alexander may have had a homosexual affair with the Persian eunuch, Bagoas, once a close companion of Darius. Alexander appears to have been physically attracted to him even though the eunuch wielded a rather malign influence.[7] Alexander's sexual orientation must be kept in perspective. In ancient Macedonian culture the distinction between homosexual and heterosexual love was not so marked whilst Alexander's attitude to sexual matters appears to be quite pragmatic. Diodorus reports how before he left for Asia, Parmenio, the senior general of the army, insisted that Alexander protect the succession by marrying and begetting a son. Alexander drily replied that he simply didn't have the time to marry, settle down and wait for the birth of a child.[8] Dominated by the formidable Olympias, Alexander, certainly on a personal level, showed great respect for women. He treated Darius' captured kinswomen with extreme chivalry whilst he gave both Sisygambis and Ada, Queen of Caria, the title of 'mother'. Alexander did, eventually, enjoy a deep intimate relationship with women, including the Athenian courtesan Thaïs. He fell in love with Barsine, the widow of his opponent, the Greek mercenary general, Memnon of Rhodes, after she was captured near Damascus following his great victory at Issus (333 BC). Barsine bore Alexander an illegitimate son, Heracles.

In the early spring of 327 BC, Alexander married Roxane ('Little Star'), daughter of the Persian satrap, Oxyartes. She became pregnant just before Alexander's death and later gave birth to a male child (Alexander IV). In 324 BC, when Alexander encouraged his own generals to take Persian wives, he took two himself: a daughter of Darius and a daughter of Artaxerxes, Darius' predecessor.[9] The all-conquering general saw his sexual preferences as a personal, very intimate matter, reserved for himself and nobody else, so woe betide anyone who tried to foist a lover on him. According to Diodorus, Alexander inherited Darius' harem

in number not less than the days of the year . . . outstanding in beauty . . . selected from all the women in Asia. Each night these paraded before the couch of the king so that he might choose one with whom he could lie.

Alexander exploited such a custom rather sparingly.[10] Plutarch also provides a telling insight into Alexander's sexual preferences and attitudes:

Philoxenus, who commanded his forces upon the coast, acquainted Alexander by letter, that there was one Theodorus, a Tarentine, with him, who had two beautiful boys to sell, and desired to know whether he chose to buy them. Alexander was so much incensed at this that he asked his friends several times, 'What base inclinations Philoxenus had ever seen in him, that he durst make him so infamous a proposal?' In his answer to the letter, which was extremely severe upon Philoxenus, he ordered him to dismiss Theodorus and his vile merchandise together. He likewise reprimanded young Agnon, for offering to purchase Crobylus for him, whose beauty was famous in Corinth. Being informed that two Macedonians, named Damon and Timotheus, had corrupted the wives of some of his mercenaries who served under Parmenio, he ordered that officer to enquire into the affair and, if they were found guilty, to put them to death, as no better than savages bent on the destruction of human kind.[11]

Nor was Alexander's drinking a nightly event. Wine certainly did not interfere with his duties as a general or as his courage as a soldier. During the siege of Tyre Alexander decided to make a night foray against some raiders who threatened his lines of communication. He took a small task force into the nearby hills. Alexander was accompanied by his old tutor Lysimachus who had encouraged Alexander in his identification as Achilles whilst Lysimachus had taken the name of Phoenix, the name of the tutor of Homer's great hero. Plutarch records what happened, giving as his source, one very close to Alexander, the chamberlain Chares.

Night came on, and, as the enemy was at no great distance, the king would not leave his teacher borne down with fatigue and the weight of years. Therefore, while Alexander was encouraging and helping Lysimachus forward, he was insensibly separated from his troops; they had a dark and very cold night to pass in an exposed and dismal situation. In this dire necessity, Alexander observed at a distance a number of scattered fires, which the enemy had lighted. So, depending upon his swiftness and activity, as well as being accustomed to extricate the Macedonians out of every difficulty by taking a share in their labour and danger, Alexander ran to the nearest fire. After having killed two of the barbarians who sat watching it, he seized a lighted brand, and hastened with it to his party, who soon kindled a great fire. The sight of this so intimidated the enemy, that many of them fled, and those who ventured to attack him, were repulsed with considerable loss.[12]

As a battlefield commander, Alexander was cunning, brilliant and composed. His conduct leading up to his great victory at Gaugamela in 331 BC depicts a general very much in control of himself, aware of what he had to achieve against a vastly superior enemy, a commander, ruthlessly determined to carry his battle plan through. Plutarch's description of Alexander on the morning of that historic battle is classic.

Alexander retired to rest in his tent, and he is said to have slept that night much sounder than usual; insomuch, that when his officers came to attend him the next day, they could not but express their surprise at it, while they were obliged themselves to give out orders to the troops to take their morning refreshment. After this, as the occasion was urgent, Parmenio entered his apartment, and standing by the bed, called him two or three times by name. When he awaked, that officer asked him, 'Why he slept like a man that had already conquered, and not rather like one who had the greatest battle the world ever heard of to fight?' Alexander smiled at the question, and said, 'In what light can you look upon us but as conquerors, when we have not now to traverse desolate countries in pursuit of Darius, and he no longer declines the battle.' In the face of such danger, Alexander showed his intrepidity and excellent judgment.[13]

Alexander's genius as a general, however, was not just his strategy, calmness or skills: what endeared him so much to his men was the way he led always from the front. He had nothing in common with those commanders who sat back and watched. Alexander, for all his drinking, was always in the heat of the frenzy. Diodorus gives a sterling account of Alexander's courage when the Macedonians were besieging a town in the province of Malli during the Indian campaign (325 BC). Alexander became impatient at his men's inability to scale and seize the walls of a town so he took charge himself. Diodorus vividly describes the violent hand-to-hand fighting which followed and nearly cost Alexander his life.

The Macedonians were still busy fighting along the wall. Alexander seized a ladder, leaned it against the walls of the citadel, and climbed up holding a light shield above his head. So quick was he that he reached the top of the wall before the defenders could prevent him. The Indians lacked the courage to close with him, but hurled javelins and fired arrows from a distance. Alexander was staggering under the weight of these blows when the Macedonians raised two ladders and swarmed up in a mass, but both ladders broke and the soldiers tumbled back upon the ground. The king was left alone, but courageously took a step which came as much a surprise as it is worthy of mention. Alexander considered it would be out of keeping with his reputation to retreat from the wall without achieving anything. Instead, he leapt down alone inside the town. The Indians thronged about him, but he confidently repelled their attack. He protected himself on the right by a tree growing close by the wall and, on the left, by the wall itself. He drove the Indians off, exhibiting such courage as would be expected from a king who had his record of success. He was determined to make this defence (if it were the last act of his life) a truly glorious one. He suffered many blows upon the helmet, not a few upon the shield. At last he was struck by an arrow below the breast and fell to one knee, overcome by the blow. Straightway the Indian who had shot him, thinking he was helpless, ran up and struck at him; Alexander thrust his sword up into the man's side, inflicting a mortal wound. The Indian fell, and the king grasped a branch close by and getting on his feet, defied the Indians to come forward and fight with him.[14]

Any warrior capable of such courage would drink to his own success and survival.

Three other factors must be taken into consideration in assessing Alexander's love of wine. First the influence of Philip and Alexander's innate rivalry with his father. Philip was a heavy drinker and reveller who openly rejoiced in the hard-drinking warrior culture of Macedon. Alexander had grown up in such an environment. He would have appreciated that such drinking bouts were a confirmation of the bonds of friendship which exist between warriors and shield comrades. When Callisthenes, Alexander's resident historian, chronicler and scribe, refused to participate in a *comus*, saying he didn't want to wake up with a hangover, such a remark was considered deeply discourteous and later held against him.[15] Secondly, Olympias' influence was also considerable. She encouraged devotion to Dionysius, God of Wine, who was also included in Alexander's ancestral tree. Devotion to Dionysius was all-pervasive in Macedon and the God of Wine was a favourite with the ordinary soldier. Time and again during his campaigns Alexander sacrificed to the God of Wine whilst he blames his terrible clash with Cleitus for not fulfilling his duties to Dionysius properly. Alexander knew the entire history of Dionysius. According to legend, the Wine God had travelled to India and the city of Nysa owned certain memorials to the God. Alexander had a 'great yearning' to see them and journeyed there with his senior officers. To their astonishment they found the garden area near the city rich with ivy so they fashioned wreaths out of this, and sang hymns to Dionysius, after which Arrian adds, 'some of the

Macedonians became possessed by Dionysius and were overwhelmed by a bacchic frenzy'. In other words, they became royally drunk.[16] Finally, these *comoi* must not be seen as a constant habitual drinking spree; neither the soldiers nor their commanders could have sustained the contrasting life of military hardship by day and heavy drinking at night. Alexander's parties, symposia or *comoi* were really what we would term the most flamboyant binges where the high command relaxed and let their hair down as the wine flowed.

On such occasions, the drinking was incessant and could be highly injurious to health and safety. After the horrors of his retreat through the Gedrosian Desert, Alexander reached the eastern province of the Persian Empire known as Carmania where, Strabo the Geographer tells us, the vineyards produce the most succulent grapes. Here, according to Diodorus, Alexander rested and, for the next week, led his troops in festive dress, feasting and drinking as they journeyed.[17] Curtius described it, 'as a seven day debauch'. The spicy details are provided by Chares, Alexander's chamberlain, and repeated by Plutarch.

> In this whole company there was not to be seen a buckler, a helmet, or spear; but, instead of them, cups, flagons and goblets. These the soldiers dipped in huge vessels of wine, and drank to each other, some as they marched along, and others seated at tables, which were placed at proper distances on the way. The whole country resounded with flutes, clarinets and songs, and with the dances and riotous frolics of the women. This disorderly and dissolute march was closed with very immodest figures, and with all the licentious ribaldry of the bacchanals, as if Bacchus himself had been present to carry on the debauch.[18]

Alexander's drinking parties, however, became increasingly dangerous, as the tensions and strains of his eleven-year campaign began to surface. Alexander and his generals faced incredible hardship and were dependent on each other for safety and security. The modern notion of 'cabin fever' would be dominant. Campaigning in unknown terrain, experiencing the savage vagaries of the weather, long periods of boredom abruptly shattered by highly dangerous, frenetic military activity would take its toll. The most serious incident was the confrontation between Alexander and 'Black' Cleitus, brother of the king's nurse. Cleitus was the king's personal bodyguard, a man who had saved Alexander's life during the Battle of the Granicus. He belonged to the old school, a gruff ruffian who didn't take too kindly to Alexander's increasingly Persian ways, his emphasis on his own grandeur and success, as well as his open declaration that Ammon was his father. In 328 BC at Samarkand, the confrontation between Alexander and Cleitus erupted. It was almost a repetition of the confrontation between Alexander and his own father at Philip's wedding party eight years earlier, only this time it ended in murder (see Part Five, p. 124 *et seq.*). Arrian claims the murder of Cleitus was down to anger and drink, and he points to the same vices when he describes the burning of Persepolis two years earlier in 330 BC.

Alexander and his army had destroyed the Persian military machine; they had swept through Darius' provinces and cities. Now they occupied the King of King's principal residence in the city of Persepolis. This palace included the Apanada, the Great Hall of Audience, which had been the very heart of the Persian Empire. Alexander and his commanders began to celebrate, and once again the drinking got out of hand. According to Diodorus, it was suggested they burn down the royal palace as an act of vengeance for the wrongs inflicted on Greece by Persia.[19] Curtius provides a graphic description of what happened next.

Inflamed with the spirit of the grape, all rose together to burn that splendid seat which they had spared when armed. The king led the destroyers, and fired the palace: then his guests, his servants, and his concubines applied their active flambeaux. The imperial structure contained a great quantity of cedar, which rapidly caught and widely communicated the flames. Now the army encamped not far from the town, perceiving the conflagration, and considering it to be accidental, hastened to give their services in extinguishing it: but when they had come to the portico of the palace, seeing the king hurling in a profusion of blazing combustibles, they dropped the water which they had brought, and augmented the fire with dry materials.[20]

Accordingly, the fatal drinking party held by Medius of Larissa in the royal palace of Babylon at the end of May 323 BC must be seen in the context of a pattern of such banquets and lavish drinking parties. By then those alcoholic carousals had acquired a sinister reputation as places where 'things might happen'. According to the sources there were two such parties on the night of 29 May: the official one to celebrate the imminent departure of Admiral Nearchus' expedition, and a second one hosted by Medius the flatterer at his own quarters in the palace. Medius was Alexander's drinking companion so his presence there was to be expected; he was also a high-ranking officer in the fleet and would have been in the company of his commander Nearchus. The other twenty guests at this private *comus* are listed in *The Alexander Romance*: Perdiccas, Meleager, Pithon, Leonnatus, Cassander, Peucestas, Lysimachus, Philip the Physician, Nearchus, Stasanor, Ptolemy, Olcias, Eumenes and Asander, Proteas, Medius, Seleucus, Antiochus, Attalus and Iolaus.[21] Alexander had retired from the earlier official banquet, a possible indication that he was feeling unwell. Arrian, quoting Aristobulus, claims that the king drank deeply because he already had a fever, but Aristobulus was Alexander's defender on the issue of alcohol. Moreover, it was common knowledge amongst the Greeks that, for someone with a fever, wine was strictly forbidden. Alexander himself had issued a similar instruction when Hephaestion had fallen ill of similar symptoms a year earlier. Of course, Alexander's fever may have broken out during the hours of feasting,[22] it might have been a viral infection or, as some have argued, a bout of malaria, picked up whilst boating through the marshy, mosquito-infested Euphrates.

It is remarkable, however, that, according to the sources, none of the other guests mentioned appear to have suffered such an infection, though commentators do point out that Alexander might have been weakened by years of war. The splendid athlete who had sprung from his flagship in the harbour of the Achaeans some eleven years earlier had suffered serious wounds. In 333 BC he had gone down with a virulent fever after bathing in the Cydnus River and had been cured by Philip the Physician. At Tyre and Gaza (332 BC), he had suffered injuries to his foot, leg and shoulder whilst a wound at Cyropolis in Samarkand had clouded his vision and given him a throat infection (328 BC). At Malli (325 BC), as we have seen, Alexander had been struck in the chest at close range by an arrow. Perdiccas had acted promptly and saved him by digging out the arrowhead with his sword, whilst the physician Critobulos had staunched the wound.[23] Psychological factors must also be taken into account as they can have a severe effect on health: particularly the sudden death of his close friend Hephaestion a year earlier, and the departure of Craterus – Alexander's lieutenant and leading commander – who was journeying back to Macedonia with 10,000 retired veterans. Both men would have played a vital role in Alexander's future plans. Hephaestion had welcomed the process of orientalization. He garbed himself in Persian dress and was Alexander's representative in dealing with his newly conquered subjects, whilst the more conservative Craterus was very popular with the Macedonians and was Alexander's mouthpiece with his troops.[24]

Alexander had other worries. In the last three years he had faced at least two serious mutinies; raising more troops was becoming increasingly difficult; there were troubles in Greece and a whole range of other problems, while, according to Plutarch, the sinister omens which had plagued the king since his arrival in Babylon would not have helped Alexander's delicately balanced state of mind. Nevertheless, Alexander's viral infection, supposed fever, or the effects of alcoholism appear to have had little influence on Alexander on that particular evening when he accepted Medius' invitation and joined in the general revelry. Athanaeus, quoting the mysterious source Nicobule, gives some insight into Alexander's state of mind during that fateful carousal.

At his very last banquet, Alexander, remembering an episode of *Andromache* by Euripides, recited it in a declaration, and then drank a cup of unmixed wine with great eagerness, and compelled all the rest to do the same.[25]

Accordingly, we have Alexander holding a banquet for his departing admiral, Nearchus. The king attends and he is about to retire when Medius of Larissa begs him to join a private party, a *comus*, in his apartment where most of Alexander's Companions have gathered. The champion Macedonian drinker, Proteas, has also been invited. Now Alexander could have been in the company of his 'Friends or Companions' when Medius issued the invitation, but the overall impression is that Medius, the professional flatterer, was the messenger boy sent to cajole Alexander to attend a surprise party where all his closest friends were gathered. As Arrian reports: some of these principal officers were about to leave within the next few days. The king seems hale and hearty. He is sober enough to consider the invitation, accept it, join in the revelry and recite, even act out, lines from a play by Euripides. He does not seem to be a man falling down drunk – especially at the beginning of Medius' party – or on the verge of some sort of serious fever, or viral infection.

What is agreed by virtually every source available is that Alexander appears to have abruptly fallen ill – and seriously so – during those celebrations in Medius' quarters. Diodorus Siculus, who rejects any suspicion of foul play, does describe a very dramatic change in this wine-quaffing king who can toast the likes of Proteas, all in the memory of Hercules, then quote from Euripides. Diodorus declares, 'filling a great cup, [Alexander] swallowed it in one gulp. Instantly he screamed aloud as if pierced by violent pain, and was escorted by his friends who led him by the hand back to his apartments.' Diodorus never mentions the word 'fever'. According to him, Alexander is not so much feverish as experiencing such hideous pain that he cannot walk straight, but has to hold the hands of his Companions, as if he had eaten or drunk something which had seriously harmed him. Diodorus is an excellent source. He ends his account proper of Alexander's life with that terrible scream, but then adds the most telling lines. 'The pains increased. The Physicians were summoned. None of these was able to assist. Alexander continued in great discomfort and acute suffering.' Justin also gives very precise symptoms which denote more than a mere fever. 'He was excruciated with such torture that he called for his sword to put an end to it, and felt pain at the touch of his attendants as if he had wounds all over' (see Justin's account in Part Three). Here we have a man who has crossed from Europe to Asia, a toughened warrior, still relatively young, a hardened drinker, but who is still capable of walking except that he has suffered shock, weakness, hideous pain and great discomfort.

Nevertheless, although the physicians are called, they appear to be baffled by these symptoms which Diodorus lists.

▶ Shock
▶ Pain
▶ Weakness
▶ Discomfort

There is no mention of fever. Plutarch had also read about this hideous scream but moved quickly to rebut it.

> Alexander drank all night. That night and the next day till he at last found a fever coming on him. It did not, however, seize him as he was drinking the cup of Hercules, nor did he experience a sudden pain in his back as if he had been pierced with a spear.

Plutarch's eagerness to reject such stories must be contrasted with Diodorus' more objective account, especially as Diodorus himself is not attempting to dramatize the situation and is equally dismissive of any foul play.

Over the years many theories have been put forward as to the cause of Alexander's death, the latest being a recent article and television programme which discount the conspiracy theory. Alexander is depicted as accidentally overdosing on the drug Hellebore. I find this difficult to accept. According to Plutarch, Alexander knew about the dangers of this drug and actually wrote to a royal physician who was treating Craterus with it to be most prudent in its use.[26]

Diodorus' description of shock, sudden pain, weakness and 'great discomfort' (which probably included vomiting and diarrhoea), however, are obvious symptoms of poisoning – arsenic poisoning to be precise – as are the symptoms which appear later: sweating, terrible thirst and skin problems (attested by Alexander's constant bathing). I shall discuss this possibility of arsenic poisoning as well as the possible dosage used, in more detail in Part Seven, but the real proof that arsenic was the cause lies in the condition of Alexander's corpse. He died in fairly hideous circumstances, at the height of a searingly hot summer in Babylon. In such an environment, any corpse would normally decompose very quickly; corruption would become obvious. Plutarch, desperate to reject the theory that his hero was murdered, makes an admission which actually proves the opposite.

Curtius reports the same:

Seven days Alexander's remains were lying trestled on a bier; the cares of the nobles diverted from his obsequies to the constitution of a government. No climate is more sultry than that of Mesopotamia; at its zenith, the festival sun kills the greater part of animals, not under shelter: so intensely torrid is the air, that every thing is scorched as by a fire: unfailing springs are so rare that the inhabitants draw from them by stealth, and conceal them by artifice from strangers. When, at length, Alexander's friends had leisure to attend the corpse, they perceived no symptom of corruption: the vivid hue of life had not left it. The Egyptians and Chaldaeans, appointed to embalm it, durst not, at first, operate on a body appearing to breathe. Afterwards, entreating that it might be unlawful for mortal hands to touch his relics, they proceeded to purify them: costly aromatics filled the coffin of gold, and the ensign of majesty was placed on the head of the embalmed.[27]

Arsenic and murder are close companions, while a strong tradition permeates the primary sources that Alexander of Macedon was assassinated and, given the evidence above, it is appropriate to study such a tradition. The accounts are as follows:

Quintus Curtius

'Most persons believed Alexander to have died from poison, and that one of the attendants of his table, Jollas [Iolaus], a son of Antipater, administered it, by his father's order. It is certain that Alexander had been frequently heard to say: "Antipater aspires after royalty: he is too powerful for a lieutenant: inflated with that mottoed plume, 'The Spartan Victory', he challenges as his due, all the honours which I bestow". It was surmised too, that the mission of Craterus, when he conducted home the band of veterans, was to remove Antipater. Such is the virus of a poison made up in Macedon, that it dissolves iron, and can be contained only in a vessel formed of a beast's hoof. The source of the pestiferous venom is the Arcadian Styx. Cassander brought some of this water, and delivered it to his brother Jollas (Iolaus), who infused it into the king's last cup. However these reports originated, they were soon stifled by the power of those whom their prevalence arraigned. For Antipater seized the kingdom of Macedon and the government of Greece; his son succeeded to his power, and slaughtered those who, by consanguinity, however remote, were allied to Alexander.'[28]

Diodorus Siculus

'Since some historians disagree about the death of Alexander, and declared this was the result of a draught of poison, it seems necessary for us to mention their account also. They claim that Antipater, who had been left by Alexander as viceroy, clashed with the king's mother Olympias. At first Antipater did not take her seriously because Alexander ignored her complaints against him but, later, as their enmity kept growing and the king showed an anxiety to gratify his mother in everything out of piety, Antipater demonstrated many indications of his disaffection. This was bad enough, but the murder of Parmenio and Philotas struck terror into Antipater as into all of Alexander's Friends. So, by the hand of his own son, who was the king's wine-pourer, he administered poison to the king. After Alexander's death, Antipater held the supreme authority in Europe and then his son Cassander took over the kingdom, so that many historians did not dare write about the drug.'[29]

Arrian

'I am aware, of course, of many other details recorded about Alexander's death; for instance, that Antipater sent him a drug, and that he died of this drug; that Aristotle concocted this drug for Antipater, already fearing Alexander on account of Callisthenes' death [executed for alleged treason against Alexander]; and that Cassander, Antipater's son, brought it. Others have even said that it was transported in a mule's hoof, and that Iolaus, Cassander's younger brother, gave it to Alexander. Iolaus was the royal cupbearer, and had some grievance against Alexander not long before his death; others, again, that Medius, due to an infatuation with Iolaus, was involved in the affair. After all, it was Medius who suggested the drinking session to Alexander. After it, Alexander had a sharp feeling of pain after drinking the cup and, on feeling this, he retired from the revelry. One writer has not even flinched from saying that Alexander, realizing he could not survive, went to throw himself into the Euphrates, so that he might disappear from the world and leave behind a tradition, more credible to posterity, that his birth was of the gods so that to the gods he returned. Roxane, his wife, however, saw that he was going out. When she prevented him, he cried aloud that she then grudged him everlasting fame as having been truly born a god. This must suffice of such stories; I merely show that I know of them, rather than because they are narratives worthy of belief.'[30]

Plutarch

'There was no suspicion of poison at the time of his death; but six years after (we are told), Olympias, upon some information, put a number of people to death, and ordered the remains of Iolaus, who was supposed to have given him the poison, to be dug out of his grave. Those who say Aristotle advised Antipater to such a horrid deed, and furnished him with the poison he sent to Babylon, allege one Agnothemis as their author, who is pretended to have had the information from King Antigonus. They add that the poison was a water of a cold and deadly quality, which distils from a rock in the territory of Nonacris; and that they receive it as they would do so many dew-drops, and keep it in an ass's hoof; its extreme coldness and acrimony being such, that it makes its way through all other vessels.[31]

Pseudo-Callisthenes

The one other source is a very famous work entitled *The Romance of Alexander the Great* by Pseudo-Callisthenes. This was probably the most popular account of Alexander's life and there are many versions in a score of different tongues. The *Romance* surrounds the life of Alexander with the most fantastic tales about his origin and life: I have studied the Armenian and Ethiopian versions. There is a great deal of similarity between them and a few notable differences. At first historians tended to regard the *Romance* for what it was: a fictional version of Alexander's life. But there is now a consensus that the *Romance*'s version of Alexander's death (as apart from the rest of the tale) is, in fact, a primary source, perhaps published and circulated somewhere between Alexander's death in 323 BC and the outbreak of hostilities between his successors in 321 BC. Robin Lane Fox, in his brilliant and lucid analysis of the *Romance* version of Alexander's death, calls it 'The Pamphlet' and subscribes to the theory that this 'Pamphlet', giving details of Alexander's death, was deliberately issued to spread the story that the Great Conqueror was poisoned. Robin Lane Fox claims 'The Pamphlet' should be regarded as one would a confidential 'official' memorandum on Stalin's death being found in a book of Russian fairy stories.[32]

'The Pamphlet' seems to have its origin in those two years between Alexander dying and his leading general Perdiccas declaring war on his rivals. Perdiccas' main rivals were Antipater, who remained as ruler of Macedon, and the latter's son Cassander. There is a great deal written about Perdiccas in the *Romance* where he is cast in a most favourable light – he is depicted as Alexander's confidant, the executor of his will, his possible successor, a man to whom Alexander entrusted his beloved Roxane. In the Armenian version, Perdiccas is described as one of those generals who attended Medius' banquet but had no knowledge of the poison plot. Others were equally innocent: Ptolemy, Olcias, Lysimachus, Eumenes and Asander. The Armenian is one of the early versions of the *Romance* and the different successors of Alexander used it to their own advantage. For example, in the Ethiopian version, Perdiccas is one of the murderers although Ptolemy remains innocent. However, the main thrust of 'The

Pamphlet' is basically the same as the poison story described by Plutarch, Diodorus Siculus and Arrian. It may be summarized as follows.

Alexander had arrived in Babylon and had been warned by the Chaldaeans that he faced great danger. A woman had given birth to a half-man monster, which she took to the Chaldaean priests who showed it to Alexander, telling him it was an evil augury; the king would die and, after his death, his generals would fall out with one another and there would be bloody slaughter. The writer goes on to describe the bitter feud raging in Macedon between the regent Antipater and Alexander's mother Olympias. She claimed that Antipater was doing what he wanted and publishing the most horrific slanders against her. Alexander, therefore, decided to go to Epirus where his mother was sheltering. In the meantime, however, Alexander sent his leading general Craterus to summon Antipater from Macedon to Alexander's court.

Antipater became aware of Alexander's plan and plotted the death of the Conqueror at the hands of his own sons. Antipater believed that the success had turned Alexander's mind and he had become highly dangerous. The *Romance* then describes how Antipater buys a gentian drug, a deadly potion so strong that it had to be boiled and stored in the hoof of a mule to preserve its potency. This was then placed in an iron box and given to Cassander, Antipater's son, to take to Babylon where Iolaus, Cassander's brother, was the king's cupbearer. Cassander arrives in Babylon. Shortly afterwards, Alexander had reason, so the *Romance* says, to strike Iolaus. This upset Medius who was Iolaus' lover.

The fatal banquet is held, some of the guests have no knowledge of the plot but the rest are all consenting. Iolaus gives Alexander the cup. 'Suddenly Alexander cries out as if he has been hit in the liver by an arrow.' For a short while Alexander could bear the pain and ordered the party to continue. He then tried to vomit and Iolaus gave him a feather, also soaked in the poison. Alexander now became very ill. Cassander and Iolaus left. Once they had, the *Romance* returns to the king's final moments. There is the story about Alexander dragging himself off to drown himself in the river but Roxane intervenes.

Alexander finally deals with his close friends, amongst whom the generals Perdiccas and Ptolemy are depicted in the best of lights. Alexander makes his will. He divides his empire, leaves instructions that his body is to be buried in Egypt and gives both his ring and Roxane to Perdiccas shortly before he expires. In many respects, 'The Pamphlet' of the *Romance* describes Alexander's death in such similar terms to the poison stories of Arrian and the rest that it may well be their source.[33]

Accordingly, there are these two conflicting traditions: the official version that Alexander of Macedon died from a mixture of high fever and alcohol, and what may be called the more dramatic version – that he was murdered by Antipater. He arranged for the poison to be given to the king through his two sons, Cassander and Iolaus who, in turn, had the secret support of certain high-ranking officers.

In the end, Plutarch, Diodorus Siculus and Arrian have carried the day with modern historians who tend to regard the stories of the king being murdered as fables or groundless propaganda.

Nevertheless, such sources must be scrutinized more closely. Diodorus Siculus, writing about 40 BC, holds the key to resolving the problems of the sources. A great deal of debate has centred upon which sources Diodorus himself used. The probable answer is that they were numerous – everything available. However, Diodorus carefully described what actually happened to Alexander: how he was drinking at Medius' party when he experienced shock, a stab of pain, weakness, increased pain and great discomfort, which puzzled his physicians. True, Diodorus does not claim Alexander was poisoned but neither does he say he was not. Diodorus' judgment remains neutral. He accepts that the poisoning story is mentioned by 'some historians' but, later on, adds the surprising statement that 'after Alexander died, many historians believed in the story that he was poisoned but dare not mention the drug out of fear of reprisal'. Diodorus, therefore, admits that many of his accounts, his primary sources, did not dare to carry the story of the poisoning out of fear of Cassander and Antipater, the very people named as part of the plot.

Quintus Curtius carries the same story, claiming that reports about Alexander being poisoned, 'were soon stifled by the power of those whom their prevalence arraigned'. Arrian simply mentions the stories to prove that he has heard of them 'rather than because they are narratives worthy of belief'. Plutarch is more vehement: 'there was no suspicion of poisoning at the time of his death.' 'The story of the poison is mere fable.'[34]

Nonetheless, Diodorus is correct. A fragment, still extant, reports that Onescritus, a naval officer who served directly under Medius, knew all about the poison plot, but dare not mention it out of fear and retaliation. The fragment reads as follows:

> It is not appropriate now to prove who they were [i.e. the partic-
> ipants at the banquet of Medius, at which Alexander was
> poisoned], whom Onescritus purposely left unmentioned,
> because he shunned their hatred. They were: Perdiccas, Medius,
> Leonnatus, etc.[35]

Macedon's old enemy, Athens, reacted with joy to news of Alexander's death. 'What!' one of its speakers declared. 'Alexander dead! Impossible! The whole world would be reeking from his corpse.' Another orator, Hyperides, moved a decree to honour Iolaus, Alexander's alleged murderer. In 321 BC, Antipater eventually overcame the Athenian army and seized the city. He sought out Hyperides, had him tortured, by cutting out his tongue, and killed him. He even refused to return his body for honourable burial in Athens.[36] The Hyperides incident demonstrates that, as early as 321 BC, the story of Alexander being poisoned by the House of Antipater was common knowledge throughout Greece, but to repeat such a story was highly dangerous, as Hyperides found to his cost. It is hardly surprising that other writers adopted a more circumspect approach. Of course Queen Olympias believed the poisoning account. In her war against the House of Antipater, she managed to seize Nicanor, Cassander's other brother, and executed him, whilst, once back in power, she dishonoured Iolaus' grave and scattered his remains.[37] However, in view of Olympias' intense hatred for Antipater, it is hardly surprising that she would accept such stories so readily.

A more considerable obstacle is the problem of Arrian and

Plutarch's resistance to the poisoning tale. Both these writers were Roman civil servants, writing in the second century AD during the reign of the benevolent and learned Emperor Hadrian. Arrian's glowing summary of Alexander's character, life and achievement borders on hero-worship. To Arrian, Alexander is the great general, the imperial statesman, the Colossus of History who possessed a vision of a universal peace in a universal state, an ideal to which the Roman Empire was also dedicated. Arrian was also conscious of the fate of Roman emperors who had been despots – Nero, Caligula and Domitian – they had all been assassinated. Tyrannicide was an accepted part of the political framework of the Ancient World. Arrian, and to a lesser extent Plutarch, could not accept that Alexander had been assassinated. Such an act might beg the question – What did Alexander do to cause such hatred and resentment as to lead to his own assassination? Of course, both Arrian and Plutarch could appeal to the sources before them but what are these? Few remain extant, only then in fragments, and they all possess one common factor: the writers are all contemporaries of Hyperides and Onescritus, and they were amongst the 'many historians' mentioned by Diodorus Siculus 'who dare not write about the "drug"'. Alexander and his successors were very interested in what was written about them, fully aware that history would judge them. At least eight of Alexander's immediate court wrote histories and memoirs;[38] Alexander himself employed Callisthenes as his official historian.

According to gossip reported by the historian Lucan, Alexander declared how he wished he could come back after death to see what people thought of all that had been written about him, whilst Lysimachus, one of the successors, had Onescritus read his memoir aloud to him and discussed a certain incident which had occurred during Alexander's reign. In such circumstances, writing history could be a very dangerous occupation. Aristobulus, one of Plutarch's sources is a case in point. Aristobulus had been an official at Alexander's court, probably an engineer or an architect. According to one source, Aristobulus lived to the age of ninety and only started writing his history when he was eighty-four years old. Now, at first glance, such a man should be trusted, yet, according to the evidence, Aristobolus, by the year 321 BC, had journeyed back to Europe and was in the service of Antipater and later his son Cassander.[39] Aristobulus was a government official, a direct witness to the savage, bloody war of the successors which broke out after Alexander's death. He would know about the fate of Hyperides and, as he entered the service of the House of Antipater, he was scarcely going to report the poison story which could reflect so badly on his master. Little wonder that Aristobulus adopts the party line that Alexander didn't even die of alcohol poisoning, let alone some secret drug. He simply contracted a fever, fell ill, and died. Aristobulus also provides verifiable evidence regarding the harsh censorship imposed about what was written on Alexander and his immediate entourage. Lysimachus was not the only one to ask an author to inform him about what had been written so that he could compare it with his own memories. During his lifetime, Alexander did the same. The Roman historian Lucan cites a very interesting story about Alexander insisting that Aristobulus read out what he had written about the Indian campaign, in particular the confrontation between Alexander and Rajah Porus. The passage is as follows:

> As it fared with Aristobulus, who wrote of a duel between Alexander and Porus and read this very passage of his work to him – he thought that he was rendering the king his greatest service by falsely ascribing some great feats to him – but Alexander took the book (and as they happened to be sailing on the river Hydaspes) and threw it over his head into the water, with the verdict: 'You ought to go the same way yourself, Aristobulus, since you are fighting such duels for me and killing elephants at one javelin throw.'

Now such an account could be rejected, but it accords with Alexander's treatment of flatterers, especially when they became too effusive. However, if the story is true, and there is no reason to ignore it, Lucan's tale demonstrates that Aristobulus was writing his history as early as 325 BC but, as Pearson points out, Aristobulus did not publish his official account for many years after Alexander's death.

The reason for the twenty-five-year gap could well be that Aristobulus, like other writers, became very cautious about what he recorded regarding the Great Conqueror and his entourage. Aristobulus was a prudent man, a careful writer who ensured that he lived to a ripe old age. What is true about Aristobulus applies to all other historians of the period and justifies the remarks of both Diodorus Siculus and Quintus Curtius that, in the years following Alexander's death, a harsh censorship prevailed against anyone putting their name to stories that the Great Conqueror had been poisoned by the House of Antipater.

Nevertheless, modern historians, in their eagerness to follow the accepted official version, have let Arrian and Plutarch off lightly. Arrian clearly discounts the poisoning story except in one little slip where Arrian describes the visit by some of Alexander's generals to the temple of Serapis. They ask whether it would be 'better' if Alexander was brought before the God? The Oracle replies that it would be 'better' if he stayed where he was. Shortly afterwards, Arrian declares, Alexander breathed his last: this, after all, being 'the better thing'. What does Arrian mean by this? That it was 'better' for his great hero to die? One possibility is that Arrian also read the sources used by Diodorus Siculus and Justin; that Alexander was in such excruciating pain, so handicapped, that death was a welcome relief. What could have caused such symptoms, so fast, that even the physicians could not help? As I shall show later, in Part Seven, arsenic poisoning is the logical answer, as it does cause excruciating pain.

Arrian touches on this but then moves on. Plutarch is even weaker. He actually cites the condition of the corpse left in the corrosive heat of a Babylon summer which, today, would certainly provoke suspicion. Moreover, Plutarch either lies, or pretends to be ignorant when he, quite categorically, states: 'There was no suspicion of poison at the time of his death.' This is simply not true: the Hyperides incident, Onescritus' statement, not to mention 'the many authors' cited by Diodorus Siculus and 'The Pamphlet' in the *Alexander Romance* tell a different tale. Plutarch, in fact, contradicts himself when he alludes to the fact that the story of the poisoning came from a primary source – Antigonus the One-eyed. The latter was present in Babylon.

He was a leading general of Alexander, a contender in the War of Succession – albeit the inveterate enemy of the House of Antipater, but still an eye-witness to what happened.[40]

Nevertheless, as historians are quick to point out, one further obstacle remains – a source shared by both Arrian and Plutarch, namely the *Ephemerides*: the so-called Royal Diaries or Journals. I do not wish to rehearse the arguments which rage about these.[41] The Royal Diaries were once accepted almost as the gospel truth, an official document describing the last days of Alexander, so bland, so anonymous that they could not lie. In the more analytical atmosphere of today, such a claim is studied with a more jaundiced eye. The position of honour given to the Royal Diaries has been considerably weakened. Apart from another section cited by Aelian, the only places where these Diaries are quoted are, in the main, the writings of Plutarch and Arrian. Critics have also declared that, for official documents, the Royal Diaries actually provide very little information about what amounts to the last two weeks of Alexander's life, meagre entries about drinking, bathing and sacrifice; where he actually stayed in the palace; that he had meetings with the likes of Nearchus and Medius, as well as briefings with other anonymous commanders. The Diaries depict Alexander as ill with a fever, which grew gradually worse, as if they were written to create the impression that it was business as usual when the king fell ill; there was no drama or conspiracy about the royal sickness; it was just one of those things. The account is so banal, suspicion is provoked that the Royal Diaries appear to have been written for this very purpose. The mystery deepens when the possible source of these diaries is traced to one of Alexander's generals, the official secretary of the army, Eumenes, who was assisted by a subordinate, Diodotus of Erithyea.[42]

One fragment describes Eumenes to be their author: 'Alexander also drank a very great deal, so that after the spree he would sleep continuously for two days and two nights. This is revealed in his *Ephemerides* [Royal Diaries], written by Eumenes of Cardia and Diodotus of Erithyea.'

Eumenes can hardly be described as an objective source. He had clashed bitterly with Hephaestion and, when the royal favourite died,

Eumenes was so terrified of Alexander recalling his former enmity with Hephaestion, that he had been the first to flatter the dead man's memory, urging Alexander and the rest of the generals to erect a lavish memorial and heap every kind of honour upon Hephaestion's memory. More importantly, Eumenes had also clashed with Alexander. Plutarch gives a vivid description of this bitter altercation.

Yet it must be acknowledged, he [Eumenes] was often in disgrace with Alexander, and once or twice in danger too, on account of Hephaestion. In the first place, Hephaestion gave a musician named Evius, the quarters which the servants of Eumenes had taken up for him. Upon this, Eumenes went in great wrath to Alexander and cried, 'The best thing they could do, was to throw away their arms, and learn to play upon the flute, or turn tragedians.' Alexander at first entered into his quarrel, and sharply rebuked Hephaestion: but he soon changed his mind, and turned the weight of his displeasure upon Eumenes; thinking he had behaved with more disrespect to him than resentment against Hephaestion. Again; when Alexander wanted to send out Nearchus with a fleet to explore the coasts of the ocean, he found his treasury low, and asked his friends for a supply. Among the rest, he applied to Eumenes for 300 talents, who offered him only 100, and assured him, at the same time, he should find it difficult to collect that sum by his stewards. Alexander refused the offer, but did not remonstrate or complain. However, he ordered his servants privately to set fire to Eumenes' tent, that he might be forced to carry out his money, and be openly convicted of the falsity. It happened that the tent was entirely consumed, and Alexander was sorry on account of the loss of his papers. There was gold and silver found melted to the amount of more than 1,000 talents, yet even then the king took none of it. And having written to all his grandees and lieutenants to send him copies of the despatches that were lost, upon their arrival, he put them again under the care of Eumenes.[43]

In the circumstances, Eumenes can hardly be described as an

untainted source. In actual fact, I doubt very much whether Eumenes was responsible for those Royal Diaries. In the Wars of Succession which followed Alexander's death, Eumenes sided with Perdiccas against Ptolemy. Eumenes was appointed as satrap of one of the provinces of Asia Minor and had little to do with Egypt after Alexander's death.[44] He apparently never went there and yet it is a reference to Ptolemaic Egypt which makes these Royal Diaries highly suspicious. The Diaries were supposed to have been drawn up in or around 323 BC, yet they mention a number of Alexander's commanders going to the temple of Serapis in Babylon for an all-night vigil before the God on behalf of their stricken master. However, Serapis is an Egyptian deity of healing; his cult was only introduced in Egypt after 301 BC by Ptolemy, who inherited Egypt following Alexander's death and fought against all-comers to keep it. Various attempts have been made to associate Serapis with some other Babylonian God but this is a 'scissors and paste' exercise and there is no archaeological or literal evidence extant of a temple to Serapis, or a cult to that God in Babylon at the time of Alexander's death in 323 BC. The introduction of Serapis as a cult into Memphis, Egypt, was, according to both Tacitus and Plutarch, the direct work of Ptolemy, who worked closely with Timotheus of Athens and the historian Manetho to found and spread the cult of the healing God–Man.[45] The reference to Serapis in the Royal Diaries, as well as in other important stories regarding Alexander's mysterious death, may not only place and date the origin of these stories but, as we shall see, be the nearest admission of direct responsibility for the Great Conqueror's assassination by the person responsible.

The Diaries also omit very important medical details. Alexander had a deep interest in medicine which he would have learnt at the hands of Aristotle. During his campaigns Alexander was wounded several times and there are a number of accounts which show the army physicians taking care of him. On other occasions Alexander is described as tending the wounds of his comrades or being interested in their injuries. Plutarch relates:

When Peucestas recovered of a dangerous illness, he [Alexander] wrote a letter with his own hand to Alexippus the physician, to thank him for his care. During the sickness of Craterus, the king had a dream, in consequence of which he offered sacrifices for his recovery, and ordered him to do the same. Upon Pausanias the physician's design to give Craterus a dose of hellebore, he wrote to him expressing his great anxiety about it, and desiring him to be particularly cautious in the use of that medicine.[46]

This is in stark contrast to what happened in Babylon. Here's the Great Conqueror, virtually the lord of the known world, very ill of a fever, but although the Royal Diaries mention certain names, there is no reference to any activity by physicians. In all the accounts of this fatal royal sickness, the only real objective reference to medical assistance being summoned is that curious entry in Diodorus where the physicians arrive but were unable to help. Now, of course, such learned men may well have been very wary of tending Alexander lest they make a mistake and be blamed for something over which they had no control. This certainly happened in Malli when Alexander was wounded in the chest. The physician became highly anxious and had to be virtually forced to give treatment to the wounded king. Of course matters would not have been helped after the death of Hephaestion. Alexander blamed the hapless physician responsible and had him summarily crucified. Nevertheless the lack of any reference in the Royal Diaries to any medical practitioners or potions being offered is singularly curious.

The same is true of Alexander's commanders – he must have been surrounded by his leading generals – Perdiccas, Ptolemy and the rest – but only two names were mentioned in the Royal Diaries as close to him, the naval commanders Nearchus and Medius, and Medius is depicted as one of the assassins by the other sources. Both are described as having briefings with Alexander. The only other names quoted by this source – Cleomenes, Pithon, Seleucus and Attalus – are those pious officers who went to seek help from the God Serapis at that mysterious temple in Babylon. In fact all these names have one thing in common: Antigonus – that old, one-eyed general of Alexander who, in the bloody War of Succession, fought for empire against Ptolemy and the latter's ally in Europe, the House of Antipater. Medius and Nearchus both served in Antiochus' Fleet,[47] the visitors to the Temple of Serapis were Antiochus' inveterate enemies; Seleucus fled to Ptolemy of Egypt for protection, whilst Pithon was responsible for the assassination of Perdiccas and betrayed his master to Ptolemy of Egypt. In my view, the Diaries are a propaganda document – issued in Egypt some time after 301, hence the reference to the temple of Serapis. They would look as if they had been published by Eumenes but were, in fact, the product of Ptolemy and his ally Cassander, hence the enigmatic reference to a second person responsible for the diaries, Diodotus of Erithyea who also held a position in Cassander's secretariat.[48]

The main purpose of these Diaries was to scotch the rumour of any poison plot. They describe Alexander's days as fairly routine, lacking any drama or mystery. They were published as part of the campaign to suppress any conspiracy theories. They also contain more sophisticated messages, including one to be discussed later.

If poison is to be mentioned, the people closeted with Alexander during his final sickness were two naval commanders, Medius and Nearchus, who later served with Antigonus against Ptolemy and Cassander. There is no mention of Perdiccas or Eumenes; by the time the Diaries were published both were dead: Perdiccas was assassinated in 321 BC, while Eumenes was executed in 317/316 BC, so the veracity of these diaries could never truly be validated. In contrast to Medius and Nearchus, the Diaries then refer to commanders who were enemies of Antigonus, supporters of Ptolemy. These are described as being quite distant from Alexander, deeply concerned about him and going to spend a night of prayer in a local temple on his behalf. It is important to recall two primary sources which have a bearing on this. Plutarch, although strident in his rejection of the poison plot, does concede that it originated, or was published abroad, by Antigonus, that enemy of the House of Antipater and its allies. Secondly, a fragment of the Royal Diaries, from about a year earlier, are quoted by the Roman author Aelian. This fragment, as we have seen, lists Alexander's movements as he attends certain drinking parties; Aelian then comments:

Accordingly, one of two conclusions must be true, either that Alexander hurt himself badly by drinking so many days in the month, or that those who wrote these things lie, so it is possible to keep in mind henceforth that the group for which Eumenes is a member make such statements.

The group, of course, consists of Alexander's generals: Eumenes was their secretary, he'd be held generally responsible for documents such as the Royal Diaries: a task easily copied by Diodotus, Cassander's man. Aelian's cynical suspicions about these so-called Diaries and their real purpose are clear: they originate from a certain group, published with an ulterior motive in mind. The conclusion is inevitable. The Royal Diaries, those excerpts describing the last days of Alexander, were a clever piece of propaganda published to show that the king suffered a fever and died of natural causes. They contain no reference to any lurid story about poison, just a boring catalogue of events. The Royal Diaries cleverly ignore any reference to the great ones – Alexander's Commanders, the 'Lords of the Purple', as Quintus Curtius describes them, who must have been close to the dying king in his final days. People would think the Diaries had been issued by Eumenes, but, by then, he and Perdiccas were dead; they were the work of this Diodotus of Erithyea. The Diaries also make a subtle point: if something nasty did happen to Alexander, then people should look to Nearchus and Medius who were closeted with the dying king, and later served with Antigonus against the legitimate rulers, Antipater and Ptolemy.

The Royal Diaries, in fact, were only part of a propaganda campaign. Writers like Onescritus and Aristobulus might be frightened of telling the truth but, there again, an anonymous pamphlet could do just as much damage. 'The Pamphlet', found in the Alexander *Romance*, originated shortly after Alexander's death and laid the blame for that event at the door of the House of Antipater. 'The Pamphlet' must have quickly spread through the Greek world and beyond, being copied and used by all parties. I have based my theories on two of the most authoritative versions, the Ethiopian and the Armenian; yet, even here, when it comes to naming the murderers, there are grave inconsistencies. The Ethiopian version, for example, depicts Perdiccas as being party to Alexander's murder; the Armenian describes him as innocent. In some versions Perdiccas appears to be the king's favourite, being nominated as a successor, given the ring and even the hand of Roxane. In the Armenian, Ptolemy is given very preferential treatment, and depicted as Alexander's legitimate successor for the kingdom of Egypt.[49]

In essence, the main thrust of the *Alexander Romance* 'Pamphlet' is that Antipater and Cassander were the murderers, and it would have been copied so many times and distributed so fast that it would be very difficult to take out the heart of the account. Had Cassander attempted to do this he would have only deepened his own guilt. His response, helped by Ptolemy, was the heavily edited Royal Diaries. It was left to the others, particularly Perdiccas and Ptolemy, to twist and turn 'The Pamphlet' story to their own advantage. The murder accounts also throw in other names for good measure. Olympias, who hated Antipater long before anything happened to her darling son, is described as one of those who waged a war of vengeance against Cassander and his family, but, there again, Olympias needed no encouragement to persecute a family she loathed. Aristotle, too, could be cited. He was Macedonian, an expert on potions, sheltered by Macedon, a prominent figure at Antipater's court, and, despite being Alexander's tutor, had good reason to resent his former protégé's execution of his nephew, the historian Callisthenes.

Accordingly, any contemporary written account about Alexander's death is dominated by fear, prejudice, propaganda, censorship or ominous omission. The primary sources are strongly influenced by three factors. First, a fear of censorship. Secondly, a school of thought hostile to Antipater such as 'The Pamphlet' in the '*Alexander Romance*', which becomes the House of Antipater for the Greek conqueror's death. Thirdly, the 'official account' deliberately fostered by the House of Antipater. Which, through the Royal Diaries', tries to depict Alexander's death as an unfortunate mishap. One person could have thrown so much light on this confusion, given a graphic description and put the record straight. Ptolemy was a writer who had no fear of retribution, He was Alexander's personal bodyguard and taster, satrap and later king of Egypt, the founder of the Serapis cult, who wrote his own accounts in the early 280s BC some forty years after Alexander's death. True, Ptolemy's account only exists in Arrian, who quite specifically declares that, apart from the facts listed, Ptolemy has nothing more to add about Alexander's death. Nevertheless, Ptolemy witnessed, at close hand, the events in Babylon. He had the opportunity to provide an eye-witness account, describe exactly what happened and even put the record straight on behalf of his old comrade-in-arms, Cassander of Macedon. Arrian had two sources: Aristobulus (who had good reason to keep silent on the matter), and Ptolemy, yet he says nothing. Ptolemy the writer, who may have been Alexander's half-brother, and was certainly his companion from youth, had served next to Alexander on the battle line, protected the royal tent and was responsible for the king's security. It is not that he lacked the opportunity to give his own account: he simply never used it. In fact Arrian is very explicit. The Roman writer claims that his description about Alexander's death is what is written in the Royal Diaries, and then adds, 'beyond this, neither Ptolemy nor Aristobulus have recorded anything'. It would seem that Ptolemy's account of Alexander's death was almost synonymous with that of the Royal Diaries, which increases the suspicion that these were, in fact, the work of Ptolemy himself. Ptolemy's silence does provoke suspicion but, there again, as we shall see, Ptolemy is a skilled hand in keeping silent when he wants to. He wrote probably just before his death, acting the bluff old soldier, confining himself, in the main, to military matters, insinuating that he was the loyal commander carrying out orders. In omitting to provide any details about that last fatal banquet at Medius' apartments, Ptolemy is simply following his usual strict policy 'least said, soonest mended'.

The poison story is remarkable in that it actually names Alexander's assassins, lists their accomplices and describes how the deed was done. But is the allegation true? The conspirators are represented as two groups: on the one hand, the House of Antipater, and, on the other, a group of powerful, high-ranking commanders, whom Antipater hadn't even seen for eleven years. Did they unite to murder Alexander? If so, why should they turn on a man who had not only let them ride like lords through Persepolis but ransack its riches before burning it to the ground? Arrian and Plutarch couldn't imagine their hero, for all his flaws, being assassinated. It begs the question – what had happened to their Great Hero, that he had to be so summarily removed? What was the motive behind his murder?

Part Five

The Motive

'Πως ὀυν ταδ' ὡς ἐιποι τις ἐξημαρτανες'

'How, indeed, did you come to commit such grave sins – as someone might regard them?'
Euripides, *Andromache* (line 929)

The Alexander of 323 BC was not, despite all that had happened, radically different from the young warrior king of 336 BC except in a shift of emphasis. The tendency to regard Alexander of Macedon as some sort of Apollo figure, the incarnation of a Greek God, Hegel's 'Hero of History', the 'Colossus who bestrode the world', is most alluring. It is so easy to depict him as the best of the west, the educated Greek soldier, law-giver and statesman bringing order and harmony as well as the benefits of western culture to the hordes of Asia. Pictorial representations of Alexander heighten the effect: the coiffed hair, the noble features, the tilted head and that dreamy girlish look are, again, most alluring. We are dazzled by the general's sheer military genius, the warrior's breathtaking courage and those high-stated occasions when Alexander could be so charming and gracious.

It's all a lie, T.S. Eliot claimed: 'We often prefer the drug of dreams to the harsh pain of reality.' This certainly applies to the study of Alexander the Great. The textbook hero is more the creation of imperialist German and English historians of the late nineteenth and early twentieth centuries, such as Wilcken and Tarn, great scholars, erudite men, but captivated by the dream, ignoring the harsh reality of a man who cut a deep, bloody swathe from the Hellespont to the borders of India.

Alexander's dependence on drink and his sexual conduct have already been discussed above, but, as he himself made very clear, such activities were subordinate to his *pothos*, his yearning to prove that he was invincible. Tens upon tens of thousands of men, women and children paid the price for this. Alexander destroyed their cities and their cultures, bringing them to an end in an orgy of rape, torture, killing or slavery. Alexander of Macedon was a killer, through and through. He extinguished Thebes, one of the eyes of Hellas, and, in his final months, seriously considered plucking out the other: waging total war against Athens.[1] Alexander pursued a policy of savage war against the Persian Empire and beyond, yet we are seduced by his occasional kindness and charm on a personal basis. Thebes is a case in point. Plutarch describes a particular incident following the sack of that city:

The calamities which that wretched city suffered were various and horrible. A party of Thracians demolished the house of Timoclea, a woman of quality and honour. The soldiers carried off the booty; and the captain, after having violated the lady, asked her whether she had not some gold and silver concealed. She said she had and, taking him alone into the garden, showed him a well, into which she told him she had thrown everything of value, when the city was taken. The officer stooped down to examine the well; upon which she pushed him in, and then despatched him with stones. The Thracians coming up, seized and bound her hands, and carried her before Alexander, who immediately perceived by her look and gait, and the fearless manner in which she followed that savage crew, that she was a

woman of quality and superior sentiments. The king demanded
who she was? She answered: 'I am the sister of Theagenes, who
in capacity of general, fought Philip for the liberty of Greece, and
fell at Chaeronea.' Alexander, admiring her answer, and the bold
action she had performed, commanded her to be set at liberty,
and her children with her.[2]

Alexander is presented as a chivalrous man, a compassionate
soldier yet, when this widow woman was making her plea, tens of
thousands of her fellow citizens were being slaughtered. As Diodorus
Siculus writes:

All the city was ransacked. Everywhere boys and girls were
hauled into captivity as they cried pitifully for their mothers . . .
As the slaughter grew, every corner of the city was piled high
with corpses . . . In the end when darkness finally fell, the houses
had been pillaged, women, children and the old who had fled
into the sanctuaries were dragged out and abused.[3]

Alexander may have shown compassion to the immediate
kinswomen of Darius; but that same chivalry, as Diodorus explains,
was not extended to other women of the court:

The lot of these captured women was pitiable in the extreme.
They who previously, from daintiness and only with reluctance,
had been transported in comfortable carriages, now rushed
crying out of the tents clad only in a single tunic, tearing their
garments, calling on the gods, and falling at the feet of the
conquerors. Their captors grabbed these unfortunates by the
hair; others, tearing off their clothing, drove them with blows of
their fists or spear-butts against their naked bodies. The women
were herded off into a terrible and humiliating captivity.[4]

Plutarch relates how Alexander could be generous and kind to
dinner guests: being so open-handed with his companions provoked a
stinging rebuke in one of Olympias' many letters to him. The same

source also describes how Alexander came across a common soldier staggering under a heavy load of treasure meant for the royal pavilion. Alexander clapped the man on the shoulder, told him to be patient but to take the treasure to his own tent.[5] Yet this was also the Alexander who decided to retreat from India, but not according to the accepted route. He had a 'yearning' to challenge the Gedrosian Desert, which had defeated former conquerors such as Cyrus and Semiramis. As a result, literally tens of thousands of his common soldiers perished in the most horrific circumstances. We are touched by Alexander's devotion to his warhorse Bucephalus. Alexander 'was plunged into grief at the horse's death and felt he had lost a friend and a comrade'. He loved his dog Peritas which he had raised as a puppy and, when the mongrel died, named a city after him. He built a shrine, at Taxila, dedicated to the Sun God, so the elephant that had borne his adversary the Rajah Porus so bravely at the Battle of the Jhelum River could spend his days in honourable retirement. Yet this was the same Alexander who had instructed his infantry at that battle to strike at the elephants in their most tender place and so bring them down.[6]

Accordingly, it would be wrong to claim that the eleven-year campaign, 334–323 BC, had radically changed Alexander. Beneath the genius, the courage, the personal charm and individual kindnesses seethed the same dark soul, an implacable personality, ruthlessly dedicated to his own ambition, determined to prove that he was invincible, resolute not to be frustrated whatever the cost might be to others. The general who destroyed Thebes, a short while later at the Battle of the Granicus, showed no mercy nor offered no terms to Greek mercenaries fighting on the Persian side. He only offered unconditional surrender, 'to Greeks fighting against Greeks' and, when they refused, ordered their total annihilation, whatever the cost to his own side. Tyre, Gaza and Persepolis were also acts of terror. The Brahmin caste of India, the Branchidae, and any other group who resisted him became the object of a genocidal campaign.[7] The primary sources list a series of brutal campaigns between 334 and 323 BC; all originate in the same cause: Alexander's total refusal to be checked, challenged or frustrated.

The Macedonians would see this ruthlessness as characteristic of a great war leader. What would concern the likes of Ptolemy was when Alexander showed a similar ruthlessness to those around him. Alexander had seized the crown after his father's brutal killing. He had executed possible opponents such as the two sons of the rival House of Aeropus; he imprisoned the third – the Lyncestian – only sparing him because he was the son-in-law of Antipater who did so much to support Alexander in his early days of kingship. Philip's leading commander Attalus, Philip's new wife Cleopatra and her small children were liquidated now, brutal though these killings were, it was to be expected in the blood-letting following any abrupt change in ruler, and was characteristic of the power struggles in the history of Macedon. What is so remarkable about Alexander is that in the years following, despite all his successes, Alexander never forgot or forgave any grievance or grudge from those around him. He demonstrated a similar intolerance to any who might falter in their unconditional support of what he wanted.

Alexander's remark when he met Diogenes, that if he were not Alexander he would be Diogenes, a hermit philosopher dependent upon no one, demonstrates a certain alienation between the king and his own environment. Alexander was a lonely man, possibly given to brooding, especially when he was opposed or criticized, a human failing but, in Alexander's case, this developed into an almost psychotic state which would brook no opposition and tolerate no criticism.

One story spans the gulf between Alexander the child and Alexander the warrior king. In 331 BC, Alexander seized Gaza, the spice capital of the Mediterranean world. He decided to send some of that precious commodity back to his family and friends in Macedon. Plutarch takes up the story:

His tutor Leonidas was not forgotten; and the present he made him had something particular in it. It consisted of 500 talents' weight of frankincense, and 100 of myrrh, and was sent upon a recollection of the hopes he had conceived when a boy. It seems Leonidas one day had observed Alexander at a sacrifice throwing incense into the fire by handfuls; upon which he said, 'Alexander, when you have conquered the country where spices grow, you may be thus liberal of your incense; but in the mean time, use what you have sparingly.' Alexander therefore wrote thus. 'I have sent you frankincense and myrrh in abundance, that you may be no longer a churl to the gods.'[8]

This is a chilling insight into Alexander's character – no criticism was ever forgotten and was always dealt with. In this case, Alexander's outstanding generosity, the cup pressed down and overflowing, was coupled with a vicious snub of a bland criticism which he'd remembered despite the passing of the years and the crises he had to face. If such an attitude could be shown to an old tutor who was simply doing his job, one can only imagine the list of enemies Alexander carried around in his head: grievances to be settled, criticism crushed and insults returned with good measure. Alexander's Companions, his military commanders, were soon exposed to this most sinister aspect of Alexander's character.

When Philip discovered Alexander's role in the Pixadorus affair, he openly berated his son in the presence of one of Alexander's Companions Philotas, who may have even betrayed Alexander's designs to the king. Philotas was the son of Parmenio, the senior general and leader of the expeditionary force Philip had sent into Asia, along with Attalus, Parmenio's kinsman by marriage, and the same individual who had taunted Alexander so cruelly at Philip's wedding feast.[9] In the opening months of his reign, Alexander had taken care of Attalus by despatching assassins who had bribed Parmenio then later dealt with Alexander's enemy. Parmenio's desertion of his hapless relative was lavishly rewarded. When the young king crossed into Asia, Parmenio became his second-in-command, whilst Philotas later assumed the senior post of commander of the companion cavalry and performed brilliant service at Gaugamela. Parmenio and his family believed they were trusted and accepted by Alexander: a costly, fatal mistake. Alexander had not forgotten that Parmenio had been brother-in-law to his enemy, Attalus. Alexander also suspected that Parmenio must have played a role in advising Philip to distance himself from Olympias and her beloved son, and in supporting the marriage to a 'true' Macedonian, Cleopatra. Nor would have Alexander forgotten the Pixadorus affair.

Parmenio and his son proved to be excellent commanders. The father was very popular with the troops, especially the old guard, though Philotas was regarded as arrogant and hot-tempered. Alexander had needed both father and son in 334 BC but, after Gaugamela in 331 BC, it was time to settle accounts. The Persian Empire was destroyed; Alexander was looking further east. The autumn of 330 BC proved to be the appropriate time the Macedonian army was planning to invade India, and had camped at Dragnia on the eastern shore of Lake Seistan. Black Cleitus, a leading member of the old guard, was absent, so was Parmenio at Ecbatana, supervising the treasury. Alexander sensed the army was growing restless over his determination to march ever east. He could not allow any focus of discontent to surface: Parmenio and his son were possibly such a focus and had to be dealt with.

Alexander had already been keeping Philotas under close observation, persuading Philotas' mistress, Antigone, to report back any treasonable 'pillow talk'. This didn't amount to much – drunken remarks made by Philotas that he and his father should bear the responsibility for Alexander's outstanding achievements. Philotas, however, had made matters worse. After Alexander returned from the Oracle at Siwah, Philotas made the mistake of congratulating the king on his divine parentage, teasingly adding that he felt for all those who were now under an authority much higher than human. A great deal of controversy exists as to whether or not Philotas was involved in any plot or, indeed, if there was a plot in the first place. Such devices are often used by those in power to remove opponents they've marked down: Alexander was determined to destroy Parmenio and his family both root and branch.[10]

The origins of the plot are obscure and begin with an aptly named Macedonian called Dimnus. According to the accepted story Dimnus and his faction were plotting to kill Alexander. Dimnus told his lover Nicomachus, who then confided in his brother Cebalinus. He, in turn, decided to share the secret with Philotas asking him to inform the king. Philotas promised he would. Cebalinus kept asking him if he had done the deed? Philotas, who saw the king at least once a day, kept reassuring him that he had the matter in hand. Eventually, Cebalinus panicked. He approached a royal page, Metron, who told all to the king. Alexander immediately had Dimnus arrested and interrogated Cebalinus personally. He accused Cebalinus of being part of the plot and ordered him to be manacled. Cebalinus screamed his innocence and, according to Curtius, blurted out the story about informing Philotas. The source of this plot, Dimnus, curiously enough, died soon after his arrest, either in a struggle with his guards, or by suicide. What is important to note is that he died before he could give a full and complete confession. Philotas was summoned to the royal quarters and asked why he hadn't passed the information on immediately. Philotas' defence was that he never believed the story in the first place and regarded it as the product of a lovers' quarrel. He conceded that he had made a mistake and begged the king to pardon him. Curtius describes Alexander extending his right hand and assuring Philotas he was forgiven. They embraced, the king declaring he fully accepted his commander's explanation.

Once Philotas was gone, Alexander summoned the rest of his Companions. He must have known the result was a foregone conclusion. Curtius describes how General Craterus, one of Alexander's favourites, became the official prosecutor. He listed a number of charges against Philotas, his boastful talk, the possibility that he was involved in the plot and the danger Philotas would pose to Alexander and his friends in both the near and distant future. Undoubtedly, Craterus' words were music to Alexander's ears. He even allowed his general to chide him gently for not discussing it with them before pardoning Philotas. Craterus then spread his net more carefully. 'Whatever happened,' he warned the king, 'from this moment on, Philotas would be his enemy and he would be supported by his powerful father Parmenio.' Sooner or later Alexander would be fighting both men: indeed, Craterus warned, the enemy within was much more dangerous than the enemy without. The veracity of Curtius' words cannot be guaranteed, but they certainly demonstrate that Alexander had decided on destroying Parmenio and Philotas. Craterus' speech could have been written by the king himself.

Craterus was speaking to the converted: jealousy amongst Alexander's leading commanders was rife and they all acted as chorus to Craterus' speech of impending doom. They insisted that Philotas be re-arrested and immediately tortured. Alexander, the consummate actor, said he would wait.

The following evening there was a banquet, feasting and revelry. Philotas was present, but the party ended early after the king's announcement that the army would move at first light. Philotas, still anxious, must have drunk deeply; he returned to his tent and fell into a deep sleep. The king immediately ordered a ring of steel to be thrown around the camp and summoned his close advisers – Hephaestion, Perdiccas, Leonnatus, Coenus and others – to his quarters. He secretly ordered the arrest of Philotas who was kicked from sleep, shackled, his head covered with a blanket and taken off to the royal tent. The next morning Alexander, following his kingdom's tradition of justice, ordered the Macedonian troops to assemble in arms. Dimnus' corpse was produced. Alexander, acting as prosecutor, delivered one of his most outstanding performances. He appreciated that, if Philotas was not popular, Parmenio certainly was, so the king presented evidence against both father and son. Alexander adopted a 'more in sorrow than anger mood', thanking the Gods that he had not been snatched from his beloved troops. Alexander declared that he was safe for the moment, able to repay his brave warriors for their outstanding courage and service. He produced a rather ambiguous letter Parmenio had sent to Philotas, choosing phrases from it to indict both father and son. Alexander then finished his speech in classic fashion. The trial of Philotas was a test of allegiance for all Macedonians. They were to be given a choice, believe him or trust Philotas. The prisoner was invited to reply but Alexander had planned well. Some of his commanders, led by Coenus, openly harangued Philotas, attacking the prisoner for his arrogance and his distaste for the accepted ways of Macedon. Philotas tried to argue back, conceding he had made a mistake in not reporting the matter immediately to the king but, of course, the result of the trial was a foregone conclusion. Philotas begged for mercy. The king's bodyguards retorted that he shouldn't have plotted against their beloved leader and he deserved the most hideous death.

Alexander, who had left the meeting, then returned. He realized that the mood of the army had yet not changed to his liking. He adjourned the assembly and ordered Philotas to be returned to the royal quarters. At the urging of Hephaestion, Craterus and Coenus, the hapless prisoner was brutally tortured. According to Plutarch Alexander listened to the whole proceedings standing behind a piece of tapestry. Alexander's commanders had little pity for their former colleague and, by the time they were finished with Philotas, he could hardly walk but they had been successful. A confession of sorts had been wrung from the prisoner. The military assembly was reconvened, the confession produced, Philotas was found guilty and promptly executed.

Others were arrested and tried with varying degrees of punishment. A soldier known as Amyntas and three of his younger brothers were indicted before the assembly; their real crime being that they were friends of Philotas but, more importantly Olympias didn't like them. Even Attalus, the man who had pursued Philip's murderer and speared him to death, fell under suspicion, but Alexander realized the dangers of a general purge. Amyntas, his three brothers and Attalus were acquitted, as was Demetrius, a member of the royal bodyguard. The relief of many of these men was short-lived; many of them died shortly afterwards, including Demetrius and Amyntas, the former being replaced amongst the royal bodyguards by Ptolemy.

Parmenio however was a different matter. Alexander, during his miniature reign of terror, recruited one of Parmenio's companions, Polydamas, who was instructed to travel to Ecbatana disguised as an Arab with an escort of native guides. Racing camels were to be used to cover the 800-mile journey. Polydamas was given secret orders to deliver instructions to Parmenio's staff officers to execute their commander. Among these was Coenus' brother, Cleander. He would carry out the task and take over Parmenio's command. Polydamas was warned to carry out his instructions faithfully; until he did so, all his kin in the camp, together with those of the native guides, would be held as hostage.

Polydamas arrived at his destination after nightfall. He first delivered Alexander's secret instructions to Cleander. The next day he handed over two letters to Parmenio, an official missive from the king, and a letter despatched under Philotas' personal seal. Parmenio, not suspecting anything, opened the king's official letter and had scarcely been reading his son's, when his staff officers, at Cleander's sign, drew their swords and stabbed the old general to death. The news of their general's sudden and brutal execution caused consternation and anger amongst the troops at Ecbatana. Cleander was able to placate the men who demanded that Parmenio's body receive an honourable burial. Cleander compromised: he agreed to burial, but cut off Parmenio's head and sent it back to Alexander as proof that his orders had been carried out. Meanwhile, back at the royal camp, Alexander had decided to complete some unfinished business: the Lyncestian, who had been in custody under house arrest since Alexander had seized power, was brought to trial on charges of treason. The Lyncestian put up a poor defence, the assembly couldn't even understand what he was saying – he was convicted and executed immediately. Alexander had removed another problem.

The proceedings against Philotas and Parmenio are extremely sinister and illustrate Alexander's paranoia and vindictiveness. Parmenio had been marked down for death as soon as Alexander assumed power but, for a while, he needed him to win support with the Macedonian army and launch his expedition against Persia. It is quite remarkable how, within one year, Parmenio and his entire family were wiped out. He and Philotas were executed whilst, in the previous year, one son Hector had died of injuries following a boating accident, whilst another, Nicanor, had succumbed to some 'fatal illness'.[11] It is indeed chilling to list the number of those who opposed Alexander, then died mysteriously a short while later. The list of Hector, Nicanor, Amyntas and Demetrius would grow even longer over the next eight years. Alexander had removed Parmenio's family and circle, while striking terror in the hearts of his other Companions. Guilty or not, the destruction of Parmenio and Philotas reeks of that terror which so characterizes the great political purges of the twentieth century – spies, torture, evidence being twisted, important witnesses disappearing, treachery, betrayal, arrest at the dead of night, show trials, the lack of any appeal and immediate execution.

Alexander had not only removed a problem but, by this show of terror, clearly demonstrated the possible fate of anyone who opposed him. In Alexander's case, time did not heal wounds, whilst pardon and forgiveness were only temporary measures. Plutarch quite categorically states 'these proceedings made Alexander terrible to his friends, particularly Antipater, who commented, when he heard of Parmenio's fate: "If Parmenio was guilty, whom do we trust? If he was guilty, what is to be done?"'[12] Of course, Alexander's persecution possessed one great weakness – Antipater wouldn't be the only person to wonder: if Parmenio and his sons were expendable then who was safe?

Antipater did not have to wait long. Philotas and Parmenio were executed in 330 BC. Alexander was not fully satisfied that that was the end of the problem. A shrewd, political animal, Alexander realized that Parmenio, in particular, was popular amongst the Macedonian troops. Once the executions were finished, Alexander, using the pretext of marching further east, encouraged his men to write home to kith and kin in Macedon, saying that their letters would be taken there by the royal messenger service. Once they were collected, those letters intended for Macedon reached only the third posting station before the messenger brought them back. Alexander and his secretariat secretly opened and scrutinized these for any disloyalty or disaffection. Any soldier guilty of complaint wasn't put on trial or disciplined but separated from his unit and became a member of a special company, quite distinct from the main host and used for particularly dangerous assignments.[13]

The letters of these 'undisciplined' men must have provided Alexander with a great source of information about how he and the high command were regarded. One senior general, Black Cleitus, had been absent during the attack on Philotas and the launch of the conspiracy to destroy Parmenio. Black Cleitus was the king's bodyguard, a gruff old Macedonian soldier, fond of the old ways and, from the evidence available, one who thought highly of both Philip and Parmenio. Alexander chose Cleitus' absence from the camp as the occasion to strike and, when Cleitus returned, gave him promotion to the vacant post. In future, he and Hephaestion would be co-commanders of the companion cavalry, the post once held by the now dead Philotas. Cleitus must have been deeply disturbed by what had happened but had the sense, at least in public, to keep quiet. Nevertheless, whether it be from the letters of the men or the reports of spies in his camp, the consequent confrontation between Cleitus and Alexander was really a logical outcome of Cleitus' attitudes and Alexander's actions. Arrian's description of the confrontation between Alexander and Cleitus in mid-summer 328 BC at the royal camp in Samarkand is most significant:

Now Cleitus for some time past had quite obviously deprecated the change in Alexander: he liked neither his move towards the manners of the East, nor the flattering expressions of his courtiers. When, therefore, Cleitus heard what was being said (he, too, had been drinking heavily), he angrily intervened, saying they grossly exaggerated the marvellous nature of Alexander's achievements, none of which were mere personal triumphs of his own; on the contrary, most of them were the work of the Macedonians as a whole. Alexander was highly offended – and I, for my part, feel that Cleitus' words were ill-judged. In view of the fact that most of the party were drunk, he could, in my opinion, have quite well avoided the shame of joining in the general flattery simply by keeping his thoughts to himself. Yet there was more to come: others of the company, hoping to curry favour with Alexander, raised the subject of Philip. They suggested, absurdly enough, that what he had done was, after all, quite ordinary and commonplace. At this, Cleitus lost all control; he began to magnify Philip's achievements and belittle Alexander's; his words came pouring out – he was, by now, very drunk indeed – and, among much else, he taunted Alexander with the reminder how he had saved his life, when they fought the Persian cavalry at the Granicus.

'This is the hand,' he cried, holding it up with a flourish, 'that saved you, Alexander, on that day.'

Alexander could stand no more drunken abuse from his friend. Angrily he leapt from his seat as if to strike him, but the others restrained him. Cleitus continued to spit out his insulting remarks so Alexander called for the Guard. No one answered.

'What?' he cried, 'have I nothing left of royalty but the name? Am I to be like Darius, bound in chains by the likes of Bessus and his cronies?'

Now nobody could hold him. Springing to his feet, Alexander snatched a spear from one of the attendants and struck Cleitus dead.

Accounts of this incident differ. Some authorities say it was not a spear but a pike; Aristobulus does not mention the occasion of the drinking bout. According to him, Cleitus need not have been killed but for his own action; for when Alexander sprang up in rage to kill him, Ptolemy, son of Lagus, a member of the king's personal guard, hurried him out of the door and over the wall and ditch of the fortress. However, Cleitus did not stay there, but went back to the banquet room and met Alexander just at the moment when he was calling his name.

'Here I am, Alexander!' he cried, and, as he spoke, the blow fell. Curtius Rufus also describes the confrontation and ends it with Alexander staring down at the dead Cleitus and whispering 'Go thou now to Philip, Parmenio and Attalus.'

According to Arrian, Alexander bitterly repented about what had happened but, once again, the Roman historian is excusing his Macedonian hero. Arrian's own report illustrates the deep resentment seething between Alexander and the old Macedonian; Cleitus' attack was upon everything Alexander had achieved since the death of his father. According to Plutarch, Cleitus also praised Parmenio and made matters worse by criticizing Alexander for the death of Attalus, Parmenio's co-general and brother-in-law who had been so summarily removed after Alexander had come to power. Cleitus represented the old school. He was fighting in Persia because he was a Macedonian officer following a plan Alexander may have implemented but which Philip had thought out. Cleitus' words clearly convey the old soldier's deep distaste for what Alexander had become and the way he acted; his speech summarizes the two schools of thought amongst the Macedonian high command: for simplicity's sake, these can be termed 'the school of Philip' as opposed to 'the school of Alexander'.

If Parmenio's death had created shock and terror, Cleitus' death would have only deepened the unease amongst the Macedonian high command. Arrian and Plutarch's assertion that Cleitus' death was just the result of a drunken quarrel appears highly unlikely. The resentments ran too deep and what we know of Alexander's mind suggests that Cleitus would never be trusted or tolerated. Shortly before this bloody confrontation, Alexander had confessed to his confidants that he had a dream where he had seen Cleitus, garbed in mourning, sitting between the dead sons of Parmenio: this simply proves how the thought is father to the deed. After Cleitus' death, Alexander acted the grieving friend, stricken to the heart, deeply penitent for what he had done. But Alexander was a talented actor: for all the dramatic gestures, the sobbing, the refusal to eat, the total withdrawal, Alexander was crying through his fingers. It's obvious from the insults which were exchanged that Cleitus deeply resented Alexander, whilst the king was highly suspicious of this member of the old guard and his sharp tongue. If he had removed Parmenio and Philotas, why should Alexander tolerate the likes of Cleitus? At one stroke he had removed a serious source of criticism and a focus of opposition. At the same time, Alexander was sending out the same messages he had after the deaths of Parmenio and Philotas. If anyone criticized the king or opposed him, friendship and camaraderie counted for nothing. Cleitus was the brother of Alexander's old nurse, a soldier who had saved his life at the Granicus. However, if Cleitus mourned Philip, Attalus and Parmenio, then Alexander would do his best to send him to join them. There is a great deal of evidence to suggest that the death of Cleitus was not just the outcome of a drunken quarrel but high drama, carefully plotted.

Once Cleitus was dead, Alexander assumed his next role, the man of sorrows. Courtiers, fearful of the king's autocratic ways, hastily assembled to perform their parts. Anaxarchus, one of the resident sophists, bluntly informed Alexander to stop grieving: he hadn't broken any law, because he was above the law. Such words comforted

the king. Alexander took his fingers from his face and dried his eyes.
The other actors in the drama emerged. Aristander and his company
of soothsayers declared Cleitus' death was simply the work of fate, a
spiteful act by the wine god Dionysius. The Macedonian army assembled and, undoubtedly, coaxed by the king's entourage, passed a
decree that Cleitus had deserved death – he was a traitor. The logic
behind this is very clear. If Cleitus was a traitor there must have been
a conspiracy which the king must have known about beforehand, so
he had every right to question the old soldier and bring about his
death.

According to Macedonian law and custom, Alexander could have
kept Cleitus' corpse unburied, but Alexander decreed otherwise. In
one swift turn, the perpetrator of murder had become the magnani-
mous victim. Alexander had got what he wanted. He had murdered
an opponent but his act was viewed on legal, moral, political and spiritual grounds as perfectly justified. The will of the prince, whatever
that will decrees, has the force of law. The deaths of Parmenio,
Philotas and Cleitus, as Curtius reports, terrified Alexander's court
and brought to an end all freedom of speech, Alexander becoming, in
Plutarch's words, 'more proud and autocratic than ever before'.[14]

Alexander was too wily, too paranoid about his own status and
power, to ignore the effects of his actions on his immediate companions, his personal entourage, the council of warriors and army
leaders who advised him. Evidence exists that even before he invaded
India, Alexander was nursing a master plan to eradicate all
Macedonian customs eventually and even replace his high command
with native recruits. Thirty thousand mature youths from the north-
east provinces of the Persian Empire were selected to join a military
academy to train as soldiers and administrators. Alexander called
them his 'Successors' and, at the same time, he began to appoint
Persians to important positions in the administration as well as absorb
Persian units into the Macedonian army. These measures went hand-
in-hand with Alexander's decision to adopt Persian ways. Plutarch
maintains that Alexander did not assume full Persian dress and
custom, but merely a mix to accommodate his newly conquered
people. Plutarch also adds that Alexander's idea of being granted the

divine honours, the process of deification were deeply practical, a device to bolster his authority and status.[15]

Alexander was too much of a realist, a pragmatic general to be lost in some idea, some dream of godhead and undoubtedly took all flattery with more than a grain of salt. On one occasion when his minor wounds were being tended during the assault on the Indian city of Massaga, the Athenian Dioxippus tried to flatter Alexander with the lines from Homer's *Iliad* about Ichor, the blood of the gods. 'Oh, shut up!' Alexander replied. 'That's not Ichor, it's blood.'[16] Such a contrasting attitude did not make Alexander any less dangerous. He could bandy words with his troops, turn flattery aside but that too was part of his acting, part of his image: the general with the common touch. The important thing was that Alexander was king, he had to be obeyed and those around him were not to criticize or oppose.

According to the geographer, Strabo, Alexander was not only a student of Homer's Achilles, but an ardent scholar of the Cyrus School of Leadership. Cyrus the Great (died 529 BC), founder of the Persian Empire, had been immortalized by Xenophon, the Greek general turned historian, who wrote of Cyrus' teachings in his book *The Cyropaedia* which describes the young Cyrus' discussions with his father Cambyses on leadership.[17] Xenophon's work has as much relevance for today's politician and businessman as it did over 2,000 years ago. Cyrus laid great emphasis on what we would term 'image': the leader must act in such a way that his subjects are almost spellbound by him. Image in Alexander's mind was all-important. On a one-to-one basis with some poor soldier, or snubbing a flatterer, Alexander could gently laugh at himself, but the public image masked an implacable will. The Macedonians could fight for him, lay down their lives for him, but must accept him completely.

This ruthless determination to enhance his image persuaded Alexander and his coterie to introduce an important Persian court ritual, *proskynesis*, full prostration by a subject before the king. The Macedonians, however, not only refused to accept such a ritual but openly ridiculed it. On one occasion Polyperchon, a leading Macedonian commander, watched a Persian official prostrate himself before Alexander. Polyperchon found it so amusing he burst out laughing and bawled, 'Come on man, bang your chin really hard! Hit the floor again.' Alexander retaliated: he struck Polyperchon, threw him to the floor and for a while placed him under house arrest.[18] Nevertheless, even such fits of anger failed to weaken the stout resistance from other quarters. Indeed, when Alexander made an attempt to introduce *proskynesis* formally, it was bitterly attacked from a surprising quarter – Callisthenes of Olynthus, Aristotle's nephew, and Alexander's official historian.

Callisthenes was not popular amongst the officer corps: he was a foreigner of a severe disposition and openly derided the coarse, heavy drinking parties of the Macedonian court. He was, in fact, regarded as a graceless snob. Callisthenes' resistance to *proskynesis* could have been the legacy of Aristotle, or an attempt by this lonely man to curry favour with Macedonian officers. When a great conference was organized, Curtius writes, so *proskynesis* could be debated, Callisthenes bitterly criticized the ritual and won the approval of the Macedonians. It was supposed to be a free debate but, 'the king was not a stranger to what happened between the different speakers for he stood behind an arras which screened the different couches'. The king was furious: Callisthenes became a marked man. A short while later Alexander trapped his opponent during a banquet for the high command. Alexander lured Callisthenes into a game of eristics where a speaker argues a case then, just as eloquently, argues against it. Alexander offered the chosen topic: the Macedonians. He knew his victim well, and after Callisthenes presented the case against the Macedonians, any good will he had earned promptly disappeared. 'He drew upon himself the implacable hatred of the Macedonians while Alexander declared that Callisthenes, in this matter, had not demonstrated an example of his eloquence but of his malice.'[19]

In the spring of 327 BC, whilst the army was in Bactria, Alexander was provided with an opportunity to settle accounts with Callisthenes. A conspiracy was discovered amongst the pages whom Callisthenes tutored, those young men of noble family who served in the royal tent. There were five conspirators in all, led by Hermolaus, a page who had been soundly beaten by Alexander for daring to kill a boar meant for the royal spear. Hermolaus, bitterly resentful, drew four others into the plot which was eventually betrayed to Ptolemy, the king's bodyguard. All five pages were tried, convicted and handed over to their respective units for excruciating execution. Callisthenes was implicated on very weak evidence that he encouraged, or at least knew of, the pages' treasonable talk and malicious designs. According to one source, Callisthenes was immediately hanged, but it would seem he was kept for a while in a cage where he died of ill use some time later. What is so remarkable about these treason trials of spring 327 is that they show that the Philip 'school of thought' was still widespread and intense. There is a strong tie connecting the young Hermolaus with the taunts of the old soldier Cleitus. The sources all depict Hermolaus voicing deep Macedonian concerns about Alexander's growing despotism and listing those who, by now, must have been regarded as 'martyrs for the cause': Philip, Attalus, Parmenio, Philotas, Cleitus and Callisthenes. What is remarkable is that, although the pages' families distanced themselves from their erring sons and kinsmen, Hermolaus' speech, whatever the changes and glosses the sources have put upon it, is a fair reflection of the widespread resentment against Alexander and his totalitarian attitude. Curtius provides a graphic account of the speech from the dock.

'Hermolaus was brought before the assembly and asked why he had contrived such a wicked plot. "You put the question, as if indeed you are ignorant of the cause . . . While stupor bound the rest in silence," Hermolaus replied: "We conspired your death, because you began to treat us, not like freeborn men, but like slaves" – His father, Sopolis, starting up, cried: "Parricide of thy parent, as well as thy king." And, laying his hand on his son's mouth, said, "That a boy, whom guilt and wretchedness rendered insane, ought not to be suffered to say any more." The king, silencing the father, commanded Hermolaus to speak what he had learned from his master Callisthenes. "Availing myself of your favour," said Hermolaus, "I shall utter what the grievances of all have taught us. What number of Macedonians survive your cruelty? How few, that are not of ignoble blood! Attalus, Philotas, Parmenio, the Lyncestian, and Cleitus, contending with the fierceness of the enemy, could live, could support the battle, could cover you with their shields, receiving wounds to purchase for you victory and glory. How illustrious your requital! The blood of one of them stains your table. Another had not, indeed, so easy a death. The conductors of your armies on the rack were a gratifying spectacle to the Persians whom they had conquered. Parmenio, by whom you had destroyed Attalus, was slaughtered without being suffered to plead. Thus you employ the hands of the wretched in dark executions, and cause the instruments of your murders to be in their turn despatched by others." Now clamours against Hermolaus swelled to uproar; and his father, with his sword, drawn and raised, would have struck him, unless he had been restrained by the king, who ordered Hermolaus to proceed, and desired the assembly patiently to hear the criminal multiply causes for his punishment.

'Hermolaus resumed: "How liberally you permit youths, unskilled in oratory, to plead their cause! But the voice of Callisthenes is immured in prison, because he alone knows how to speak. Why is he not brought forth, while even avowed conspirators are heard? You shrink from the free speech of that innocent man; you could not bear his look. I strenuously maintain that he had done nothing. Here they stand, who meditated with me the glorious stroke. Not one of us can allege that Callisthenes was privy to our design; however long he may have been devoted to death by a most unjust and most unforgiving king. Of the Macedonians, whose blood you waste as though it were superfluous and worthless, these are the rewards. But you possess captured treasures, which are transported by 30,000 mules, while your soldiers have nothing to take home . . . All these ills we could, however, endure, till you surrendered us to the Barbarians, and, by a new procedure, subjected the victorious to the yoke. The Persian garb and discipline delight you: your country's manners you detest. It was therefore, the king of the Persians, not of the Macedonians, that we would have killed; we arraign you as a deserter, by the rules of war. To Thee, thou has required the Macedonians to kneel as to a god. You renounce your father Philip; and were any of the gods esteemed greater than the Thunderer, thou wouldst discard Jupiter. Is it strange that the freeborn cannot brook your arrogance? In you what trust can be reposed by us, who must either die innocent victims, or, which were worse, like slaves? If your amendment be practicable, you are indebted to me, since I have first dared to tell you what free minds cannot submit to. I will kneel to you to spare our parents: Oh! Do not load with torments, your old soldiers bereaved of offspring. As for ourselves, lead us to execution, that we may obtain by our own death, the release from slavery which we proposed from yours.'''[20]

Hermolaus' speech is basically the 'School of Philip' manifesto and, despite the interruptions and cries of protest, the speech at least represents Macedonian intransigence to Alexander's high-handed ways. The speech is also very important because it demonstrates, despite all Alexander's propaganda, high drama and sheer terror, the deaths of Parmenio and others were bitterly resented. In my view the speech is historically correct and would have done little to curb Alexander's growing paranoia. The main thesis of Hermolaus' speech was that the discontent was widespread. Alexander must have brooded on that. According to Plutarch after the pages were executed and Callisthenes removed, Alexander wrote to Antipater, his regent in Macedon, 'the Macedonians . . . have stoned the young men to death. As for the sophist [i.e. Callisthenes] I shall punish him myself *and those that sent him too nor shall the towns which harboured the conspirators escape.*'[21] The last phrase is enigmatic but the words seethe with a bloody menace perhaps against Antipater himself, certainly against Aristotle who probably secured Callisthenes' position in the army. Alexander is also insinuating that there was more to the pages' plot than meets the eye. In the end, it was not Alexander's Oriental innovations which brought his 'anabasis, his ever-going forth' to an end but a dramatic clash between his implacable will, his determination to do what he wanted and the army in general.

Alexander launched the Indian expedition in the spring of 327 BC; by autumn 326 BC, his troops had taken enough. They had journeyed hundreds of miles, campaigned against a ferocious enemy, sustained hideous losses, confronted the terrifying war elephants of Rajah Porus, faced the implacable opposition of the Brahmin priests and suffered the enervating heat and treacherous monsoons of what is now western Pakistan and the Hindu Kush. In the last months of 326 BC at the Beas River, the Macedonians, despite Alexander's bribes, threats and tantrums, declared they would go no further and were not even prepared to discuss the matter. Alexander called a crisis meeting of his high command. He pleaded, he bribed, he urged them to follow him deeper into India, only to be met with a stony silence: they, too, would not be persuaded.

At last General Coenus, who had been so instrumental in the destruction of Parmenio and Philotas, plucked up courage and explained the mood of the army. There is very little evidence to suggest that Coenus actually delivered the speech reported – it was more the work of Ptolemy who provides an important and clear picture of army thinking by the autumn of 326 BC. Coenus' speech is a model of diplomacy and tact. He first concedes that Alexander does not demand 'unreasoning obedience' and that he would only act if he had their full consent (in view of what had gone on before, Ptolemy must have had his tongue firmly in his cheek). Coenus explains he is not really speaking for the officer corps but for the common soldiers. He then bluntly informs Alexander that if the troops don't want to go on he must accept it. He actually advises Alexander to go home to his mother in Macedon. Once there, Alexander could raise new troops for his new conquests, be it against the Scythians around the Black Sea or along the coast of Africa, conquering the kingdoms of Carthage and Libya. He would be able to recruit fresh young men bursting with energy rather than lead veterans who simply wanted to go home. Coenus adds that a successful man should know when to stop. The army had full confidence in Alexander and his famous luck, but fortune could change.

According to Arrian, echoing Ptolemy, Coenus' words were greeted with applause and even tears. Alexander however withdrew, seething with anger. He tried to hold out but neither the army nor the high command could be moved. Eventually Alexander made a sacrifice. He found the auspices for any further advance highly unfavourable and, with that face-saving device, Alexander told a rapturous army that they would withdraw.

Coenus' speech is very important. Many historians regard it as a simple defiance to any further advance. In fact, it is more than this. It is the manifesto by Ptolemy the author, one of Alexander's generals, not just about retreating from India but any further conquest. There is no doubt, however, that Coenus led the opposition, but he did not live long enough to enjoy the good will of his colleagues. Shortly afterwards he died mysteriously, perhaps of a sickness and a fever but, there again, by 326 BC even the most right-minded observer must have been struck by how many who opposed Alexander did not survive long.[22]

The Great Conqueror was undoubtedly furious and the consequent retreat in 325 BC through the Gedrosian Desert – now called the Makran, which divides western Pakistan from Iran – may have been the result of a mistake or something more sinister. According to Strabo, quoting Nearchus:

> Alexander conceived an ambition to lead his army through Gedrosia after when he learned that both Semiramis and Cyrus (previous Persian rulers) had made an expedition against the Indians, and that Semiramis had turned back in flight with only twenty people and Cyrus with seven; and that Alexander thought how grand it would be, when those had met with such reverses, if he himself should lead a whole victorious army safely through the same tribes and regions.[23]

Alexander may have been determined to surpass previous conquerors, he may also have been utterly furious, and decided to punish and purge an army which had dared to oppose him. Either way the result was the same. Tens upon tens of thousands of his soldiers perished in the boiling desert cauldron. Some sank into the sand, others were caught in flash floods, many died of thirst, heat stroke or poisonous snakes. Ptolemy himself was stricken and, according to sources, healed by a certain medicine Alexander himself discovered. According to Arrian, when Alexander came out of the Gedrosian Desert he had lost more men during that 60-mile trek than through all his campaigns – some estimate only 15,000 out of 70,000 survived.[24]

Alexander, however, was neither chastened nor humbled but even more implacable. He arrived back in the eastern provinces of his Persian Empire and launched what the historian Badian called, 'a reign of terror', a brutal purge of any opposition at every level, before he prepared his new great *anabasis*, or going-forth. Undoubtedly, things had become slack whilst Alexander had been in India but, in the short space of two years between coming out of the Gedrosian Desert and his death in Babylon, Alexander threw himself into this purge with unrestrained vigour. Harpalus, a boyhood friend and colleague of Alexander who, on account of certain disabilities, served as treasurer, had lived like a sultan during Alexander's absence in India. Harpalus had brought his concubines to stay and treated them like queens, embezzling state funds to keep himself and them. On Alexander's return Harpalus decided to abscond with part of the treasure he was supposed to be guarding. For a while he made himself a thorough-going nuisance as he fled from one city in Greece to another. Eventually he was hunted down and assassinated in Crete.[25]

Nor did Alexander lack other victims for his angry paranoia. Astaspes, satrap of Carmania, one of the first eastern provinces Alexander entered after his return from India, was accused of high treason, and summarily executed for not providing enough help to Alexander during the king's trek through the desert. High-ranking Greek officers Sitalces, Cleander (the general who had executed Parmenio), Heracon and Agathon were also summoned to court, accused of various crimes including rape and embezzlement, and promptly executed. The generals were accompanied by 6,000 troops and Alexander ordered 600 of these to be killed in a brutal decimation. The fact that Cleander was Coenus' brother certainly wouldn't have helped his case before the king. Two further satraps, father and son, Abulites and Oxarthes, were also executed, ostensibly for not helping Alexander during his recent campaign. Abulites, fearing the worst, had brought 3,000 talents with him to temper the king's rage. Alexander took the treasure and threw it down in front of his horses. Of course the animals refused to touch it. 'What use is that?' Alexander screamed. Oxarthes must have infuriated Alexander with his excuses, for the king himself grasped a pike and ran the man through on the spot. Orsines, satrap of Persis, brought the king gifts but neglected Alexander's Persian favourite, the beautiful but vicious Bagoas. The satrap informed the favourite that he would always have presents for the king, but not for his whores. A short while later, Orsines faced a litany of charges, in which Bagoas had a hand, as did the Macedonian Polymachus who had fallen foul of this autocratic king: both were executed.[26]

Alexander was also resolute in his attempt to push on with his Persianization programme. He took two further wives, the daughters of previous Persian kings, and virtually obliged every single member of the high command to take a Persian wife as well. Ostensibly it was a festive event, but these forced marriages were highly resented. Once Alexander was dead his commanders, with the exception of Seleucus, repudiated their Persian wives. Historians have hailed these forced marriages as a bold attempt by Alexander to unite two cultures. However, these must have been, by virtue of their later repudiation, fiercely resented by his generals – they were Macedonian warriors who would want to choose their own wives. Moreover, Alexander's marriage strategy may have had a more sinister purpose. Philotas had been betrayed by his mistress Antigone. The Persian noble women, as exemplified by Sisygambis and Roxane, were devoted to Alexander. Forcing his senior commanders to take Persian wives was also a security measure: Alexander would have a spy in every household.[27]

Alexander also moved to strengthen the Persian contingent of his army, brigading Persian soldiers alongside Greek. One of Alexander's early initiatives in this policy of military replenishment now came to fruition. The 30,000 Persian youths from the north-east provinces, selected and trained in what amounted to an exclusive military academy, arrived in Susa during the summer of 324 BC. These young warriors, whom Alexander called the *Epigonoi*, the 'Successors', arrived kitted out, trained, and ready for battle. The Macedonians ridiculed them, calling them 'young war dancers', but they were deeply disturbed. These *epigonoi* would be the nucleus of a Praetorian guard, the core of a new model army.[28]

Undoubtedly, the arrival of these young warriors, together with the mutiny in India, the disastrous retreat through the desert, and the brutal purge which had followed, had created a deep rift between Alexander and the rank-and-file. At Susa, shortly after the great wedding feast between Macedonian and Persian, Alexander offered to settle all the debts of his soldiers. These were burdensome on the troops who often had to pawn or sell plunder to the merchants and quartermasters who followed any army. Arrian reports that the soldiers refused to comply. They did not trust the king and believed that all he wanted was a list of those who were in debt. Alexander chided them and, innocent-eyed, issued a statement that he was a king, and kings always spoke the truth to their subjects. He then added that he didn't need their names, just the pawn tickets and the IOUs they held. The troops of course responded eagerly.[29] In fact, this debt-cancelling operation masked Alexander's intended policy to purge his army which had mutinied against him in India and ensure they went nowhere else. On his return to Persia, Alexander issued an imperial decree ordering all satraps and governors to disband their private armies. In essence, this meant that thousands upon thousands of Greek mercenaries were thrown out of work and left to their own devices. Such men, trained and bloodied in war, often exiles from their own cities, knew only one trade: fighting. On the one hand, Alexander had weakened the strength of provincial governors and their ability to conspire or rebel. Yet he also realized that the disbanded mercenaries could, in time, become a very real threat with bands of armed men drifting across his empire. At Susa, a second decree was issued, ordering all Greek states to repatriate their exiles. By this complex measure, Alexander thought he would not only rid himself of these expatriates but also dry up the pool of mercenaries for hire, as well as keep each city-state busy with its own problems for the foreseeable future. Many of these exiles were fiercely resented, they had blood feuds against those who had expelled them and there was always the complicated question of forfeited property and goods.

Alexander issued such decrees at what he considered a most appropriate time. Since his return from India, the League of Corinth and other city-states, including those in North Africa and Italy, had despatched embassies to him to pay respects and affirm their loyalty. Many envoys were both cautious and frightened, fearful of Alexander's anger and suspicions. The League of Corinth's envoys came wreathed in garlands as if approaching a god, carrying gold crowns from their cities, the highest honour which could be bestowed. Consequently the arrival of these envoys was an opportune occasion for Alexander to continue his programme of confirming and strengthening his authority. The prohibition of private armies and the Exiles Decree was followed by a third one: in future, divine honours would be accorded to Alexander, a move which would elevate opposition and conspiracy against Alexander from high treason to the most horrid blasphemy.[30]

During these two years, 325–323 BC, Alexander also drew up plans for future expeditions and glorious projects. Some historians have disputed the long list of these projects given by Diodorus Siculus, though many of them do seem possible and viable. Arrian talks of plans to send a naval expedition around Africa and so enter the western Mediterranean as part of a pincer movement against the independent states of Carthage and Libya. Other plans included striking north to the Black Sea and launching a military campaign against the Scythians. Plutarch and Curtius specifically mention a North African campaign which would have involved building roads, harbours and fleets. Alexander was certainly eager for fresh wars – in the first instance against Arabia, which would entail the construction of a new war port at Babylon, big enough to contain a battle fleet of 1,000 ships. Nearchus was appointed to lead a naval contingent into Arabian waters to explore and gather information. Whatever had happened in the past, Alexander was determined on war, but this time there would be a new army, a force personally loyal to him. There would be no more mutinies, no more resistance.[31]

At Opis in the late summer of 324 BC, Alexander moved into what he must have considered as his end game. He called a general assembly of the Macedonian army and delivered his thunderbolt. He had decided to pension-off some 10,000 of the veterans no longer fit for active service. What the Gedrosian Desert had begun, Alexander was determined to finish. The army saw through his plan: Alexander was purging his forces. His declaration was met with boos, catcalls and cries that he should send them all home and continue his fight with help from his new-found father Ammon and his Persian war dancers. Alexander's state of mind can be judged by his reaction: a highly dangerous, but even more courageous, confrontation with his soldiers. He jumped down from the rostrum and charged into the ranks, personally pulling out the most vociferous speakers and handing them over to his Persian bodyguard for immediate execution. Over a dozen soldiers faced summary capital punishment then Alexander returned to the attack. What is obvious from the speech which followed was that the mutiny in India rankled deeply; this was in the forefront of Alexander's mind. He personally accused the troops of deserting him, of leaving him with no choice but to turn 'to the Barbarians'. Alexander stormed from the platform, he sulked like Achilles in his tent, then issued a series of orders. Persian troops would replace Macedonian units; their brigade commanders would be Persian whilst certain high-ranking Persian nobles would be amongst his Companions.

It is interesting to note that none of Alexander's military command sided with the troops. This time there was no Coenus, no honest and blunt speeches from the heart. They were probably too frightened. The Macedonian rank-and-file were by themselves. The troops sent a delegation, weeping and wailing, to offer their most profuse apologies. Alexander, the actor, met them, his eyes brimming with tears and exchanged with some of them the kiss of peace. A great feast was organized at Opis to commemorate the reconciliation between the king and 'his children', between Macedonian and Persian. Some historians used to hail this as a great gesture of unity: in truth Alexander smiled and toasted the Macedonians but he hadn't changed. The purge continued, though this time the pill was heavily coated with honey. Discharged Macedonians would receive back pay, travelling expenses and the most generous bonus of one talent. One slight sting in the tail: they would have to leave their Persian wives behind and any children they may have had by them. Alexander, all kind and paternalistic, promised that he would look after such children himself. The king was ridding himself of troublemakers, punishing them whilst at the same time rewarding them. These troops would go back to Macedonia, and he chose his most loyal general, Craterus, a man popular with the troops, to lead them. Craterus would ensure their good behaviour whilst, in his knapsack, he had secret instructions to deal with Antipater once he was back in Pella. (Antipater had been regent in Macedon since Alexander had left eleven years before.) Craterus left, taking 10,000 veterans with him; he and Alexander would never meet again.[32]

No evidence exists of one other group that Alexander must have regarded ready for purging – his Companions, all leading generals, the brigade commanders and cavalry leaders. The only hint we have of Alexander's displeasure is their absolute silence during these two years of terror. Alexander had not forgotten the mutiny in India, or their stony silence when he had asked for their support, or the way they had applauded Coenus' speech. These Lords of the Purple, these panthers who supped with the king, must surely have fallen under Alexander's paranoid scrutiny. The incident at Opis certainly provided an insight. When Alexander retreated to sulk in his tent, one of the measures which he published was that Persian nobles would join his group of Companions. In truth, Alexander must have been furious with the likes of Perdiccas, Ptolemy and the rest.

In his speech at Opis Alexander had brutally reminded his troops of the great rewards he had earned for them. According to Plutarch, Alexander had done the same for these Companions, the senior military commanders. Alexander had lavishly rewarded them, person-ally looked after them and often lectured them on their growing softness. Plutarch reports:

> He found that his great officers set no bounds to their luxury, that they were most extravagantly delicate in their diet, and profuse in other respects; insomuch that Agnon of Teos wore silver nails in his shoes, Leonnatus had many camel loads of earth brought from Egypt to rub himself with when he went to the wrestling-ring, Philotas had hunting-nets that would enclose the space of an hundred furlongs; more made use of rich essences than oil after bathing, and had their grooms of the bath, as well as chamberlains who excelled in bed-making. This degeneracy Alexander reproved with all the temper of a philosopher. He told them, 'It was very strange to him that, after having undergone so many glorious conflicts, they did not remember that those who

come from labour and exercise always sleep more sweetly than the inactive and effeminate; and that in comparing the Persian manners with the Macedonian, they did not perceive that nothing was more servile than the love of pleasure, or more princely than life of toil. How will that man' continued he, 'take care of his own horse, furbish his lance and helmet, whose hands are too delicate to wait on his own dear person? Know you not that the end of conquest is, not to do what the conquered have done, but something greatly superior?' Thus Alexander hazarded his person, by way of exercise for himself, and example to others. But his friends, in the pride of wealth, were so devoted to luxury and ease, that they considered long marches and campaigns as a burden, and by degrees came to murmur and speak ill of the king. At first he bore their censures with great moderation, and used to say, 'There was something noble in hearing himself ill spoken of while he was doing well.'[33]

Plutarch's account is most remarkable and significant. It reveals Alexander's attitude to his commanders, certainly before his invasion of India. He is very paternalistic – he would intervene on their behalf but he was wary of their sluggishness, their eagerness to rest on their laurels and enjoy the fruits of their conquests. Such an attitude amongst Alexander's high command is understandable. By the time Persepolis was burnt they had plucked the heart out of the Persian Empire, avenged all wrongs, amassed a king's fortune. The prospect of marching to the winking rim of the world no longer seemed attractive. Like soldiers the world over, in any age, they believed they had fulfilled their job descriptions and wanted to go home. The vision of Isocrates as expressed in his 'Address to Philip' had been fulfilled. Such sentiments would be totally alien to Alexander and, coupled with his growing paranoia, his determination to have his way, a dangerous brew was concocted.

By the time the Indian expedition was over – so Coenus summarized the high command's attitude – they had had enough, they wanted to go home, they wanted to enjoy the fruits of their labours. If Alexander wanted to continue to fight, then he should go home, raise a new army and go where he wished. Coenus' sentiments were echoed in a minor confrontation between Alexander and one of his brigade commanders, Meleager. Alexander had just given lavish gifts to the Indian prince, Taxiles. Meleager commented that it was a pity Alexander had to travel all the way to India to give any man such lavish rewards. Alexander retorted that envious men only hurt themselves. It was a bitter exchange involving a high-ranking officer who'd reached the point of frustration that he actually believed enemy commanders were being treated better than he, campaigning on Alexander's behalf.[34]

Despite his paranoia and fury at what had happened, Alexander, on his return to Persia, during those two years before his death (325–323 BC), would have been cunning enough to understand that the hearts of his commanders, men like Meleager, did not beat the same as his. They had fought for nine years, seen comrades die in battle, suffered the horrors of the Gedrosian Desert. Above all, they had seen former comrades – Parmenio, Philotas, possibly Parmenio's two other sons, Cleitus, Callisthenes, Coenus, Cleander and the rest, men who had performed outstanding tasks for Alexander – fall abruptly from grace when they had stopped pleasing their king. They had witnessed the purges after Alexander's return to India, and the king's ominous threats at Opis to replace the entire army structure with Barbarians. Nor was there any end in sight. Alexander was planning further wars and, apart from Craterus, none of Alexander's immediate entourage had been provided with opulent high office as satrap or governor. True, Alexander may have needed the Macedonian high command, but there is no doubt that he distrusted them. If they continued to follow Alexander the way forward was well mapped out for them: the usual drinking parties in the flesh pots of Babylon, followed by more hard knocks if they were not replaced by Persians or did something to displease Alexander. They would certainly agree with Arrian's remark that Alexander's thirst for conquest was insatiable.

Plutarch clearly states that, by the time Alexander entered Babylon in 323 BC, he no longer trusted his Companions. The feeling was certainly mutual.[35] The mutiny near the Jhelum (Beas) River may not have begun the rot; it certainly hastened it. Shortly afterwards, when

Alexander was planning his withdrawal from India by land and sea, he discussed with Nearchus who would command the fleet which would sail out into the Indian Ocean. According to Nearchus, albeit a biased source, for the admiral was bent on his own aggrandizement, the king was not sure to whom he could entrust such an important mission.

> Nearchus says that Alexander discussed with him whom he should select to be admiral of this fleet; but as mention was made of one and another, Alexander rejected some as not willing to risk themselves for his sake, others as chicken-hearted, others as consumed by desire for home, so finding some objection to each.[36]

The report may, in fact, be accurate. Alexander's discussion with Nearchus is a reflection of Coenus' words at that fatal council meeting and Alexander's own speech when he addressed the Macedonian assembly at Opis in 324 BC. They both had their origin in the above-mentioned description by Plutarch where Alexander has serious reservations about what he calls his 'luxury-loving high command'. Alexander was also suspicious and jealous of his colleagues. One constant thread, amongst many, which links the opposition of Philotas, Cleitus and Hermolaus, is that Alexander had a tendency to claim all the glory for himself and not acknowledge the contribution of others. It is no coincidence that Ptolemy, one of Arrian's principal sources, is not shy in putting forward his own achievements when he served under the Great Conqueror. In fact, even the ancient sources record the tension between Alexander and his Companions. The Roman historian Aelian in his *Historia Varia* provides a fragment which contains an assessment by Alexander of his high command. It is not very flattering.

> Alexander, son of Philip, is said to have been very jealous of his friends and envious of them all, though not for identical reasons. He disliked Perdiccas for being a born soldier, Lysim[m]achus because he had a good reputation as a general, and Seleucus for

his bravery. Antigonus' ambition pained him; he disliked Antipater's quality of leadership, was suspicious of Ptolemy's cunning, and feared Attalus' insubordination, not to mention Pithon's revolutionary instinct.[37]

Accordingly, Alexander may have lavishly rewarded his Companions, but he believed he owned them body and soul. Even so, he was wary of them whilst his seething fury at their laxity or opposition was never far beneath the surface. As we have seen, when Polyperchon laughed out loud at Persians prostrating themselves before the king, Quintus Curtius reports 'how Alexander leapt to his feet, struck the general, threw him to the ground and told him to lie there like the rest'. Eumenes, the head of the army secretariat, was asked by the king for a loan, and when he made a niggardly response, Alexander's fury literally blazed out and he ordered Eumenes' tent to be burnt. The king committed a similar sort of arson before he set out to India: in order to strip himself of all the unnecessary baggage, as well as to demonstrate his determination on fresh conquest, Alexander burnt his own treasure wagons and then did the same for those of his Companions.[38] Alexander ruled his colleagues with a rod of iron. When Hephaestion and Craterus quarrelled and drew swords on each other, Alexander intervened and swore that if it happened again he would personally kill the person responsible for starting the argument. Ephippus claims that Alexander 'was a very violent man with no regard for human life'.[39]

The sudden death of his favourite Hephaestion at Ecbatana in the summer of 324 BC only darkened the king's soul. The entire high command, some of whom had quarrelled with Hephaestion, were absolutely terrified that Alexander, 'frenetic with grief', might recall their own quarrels with the dead favourite. They competed with each other to accord Hephaestion's memory every favour. Eumenes, as Plutarch relates, led the rush. Quintus Curtius reports the same; he adds that the tears of an officer as he passed Hephaestion's grave could have been misunderstood by the 'frenetic' king, so Perdiccas, one of the senior commanders, had to intervene swiftly to explain the officer's conduct. As we shall see, though, Alexander's grief over the death of his favourite may not have only been rooted in sorrow, but anger and suspicion. He crucified the physician who had been supervising Hephaestion, the usual Persian punishment for treachery and treason.[40]

By the time he approached Babylon, Alexander had lost his two favourite commanders. Hephaestion had moved on to be a god whilst Craterus was busy leading 10,000 veterans home to Macedon, carrying secret instructions of his own to replace Antipater. The senior commanders, bearing in mind the king's words at Opis, must have wondered if Antipater was next on the list of proscribed. In 334 BC, this veteran general of Philip's army had played a most significant role in Alexander's seizure of power. Antipater had presented Alexander to the Macedonian assembly as well as closely cooperated with the new king in the destruction of Attalus, and in the military operations preparatory to Alexander crossing the Hellespont. Alexander had left Antipater virtually king of Macedon, along with his murderous queen mother, who was probably given a watching brief. It was a fine balancing act. Antipater and Olympias fought each other until the queen mother and her daughter could take no more and went into self-imposed exile in her native kingdom of Epirus.

At first Alexander seemed to have accepted such quarrelling as part and parcel of the political fabric. He knew his mother. Moreover, Antipater had played a vital role and did a splendid job whilst the Macedonian wolf was ravaging the Persian Empire. Antipater had protected Alexander's back when Darius, on the advice of the astute mercenary general Memnon of Rhodes, had evolved a two-fold strategy to counter the Macedonian invasion. The Persian king had hoped to cut off Alexander from his base in Macedonia and open a second front in Greece. The Persians had sent money, ships and men to Aegis of Sparta, the one-city ruler who had refused to accept Macedonian supremacy. Antipater, despite his constant disputes with Olympias, solved the problem brilliantly, scoring a splendid victory in 331 BC outside the walls of Megalopolis, utterly defeating Aegis and his Greek insurgents. Alexander should have been pleased but, never one to extol the achievements of others, he dismissed Antipater's victory as a 'battle of mice'.

Olympias kept up her flood of letters which, according to Plutarch, the king read tongue in cheek. However, the situation changed dramatically with the death of Parmenio and the execution of Antipater's son-in-law, the Lyncestian. Antipater's response to the destruction of the Parmenio clan was cited by Plutarch in his *Moralia*: 'if Parmenio plotted against Alexander who is to be trusted? And if he did not, what is to be done?' Antipater was politically astute enough to realize that Parmenio's death meant that no one was safe, so he focused on the second part of his question, and immediately opened up secret negotiations with the Aetolians, another source of opposition to Alexander in Greece. Cleitus' death terrified Antipater further, and Alexander, through his spies, as well as his beloved mother, must have sensed the change in mood. Antipater was certainly high on his list of priorities when Alexander emerged from the Gedrosian Desert. He now listened to Olympias' complaints as well as the envoys she despatched to him. He suspected that Antipater was no longer the honest steward and began to voice such suspicions publicly. When someone was stupid enough to praise the old general in Macedon, Alexander snarled, 'although Antipater's exterior appeared to be white, he was decidedly purple on the inside'. In other words Antipater had imperial yearnings and Alexander decided to take him to task. The 10,000 veterans who accompanied Craterus home were a powerful strike force to take care of any opposition in a kingdom where manpower, due to Alexander's wars, was becoming an increasingly precious resource. Craterus was also to take over the regency. In his letter to Antipater and Aristotle, Alexander had hinted that Callisthenes' treachery had its roots elsewhere, a veiled warning to his regent.[41] It is interesting to speculate what was intended. On his deathbed, when Alexander was asked to whom he was leaving his empire, he replied, 'Kratisto – to the strongest' but he may have meant Kratero – to Craterus his favourite general now on his way back to Macedon.

In his paranoid state, Alexander may have truly believed that Antipater, the colleague of Parmenio, Cleitus and Coenus, was the root cause of all conspiracy and a possible source of serious trouble in the future. If Antipater was removed and Craterus took over as viceroy, Alexander would have secured his home base, tightened his control over Greece, and kept a watching brief on the families and supporters of his close Companions. At the same time, Antipater was invited to court and, after the two-year purge, many must have thought that Antipater's arrival in Babylon would be followed by his swift execution. Antipater realized the danger, he prevaricated, compromised and despatched his son Cassander, a Companion of Alexander from the king's days in the Groves of Mieza.

Cassander, no friend of Alexander, arrived early in 323 BC and immediately moved into confrontation with the king over his own attitude as well as that of his entire family. Plutarch provides the details of what happened.

Alexander was most afraid of Antipater and his sons; one of whom, named Iolaus, was his cupbearer; the other, named Cassander, was lately arrived from Macedonia and happened to see some barbarians prostrate themselves before the King. Like a man accustomed only to the Grecian manners, and a stranger to such a sight, he burst out into a loud laugh. Alexander, enraged at the affront, seized him by the hair, and with both hands dashed his head against the wall. Cassander afterwards attempted to vindicate his father against his accusers, which greatly irritated the king. 'What is this talk of thine?' said he, 'dost thou think that men who had suffered no injury, would come so far to bring a false charge?' 'Their coming so far,' replied Cassander, 'is an argument that the charge is false, because they are at a distance from those who are able to contradict them.' At this Alexander smiled, and said, 'These are some of Aristotle's sophisms, which make equally for either side of the question. But be assured I will make you repent it, if these men have had the least injustice done them.' This, and other menaces, left such a terror upon Cassander, and made so lasting an impression upon his mind, that many years after, when king of Macedon, and master of all Greece, as he was walking about at Delphi, and taking a view of the statues, the sudden sight of that of Alexander is said to have struck him with such horror, that he trembled all over, and it was with difficulty he recovered of the giddiness it caused in his brain.

Cassander arrived at a court tense with fear where resentments, grudges and grievances festered beneath the protocol and etiquette.[42] Alexander's Companions must have been afraid, terrified of their king – but does this mean, according to the sources, they were willing to enter a full-blown conspiracy against him? To put their trust in Antipater, a general they hadn't seen for eleven years? Against whom, some of them, within two years of Alexander's death, would be locked in a fight to the death?

Part Six

The Conspirators?

'θεου γαρ ἀισα θεος ἐκρανε συμφοραν'

'This doom was created by God, this disaster is the work of a God'
Euripides, *Andromache* (line 1202)

Alexander's Companions were hardly 'a band of brothers' dedicated to the one vision. They were a disparate group united under Alexander, yet riven by jealousies, rivalries and differences. Alexander was young and there is a mistaken belief that his Companions or Friends, those senior military commanders who surrounded him, were also young. In fact, they were of various backgrounds and ages. Parmenio, Antipater and Antigonus the One-eyed were all close to sixty and had seen long military service under Philip. Ptolemy, by 323 BC, was about forty-four years of age while Eumenes was old enough to have served Philip. More importantly, Eumenes was allegedly of common birth from Cardia in Thrace: two major handicaps in the Macedonian court with its xenophobic tendencies and its emphasis on noble blood and descent. During the palace brawl which immediately followed Alexander's death, Eumenes felt he should stay out of the quarrel because he was not of Macedonian origin; a fact he was consistently reminded of during the subsequent War of the Successors, which broke out amongst Alexander's Companions two years after his death. Nearchus, Alexander's admiral, who was so royally feasted in the last few days of the king's life, was Cretan but still liked to emphasize his achievements and his standing with the king as compared with others. Men like Perdiccas and Attalus were brothers-in-law and, together with Leonnatus, came from the out kingdom of Orestis.

Apart from Ptolemy such men tend to be shadowy figures, kept in the shadows by Alexander. Some hardly survived in the harsh sunlight of battle and intrigue once the Great Conqueror had gone. Diodorus, later in his account, calls Perdiccas, 'a man of blood' and this description would fit them all. They were warriors: to dine with them was truly to sup with panthers. Curtius grandly calls them 'Lords of the Purple'; other sources the *diadochoi* – the Successors. Within five years of Alexander's death they were tearing each other apart; they were panthers and Alexander was master of them all. They would band against a common enemy and, when circumstances changed, turn upon each other.[1]

In 321 BC, circumstances abruptly changed when Perdiccas made a bid for empire and the blood spilling began in earnest. Even before Alexander's death and the subsequent civil war, the tensions between them must have been intense. One brigade commander Neoptolemus used to ridicule Eumenes as someone who 'followed Alexander from behind a desk'. Little wonder that when the panthers clashed in the Wars of Succession, Eumenes and his taunter were on opposing sides and both sought out each other in battle. Plutarch provides the details.

> In the meantime, Neoptolemus engaged Eumenes. The most violent hatred had long subsisted between them, and this day added stings to it. They knew not one another in the two first encounters, but in the third they did; and then they rushed forward impetuously with swords drawn and loud shouts. The shock their horses met with was so violent, that it resembled that of two galleys. The fierce antagonists quitted the bridles, and laid

hold on each other; each endeavouring to tear off the helmet or the breastplate of his enemy. While their hands were thus engaged, their horses went from under them; and as they fell to the ground without quitting their hold, they wrestled for the advantage. Neoptolemus was beginning to rise first, when Eumenes wounded him in the leg, and by that means got upon his feet before him. Neoptolemus being wounded in one knee, supported himself upon the other, and fought with great courage underneath, but was not able to deal his adversary a mortal blow. At last receiving a wound in the neck, he grew faint, and stretched himself upon the ground. Eumenes, with all the eagerness of inveterate hatred, hastening to strip him of his arms, and loading him with reproaches, did not observe that his sword was still in his hands, so Neoptolemus wounded him under the cuirass, where it touches upon the groin. However, as the stroke was but feeble, the apprehensions it gave him were greater than the real hurt.[2]

Eumenes had also had serious clashes with Hephaestion, as did Craterus who went at the royal favourite with drawn sword. Plutarch reports 'a hunting accident' when Craterus was wounded in the leg by Perdiccas's lance. It could have been an accident or an opportune occasion to give vent to the rivalries between such men.[3] Nothing underlines the quite sinister nature of these panthers more than the fall of Philotas from power. Philotas was a Macedonian, a superb cavalry commander, a battle-line colleague who had made an important contribution to Alexander's victories against Persia. He was suddenly arraigned for treason on the flimsiest of evidence. According to the sources no one speaks for him; indeed the opposite. Quintus Curtius provides a compelling insight into the rivalries between Alexander's so-called friends who positively jumped at the chance to destroy Philotas.

Craterus, one of a few in select favour with Alexander, envied the distinguished confidence enjoyed by Philotas. He was not ignorant that the latter was ever filling the king's ear with vaunting exaggerations of his own bravery and services; which was ascribed either to a design to depress others, or to gross arrogance. Persuaded that a more available opportunity to crush his rival could not occur, Craterus masked hatred of a brother officer under attachment to his prince.

What followed reads like the account of Mafiosi gang leaders turning on one of their own kind, made vulnerable and weak. Curtius reports.

Hephaestion, Craterus, and Coenus contended that the truth ought to be wrung from him by torture; and the others came over to their opinion. The council dissolved; Hephaestion, Craterus, and Coenus rose together to go and press the question on Philotas. The king sent for Craterus, had a conversation with him, of which the tenor is unknown, and then retired to his closet, where in solitude for a great part of the night, he waited the result of the inquisition . . . The executioners displayed before Philotas all the instruments of cruelty. 'Why do you delay,' he exclaimed impulsively, 'to kill the king's enemy and murderer, now confessing? What need for torture? I contrived, I willed the mischief.' Craterus required that he should repeat that avowal on the rack. Philotas, as they were haling him, stripping him, and filleting his eyes, appealed to remorseless ears, by the Gods of his country, and the laws of nations. As though he were already condemned, he was made to suffer the last resources of excruciation; he was deplorably lacerated by his persecuting enemies affecting zeal for the king. Notwithstanding they employed, alternately, fire and the scourge, less for the purpose of examination than punishment, he forbore to utter either a cry or a groan. But afterwards, his body swelling with ulcers, while lashing whips furrowed him to the bone; unable to support the agony, he promised, 'If the torments were discontinued, to communicate what they should demand to know.'

Even then they weren't satisfied but wanted more: 'They again applied to him the instruments of torture, themselves also striking his face and eyes with their lances, in order to extort a confession of his crime.'[4]

In the bitter Wars of Succession such cruelty amongst Alexander's former Friends and Companions was commonplace. Antigonus the One-eyed starved Eumenes to death; Craterus was knifed in battle; Perdiccas was assassinated by his own men.[5] Alexander sensed this would happen. On his deathbed he prophesied that there would be great debate amongst them and lavish funeral games – which would entail them fighting each other to the death.[6] The Roman historian Justin quite rightly reports after Alexander's death:

> The chiefs . . . were looking to sovereigns and thrones . . . for they were men of such ability and authority, that each of them might have been taken for a king. Such was the personal gracefulness, the commanding stature, and the eminent powers of body and mind, apparent in all of them, that whoever did not know them would have thought that they had been selected, not from one nation, but from the whole earth. Never before, indeed, did Macedonia, or any other country, abound with such a multitude of distinguished men, whom Philip first, and afterwards Alexander, had selected with such skill that they seemed to have been chosen, not so much to attend them to war, as to succeed them on the throne. Who then can wonder that the world was conquered by such officers, when the army of the Macedonians appeared to be commanded, not by generals, but by princes? – Men who would never have found antagonists to cope with them, if they had not quarrelled with one another; while Macedonia would have had many Alexanders instead of one, had not Fortune inspired them with mutual emulation for their mutual destruction.[7]

By 323 BC in Babylon, the tensions in such a high command must have been palpable. The generals, wary of their suspicious king who, deeply embittered after the mutiny in India, responded with equal distrust for a group of men upon whom he felt he could no longer rely.

Back home in Macedon, Antipater, fearful of what was about to happen, and realizing that he could suffer the same fate as Parmenio and the rest, did initiate a conspiracy against Alexander. Virtually every single source names Antipater and his son Cassander. Cassander was personally abused by Alexander and for the rest of his life nourished an intense hatred for all Alexander's immediate family as well as the king's memory.[8] Cassander arrived at Alexander's court in 323 BC, in circumstances where he would be zealously watched, as would all members of his family, including his brother the 'cupbearer Iolaus'. Alexander was a born intriguer: he would keep the House of Antipater at a good arm's length and under close scrutiny. Plutarch provides proof of this. In his *Moralia*, he reports how, when Cassander arrived in court, he tried to seduce a musician, Evius, which brought down on him Alexander's anger and vituperation: Cassander was, therefore, closely watched and the same would be true of his brother Iolaus.[9]

Given such intense rivalries, Antipater, the old fox, would never entrust his life, and those of his family, to a group of commanders he hadn't seen for eleven years, men who had participated in the destruction of comrades such as Parmenio, Philotas, Cleitus, not to mention his own son-in-law, the Lyncestian. This was too dangerous. Virtually every plot against Alexander was always betrayed by someone in the know. Such a conspiracy, with others of Alexander's generals, would be open to easy penetration at a court seething with spies and mutual animosities. Antipater and Cassander would look for someone they could trust and who better than Alexander's personal bodyguard, his steward, his taster, that old friend of Cleitus, the illegitimate son of Philip of Macedon, a general very popular with his troops: Ptolemy, son of Lagus.

Part Seven

Ptolemy the Assassin?

'σοι δ'ην τις ὁστις τουδ' ἐκοινωνει φονου'

'Was there someone who shared this murder with you?'
Euripides, *Andromache* (line 915)

Ptolemy, son of Lagus, was about forty-four years of age when Alexander died in Babylon in June 323 BC. He was Macedonian by birth, the son of a noblewoman Arsinoë, but his paternity is in doubt. Quintus Curtius mentions a well-attested rumour that Ptolemy was the illegitimate son of Philip by Arsinoë, who was quickly married off during her pregnancy to Lagus, a distant kinsman of the king.[1] This is reported by the Roman writer Pausanias: 'The Macedonians consider Ptolemy to be the son of Philip, though putatively the son of Lagus, asserting that his mother was with child by Philip when she was married to Lagus.' Philip probably was Ptolemy's father. A silver tetradracham, minted at Alexandria eighteen years after Ptolemy seized the Egyptian throne (in 305), displays his features which are very similar to those of Philip carved on the ivory funeral statuettes of Philip found in his tomb at Vergine: the curly hair, the large boxer's nose, the strong slightly upturned chin, the sensuous lips, the drooping eyes with their amused cynical gaze. Philip's stepfather had been called Ptolemy and the name, together with the strong physical likeness, does hint at the possibility that Ptolemy was Philip's illegitimate issue.[2] This also explains Ptolemy's later closeness to Alexander as well as his popularity with the rank-and-file of the Macedonian army, as Ptolemy seems to have inherited his natural father's lazy charm, good nature and open-handed generosity. He'd also inherited Philip's cunning and his prowess both as a warrior and as a commander.

There is every likelihood that Ptolemy was kept in the background during the early years of Alexander's life to protect him against Olympias' homicidal jealousy. The fate of Arridhaeus, not to mention the death of the baby Caranus, provide powerful testimony to Olympias' murderous hatred towards any prince, with royal blood, who might pose a threat to her beloved son Alexander. A rather obscure source claims that when Lagus found out that a 'cuckoo' had been placed in the family nest, he exposed the infant who would have died of exposure had he not been saved by the intervention of that most imperious of birds, the eagle, which would account for its appearance on some of the coinage issued by Ptolemy's mint during his forty-year rule of Egypt.[3] Of course, there is every likelihood that tales about Ptolemy's paternity were the stuff of legends and Ptolemy would certainly not have been averse to promoting such stories.

In his *Moralia* Plutarch records a story about how, when he became lord of Egypt after Alexander's death, Ptolemy was laughing at a rather ignorant grammarian who couldn't tell him who Peleus' father was. The grammarian furiously retorted that he would answer Ptolemy's question, if Ptolemy could tell him who his (Ptolemy's) true father was. Ptolemy simply burst out laughing and turned away.[4] There is no doubt that Philip had a high regard for Ptolemy. Some eleven years older than his legitimate first born, Ptolemy was included amongst Alexander's Companions at Aristotle's academy in the Groves of Mieza.[5] Ptolemy must have been greatly influenced by this experience: as lord of the Two Lands (as Egypt was known), Ptolemy won a reputation as a notable patron of the arts, the sponsor of painters and artists and the founder of the great museum and library at Alexandria. Although Ptolemy was considerably older than Aristotle's principal scholar, his inclusion could also have been on the grounds of security. In later life, Ptolemy was to assume the role of Alexander's personal bodyguard, his head of security, the supervisor of his meals, which would give him so much influence and access to Alexander at that fateful banquet held by Medius on 29 May 323 BC.

Ptolemy was certainly seen as a member of Alexander's entourage but, unlike Philotas, he probably didn't act as Philip's spy so, when Alexander was punished over the Pixadorus affair (338 BC), Ptolemy, along with others from Alexander's immediate retinue, was sent into exile.[6] Accordingly, he was absent from Macedonia when Philip was murdered and returned after Alexander assumed the reins of power. Undoubtedly Ptolemy also served with Alexander in those military campaigns before the great expedition across the Hellespont. When the royal army did cross in 334 BC, Ptolemy could be described as royal friend or companion, although he appears to have held no independent command. Arrian, who based his own account on Ptolemy's later writings, claims that Ptolemy was enrolled in the bodyguard immediately but other sources indicate that this happened only after the fall of Philotas.[7] The reason for this confusion will be discussed later.

After the king's great victory at Gaugamela (331 BC) Ptolemy received military promotion and was entrusted with a brigade of 3,000 infantry in the mopping-up operations following the king's outstanding victory. Ptolemy is never averse to dropping hints at how skilled he was, and Arrian includes this in his account. During these military sweeps, Ptolemy and his men were engaged in 'some close fighting' but cut the greater part of the enemy in pieces. Ptolemy, therefore, seems to have enjoyed a double role: Alexander's personal security officer and what would now be termed Commander of Special Forces.

After the Gaugamela campaign, Alexander became engaged in a strenuous struggle against the different satraps or governors of certain Persian provinces who refused to accept Macedonian domination. One of Alexander's most ardent Persian opponents was the satrap

Bessus who had been involved in the capture, deposition and murder of his former ruler, the King of Kings, Darius. Once Darius had been assassinated and removed from the scene, Bessus proclaimed himself as his legitimate successor, taking the title of Artaxerxes V. Alexander was determined to capture Darius' murderer and self-proclaimed successor. In 329 BC he crossed the Oxus River and hotly pursued Bessus, who now retreated back into the mountainous provinces of the Persian Empire. Alexander announced that his quarrel was with Bessus alone, a clever move to detach the Persian rebel from any support he might enjoy amongst the provincial nobles of Sogdiana. Two of Bessus' lieutenants, Spitamenes and Dataphernes, responded by placing Bessus under house arrest and invited Alexander to take him. Arrian, following Ptolemy, describes how Alexander sent a flying column under Ptolemy to Spitamenes' camp to seize the prisoner. Ptolemy surpassed himself, accomplishing in four days, as he proudly writes, what would have taken another commander ten. He arrived at the Persian camp only to discover Spitamenes and Dataphernes had second thoughts. They'd up-camped and left, though not taken Bessus with them: he was still under house arrest at a nearby village. Ptolemy immediately took a cavalry force, hastened to the village, sealed it off, and captured Bessus in what only can be described as a 'snatch operation'. Ptolemy, the ever-faithful commander, then sent a letter to Alexander asking what should be done with the prisoner. Alexander replied that Bessus was to be accorded no honours, he was to be stripped naked, a dog collar put round his neck and forced to stand by the side of the road until Alexander arrived. Ptolemy duly carried this out. When Alexander reached the place he climbed down from his chariot and interrogated the prisoner, accusing him of being a regicide and a usurper. Bessus was ordered to be flogged, his face mutilated, and then he was despatched back into the Persian Empire for public display before gruesome execution.

The Bessus story certainly enhances Ptolemy's reputation as a shrewd military commander and loyal subordinate. Perhaps Arrian himself had suspicions because he mentions another source, Aristobulus, who claims that Bessus was simply handed over to Alexander by other satraps. If the story were embroidered by Ptolemy many years after Alexander's death, then it provokes a suspicion that while the Great Conqueror was alive, Ptolemy was not averse to emphasizing his own military skill through subtle propaganda. Little wonder, as Aelian reports, that Alexander regarded Ptolemy as devious.[8]

Ptolemy was never far from the king's person. He accompanied Alexander on his remarkable journey to the Oracle of Ammon at Siwah across the Libyan Desert in the late spring of 331. During the rest of Alexander's reign, Ptolemy continued his double role of task force commander and head of security. When a spring of miraculous oil (actually petroleum) was discovered near the Oxus River, the find was immediately reported to Ptolemy who told Alexander, so that the king could consult his soothsayers. They declared it a most auspicious sign for the coming campaign, Alexander's invasion of the north Persian province of Sogdiana, to defeat certain rebels as well as their wild Scythian allies.

During the subsequent campaign, Ptolemy commanded a division as he did in India. Here, Ptolemy excelled himself. Arrian describes a dramatic scene of Homeric proportions, hand-to-hand combat between Ptolemy and an Indian chief.

During the pursuit, Ptolemy, son of Lagus, actually spotted the chief of the Indians of this area; he had already reached a hill and was trying to escape with some of his guards. Ptolemy, though he had a much inferior force, nevertheless charged for him; but the going was too steep and rough for his horse, so he dismounted, gave it to a man to lead, and continued to chase the Indian on foot. Seeing him coming, the Indian and his guards turned to face him. They met. The chief struck Ptolemy in the chest with his long spear, which pierced his armour but did not penetrate his body. With a blow clean through the Indian's thigh, Ptolemy laid him flat, and began to strip him, whereupon his guards, seeing their chief was down, turned and fled. Other Indians, however, on the nearby hills, grieved at the sight of their leader's body being carried off by the enemy. They hurried down and a fierce struggle ensued over the corpse. By then Alexander and his cavalrymen, now dismounted, were not far from the hill; they joined in the mêlée and finally succeeded in driving the Indians into the hills and getting possession of the body.[9]

It is rather remarkable how Ptolemy emerges as a great hero during the Indian campaign – a military expedition highly unpopular amongst Alexander's high command. Undoubtedly, the descriptions of Ptolemy's derring-do are the result of clever propaganda. Others may have resented the campaign and viewed it as harsh, but Ptolemy excelled himself there. Time and again, particularly in Arrian, we have Ptolemy helping to seize an impregnable Indian position, leading a flying column of mixed military units to harass the enemy, be it in the open or at the fortress of Sangala. If Alexander was Achilles, it is not Hephaestion who emerges as Patroclus but Ptolemy. In the closing weeks of the Indian campaign, Alexander had to face fierce resistance led by the Brahmin priests who fought with poisoned swords. Ptolemy was involved in the savage hand-to-hand fighting and received a potentially fatal wound. Quintus Curtius describes the scene in language worthy of Homer, where the wounded Ptolemy portrayed as the greatest of heroes, is actually healed by Alexander who finds an antidote for the poison in a remarkable dream from the gods.

Ptolemy, wounded in the left shoulder, not indeed deeply, but, it was evident, dangerously, attracted the chief anxiety of the king. Related by consanguinity to Alexander, he was considered by some as a son of Philip, having been born of one of his concubines (given, when pregnant, in marriage to Lagus). A guard of the presence, a most intrepid soldier, yet more highly accomplished in the arts of peace, of moderate and courteous manners, liberal in the highest degree, easy of access, he [Ptolemy] had assumed nothing of princely state. It was problematical whether these qualities endeared him more to the king or to the common soldiery. On this critical occasion, was first expressed the affection of his fellow-countrymen. A prophecy of his subsequent elevation, the care of the Macedonian soldiers for Ptolemy was like that of the king; who, overcome by the labours of the field and by anxiety, in order to remain in the apartment with the patient, caused his own couch to be lifted in. As soon as he had extended himself on it, Alexander sunk into a profound sleep. He declared, on awaking, 'That, in a dream, a dragon had appeared to him, presenting a herb in its mouth, as an antidote to the poison.' He described the colour of the plant, affirming his readiness to identify, if anyone should find it. The search, prosecuted at once by numbers, was not unsuccessful; and the king applied the remedy. Ptolemy's wound became immediately divested of anguish, and in a short time was perfectly healed.[10]

This story is repeated in other sources, which provide both a different location and cause for the wound, yet the ingredients would do justice to any epic tale of Ancient Greece. Ptolemy, the beloved of the king, the Gods and the army, is grievously wounded. Alexander is worried sick and tends him personally, a remedy is provided where a dragon (or a snake) leads Alexander to some precious antidote which saves the hero's life. It is a fine piece of propaganda which demonstrates that Ptolemy also knew his Homer. There's very little mention of Hephaestion, it is Ptolemy who is the king's companion, who's tended by the warrior king and saved by the Gods. The references to snakes or dragons revealing the cure would be very useful additions for Ptolemy's Egyptian subjects who regarded both as sacred, being messengers of the God. Ptolemy, as ruler of Egypt, laid great emphasis on himself being Alexander's direct heir to this kingdom of the Two Lands, the burier of the Great Conqueror and the guardian of his shrine. Such a story, describing Ptolemy as the brave, divinely touched warrior, tended lovingly by Alexander, would have enhanced Ptolemy's status in both Egypt and the Greek-speaking world.

Ptolemy certainly recovered from his wounds to continue Alexander's bloody work after the retreat through the Gedrosian Desert. When Alexander returns to the western Persian provinces, it is Ptolemy who is appointed to supervise the building of a funeral pyre for Calanus, the Indian wise man and friend of Alexander. When

Hephaestion dies, once again Ptolemy assumes the role of Patroclus, joining the royal Achilles in a final bloody raid against the Cosseans, a tribe which threatened Alexander's communications – the war was short and brutal, a fitting tribute to Hephaestion's shade. At the end of that campaign Arrian, who seemed to have admired Ptolemy as much as he did Alexander, closes Ptolemy's career as a military commander under Alexander with the most fitting epitaph. 'It was winter . . . when Alexander made his raid but then Alexander would never be put off by inclement weather or tough terrain and the same may be said of Ptolemy, son of Lagus, who commanded part of the expedition.'[11]

Accordingly, Ptolemy emerges from these references to his career as a senior general before Alexander's death as highly trusted and loved by Alexander, a brave warrior responsible for special operations who played a key role in guarding the king. There is no doubt that Ptolemy, after he became ruler of Egypt, was a most skilled hand at enhancing his status with a subtle flow of propaganda, both in his own writings and those of others, such as what Robin Lane Fox calls 'The Pamphlet', the *Alexander Romance*. This propaganda permeates Arrian, the *Alexander Romance*, Quintus Curtius and Diodorus. That all sources repeat the same story line points to a common origin: Ptolemy's court in Egypt. In describing the last days of the Indian campaign and Ptolemy's wounds, Diodorus writes:

> So the wounded were dying in this fashion, and for the rest Alexander was not so much concerned, but he was deeply distressed for Ptolemy, the future king, who was much beloved by him. An interesting and quite extraordinary event occurred in the case of Ptolemy, which some attributed to divine Providence. He was loved by all because of his character and kindness to all; and he obtained a succour appropriate to his good deeds. The king saw a vision in his sleep. It seemed to him that a snake appeared carrying a plant in its mouth, and showed him its nature and efficacy and the place where it grew. When Alexander awoke, he sought out the plant, and grinding it up plastered it on Ptolemy's body. He also prepared an infusion of

the plant and gave Ptolemy a drink of it. This restored him to health.[12]

In his accounts of Ptolemy after Alexander's death, Diodorus must have had access to the same propaganda where, once again, Ptolemy is depicted as Alexander's loyal friend, a wily general, and a brave warrior, much loved by everyone. Nevertheless there is a paradox here. What is remarkable is what Ptolemy doesn't say about himself which he could have done to emphasize his closeness to the king. Undoubtedly, Ptolemy was a most capable field commander but he was also responsible for the king's security.[13] Probably soon after Hephaestion's death, Ptolemy was promoted to be both the king's taster and steward, directly responsible for what the king ate and drank. He would, therefore, have played a key role at Medius' surprise party at the end of May 329 BC.

The source for this very important position is extremely good, Athenaeus quoting Chares, Alexander's Chamberlain:

> In our day the eater [i.e. the taster] had become the super-intendent of the entire service; his office was distinguished and honourable. Chares, at any rate, in the third book of his histories, says that Ptolemy was appointed taster for Alexander.[14]

Ptolemy, therefore, was Alexander's intelligence officer, collecting information, be it a spring of miraculous oil or rumours that Hermolaus and the pages were conspiring to kill Alexander. He was so close to Alexander, so trusted, he even supervised the king's food and drink. He, not Iolaus, the member of a disgraced clan, would be measuring out Alexander's wine and food. Above all, given Alexander's state of mind in 323 BC and the possibility of serious conspiracy, Ptolemy must have been very close to him both at Medius' banquet and those snacks allegedly Alexander ate as he lay by the pool in that bathhouse. Nevertheless, it is truly remarkable that Ptolemy himself never, either in any fragments or through Arrian, describes such closeness to the king in a personal and very intimate way. True, Ptolemy's history is lost, but Arrian read it: he was an ardent admirer

of both Ptolemy and Alexander, yet remains so silent on those last
days of the Great Conqueror. The same silence shrouds important
incidents such as Cleitus' fatal argument with Alexander or the latter's
great act of arson at Persepolis. More importantly, Ptolemy was at
Medius' party. He must have been close to the king during the last ten
days of his life, yet never refers to any ailments, rumours of treason or
what happened immediately afterwards. Ptolemy, through Arrian, is
silent about so many things. He seems wholly determined to portray
himself as a loyal friend, the effective field commander quite distant
from the seamy court politics of Alexander's court and camp.

The only conclusion I can draw is that Ptolemy's lack of reference
about such personal intimacy to the king was for good reason – if
Alexander was murdered, then what role did Ptolemy play? Was he
guilty of a lapse of security, or did he play a more active role? I firmly
believe in the latter.

Ptolemy must have been about thirty-one years old when his
natural father Philip died. Ptolemy had been exiled from Macedon
and had little to do with the assassination of the king. However, if
Alexander was involved in Philip's murder, and there is considerable
evidence that this is so, Ptolemy must have had a view on his half-
brother's participation in the assassination of the old king. The
circumstances surrounding Philip's death are highly suspicious,
particularly the way three of Alexander's personal guards were the
ones who pursued Pausanias and speared him to death. In the War of
Succession which followed Alexander's death, Ptolemy had no time
for Perdiccas, Attalus and Leonnatus, the killers of Philip's assassin. In
his eighteenth book, Diodorus describes Ptolemy after Alexander's
death as 'utterly hostile to Perdiccas'. And he and this important
general were soon at each other's throats in a fight to the death.[15]
Ptolemy certainly would have had suspicions about the involvement of
Alexander, Olympias and others of their entourage in Philip's murder,
enough to invoke and nourish, according to the Macedonian custom,
a blood feud.

Ptolemy was not a young man when Alexander succeeded to the
throne. In age, he was midway between younger members of
Alexander's retinue and the likes of conservative Macedonians such as

Cleitus, Antipater and Parmenio. In my view, he strongly sympathized with the latter. When Cleitus had his violent confrontation with the king, that well-placed source Aristobulus claims Ptolemy grasped Cleitus, dragged him from the royal tent and pushed him into the cold dark night, even to beyond the confines of the camp.[16] Quintus Curtius is not so detailed but he does relate how Ptolemy was one of those who pleaded on Cleitus' behalf. Aristobulus, however, was a first-hand witness, a primary source, and his description of what happened requires careful analysis. Here we have Ptolemy, only recently promoted to the king's personal bodyguard, virtually manhandling Cleitus, a gruff old bear of a man, Alexander's senior commander. Cleitus was beside himself with rage and very drunk, yet Ptolemy can drag him out of the tent and push him into the night. Cleitus would have hardly allowed what he considered one of Alexander's 'toadies' to lay violent hands on him, especially when he was brimming with anger and drink. He must, therefore, have enjoyed a close relationship with Ptolemy, accepting the king's bodyguard as a friend, sharing common values and, in particular, a mutual distaste for Alexander's increasing Oriental despotism. Significantly, Ptolemy, through Arrian, never praises Alexander's Persianizatian nor does he depict himself as a fervent supporter of Alexander's increasing absolutism.

Another important incident underlines Ptolemy's conservative views. In his description of the burning of Persepolis, Ptolemy, through Arrian, simply describes it as the result of a strategic decision, a body blow to the power of Persia. The total destruction of the great Hall of Audience is depicted as almost sacred, a symbolic act, just punishment for all the sins Persia's King of Kings had committed against the Greeks.[17] Plutarch, however, provides a different story. He alleges that Alexander became drunk and was incited into the arson by Thaïs, an Athenian courtesan, who also became Ptolemy's mistress and, in time, mother of three of his children. Thaïs must have had her lover's support, she must have reflected Ptolemy's mood. She voiced the vision of conservative Macedonians, such as Ptolemy, to strike at the heart of Persia and destroy its culture with fire and sword. Thaïs is an interesting character. An Athenian courtesan, she must have met

Alexander when he visited Athens after the great victory of Chaeronea and, with other hetaira such as Glycera, Harpalus' mistress, joined the court of Macedon. Thaïs' relationship with Alexander, then Ptolemy, fuels all kinds of speculation. Her involvement in the burning of Persepolis is a reflection of what others were thinking – as was her remark – ignored by historians – yet reported by Plutarch. In prompting Alexander to commit arson, Thaïs declares: 'I have undergone great fatigues wandering about Asia.' It's a perceptive comment which shows that, as early as 330 BC, four years before the mutiny at the Jhelum (Beas) River in India, some of Alexander's elitist entourage had already had their fill 'of wandering about'. Thaïs was one and, more importantly, Ptolemy was another.[18]

Before he launched his Indian campaign Alexander understood the resentment of his army about advancing further east. He encouraged them with speeches, flattery and bribes, but this all abruptly ended. The army refused to move any further and Coenus, in Arrian's account, delivers the speech of defiance which wins such rapturous support from his comrades and provoked the anger of the king. Ptolemy, by his own admission, was a leading commander. He must have been present at that fateful council meeting. I believe Coenus' speech, as reported by Arrian, was more Ptolemy's work, the publication of the Macedonian manifesto which can be starkly summarized as follows: Alexander's troops, including his commanders, had campaigned and fought long enough. They wanted to go home and, if the king wished to continue his military expedition, then he should raise a new army. Ptolemy certainly does not disassociate himself from this speech. Usually he is so quiet in such matters, but here, instead, he lays great emphasis on Coenus' words and the support they won from everyone except the king. Coenus died shortly afterwards. However, in his speech, Coenus talks of Alexander's plans against the Scythians around the Caspian Sea, as well as expeditions against the city-states of Libya and Carthage in North Africa, plans Alexander only considered a long time later; he was actually preparing to implement them just before his sudden death in Babylon. Coenus' is voicing Ptolemy's thoughts at the time but embroidered to include plans not laid out until three years later. In brief, Ptolemy's attitude, which reflected that of Thaïs, can be summarized as follows: Persia should be punished, the king should be faithful to Macedonian traditions, the army had achieved enough and it was time to rest on their laurels and enjoy the spoils of victory.[19]

Such views certainly surfaced soon after Alexander's death when the leading generals gathered to discuss the succession. The account given by Curtius is remarkable. Ptolemy, for all his closeness to Alexander and the propaganda about his being the Great Conqueror's legitimate successor in Egypt, is the one general who totally rejects any idea of Alexander's children by a Persian princess being allowed to rule Macedonians. Ptolemy's speech stands in stark contrast to the manifestos of the others. Curtius' summary is crucial:

'At Babylon, whence began our digression, the guards of the presence convened, in the palace, the principal courtiers and leaders of the army: there followed a concourse of soldiers, eager to know on whom Alexander's dominion would devolve. As an impenetrable crowd excluded many officers from admission, a herald proclaimed that no one should approach besides those called by name but this regulation was despised. A strong wailing burst out, subsided, and was re-excited. At length, the tears of the multitude subsided, expectation held them silent. The regal chair, in which were the diadem, the robes, and the arms of Alexander, were exposed to public view, Perdiccas then deposited in the chair the signet which the king had given him the day before. On seeing these vacant ensigns, the assembly once more wept.

'"I here," said Perdiccas, "surrender to you the ring delivered by the king himself to me, with which he was used to seal his acts of power. To match the calamity with which we are afflicted, not one could be devised by incensed gods. The vastness of his achievements justifies us in believing that the Celestials lent such a man to human affairs, and that, their designs accomplished, they have suddenly taken back their offspring. Since, therefore, nothing remains of him, more than is always shut out from immortality, let us, as soon as possible, discharge the last duties to his corpse and name; mindful in what city, among what people, we are, and of what a king and champion we have been deprived. Our present deliberations, fellow-soldiers, must embrace measures to keep the conquest won among the conquerors. A head is indispensable: to constitute this, either single or multifold, is now in your power. But it behoves you to know that a military mass without a leader is a body without the intelligent principle. Roxane's declared pregnancy has proceeded six months: we pray that she may bear a son: become an adult; his shall be the kingdom, the gods assenting. By whom ye will be governed meanwhile, now determine." Thus Perdiccas.

'Then Nearchus spoke: "That the blood and lineage of Alexander will alone grace the imperial dignity, no one can deny . . . But to wait for a king not yet born, and to pass by one already in existence, suits neither the inclination of the Macedonians, nor this crisis: there is a son of the king by Barsine [Hercules]: to him let us yield the diadem." This speech pleased no one: the soldiers therefore, in their manner, clashing their spears and shields, perseveringly interrupted it. They nearly proceeded to tumult, as Nearchus stubbornly maintained his opinion.

'"An offspring entirely worthy to rule the Macedonian nation," then observed Ptolemy, "is the son neither of Roxane or Barsine! It will irritate Europe to pronounce the name of a king having so much captive blood in his composition. Have we subdued the Persians to serve their progeny; which those rightful lords of the East, Xerxes and Darius, with armed myriads, and powerful fleets, in vain required us to do? My proposition is that Alexander's throne be fixed in his pavilion, those who were associated to his councils there meet, as often as it be needful to deliberate in common: and as to any point which the majority of these decree, let it stand a sovereign act: let the generals and viceroys obey these." With Ptolemy some agreed, but the greater number with Perdiccas.

'Then Aristonus arose to speak: "When consulted as to whom he left the kingdom, Alexander willed that the most worthy should be elected: his disposal of the signet shows that himself adjudged Perdiccas the most worthy. Nor was this companion of the dying king alone with him: but the king, casting his eyes round, singled, from a crowd of friends, this man to whom he delivered his ring. It pleased him, therefore, to confer the supremacy on Perdiccas."

'The assembly entertained no doubt that Aristonus had rightly construed Alexander's last act; they therefore unanimously desired Perdiccas to step forth, and take the royal signet. Perdiccas hesitated between avidity and bashfulness. He imagined that the more modestly he approached the object which his wishes were embracing, the more it would be pressed upon his acceptance. After lingering, long undetermined how to act, he retired behind his companions.

'Meleager, one of the captains, whom the indecision of Perdiccas had elated, began with fortified spirit: "The gods can never permit the fortune of Alexander, the dignity of such power, to descend on those shoulders: men, assuredly, will never suffer it. I speak not of individuals more ennobled than he is. Nor does it concern us, whether we have, for a king, the son of Roxane, whenever he shall be produced, or Perdiccas, since the latter, under the title of protector, will seize the sovereignty. Hence it is, that he will hear of no king, unless it be one in embryo and while it were just and requisite that all things be expeditiously settled, he alone is waiting the full term of months, having already divined that a boy is conceived: do you doubt that Perdiccas is prepared at least to substitute one? If solemnly adjuring us, Alexander had left us this man for a king, this alone of all his commands, I should judge it right to disobey. Why, Macedonians, do you not separate to pillage the treasuries? To these imperial riches the people is heir!" Having thus spoken, Meleager broke away through the armed crowd, those who had opened for him to pass, followed to the promised spoil.'[20]

Curtius' account is remarkable because it shows Ptolemy in a totally uncompromising attitude compared with the rest. He wants nothing to do with Persian rulers, he regards the Persian Empire as the spoils of conquest. He depicts the King of Kings as Greece's natural enemy and he wants a Council of Regency even without the viceroy Perdiccas. Ptolemy is totally at odds with many of his colleagues. Now, it would be easy to reject Quintus Curtius' description as a product of a later historian's fertile imagination yet Curtius' account faithfully reflects Ptolemy's attitude in the forty years following Alexander's death. Ptolemy attempted to stay on good terms with his colleagues but he accepted no central command; as Diodorus relates, Ptolemy took Egypt and held it as a prize of war against all comers. Ptolemy made great play of being Alexander's heir and the custodian of his corpse but, apart from a possible marriage alliance with Alexander's half-sister Cleopatra, he showed little regard for Alexander's wives or children. The Greek writer, Pausanias, in his *Description of Greece* corroborates Curtius' account. Pausanias declares that Ptolemy's opposition to a central ruler conflicted with the views of others, and that Ptolemy was 'chiefly responsible' for the consequent division of the empire.[21]

Ptolemy made himself ruler and master of Egypt. Curtius' and Pausanias' accounts, it is even more surprising that Ptolemy, so out of step with other Lords of the Purple, should have acquired so easily such a powerful prize, especially in view of the hostility between him and Perdiccas who, within eighteen months of these events in Babylon, was conspiring to wrest Egypt from Ptolemy.[22] In fact, Egypt is the key to the events of June 323 BC. Ptolemy never describes, nor does any other source, how Ptolemy, one general amongst many, became ruler of Egypt. True, there are the stories in the *Alexander Romance* and elsewhere about Alexander leaving a will, of entrusting Egypt to Ptolemy but there is no other evidence for this. Such remarks were the work of Ptolemy's fertile imagination.[23]

The kingdom of the Two Lands was a great prize. It was a sovereign state with a history stretching back thousands of years. It had natural borders easy to defend and, according to Diodorus, was the richest province of the Macedonian Empire. Egypt was one of the few countries to welcome Alexander's invasion with open arms and support his cause against the hated Persians. Egypt remained relatively loyal for the rest of Alexander's reign. More importantly, it was one of the few provinces not to rebel or be torn by civil war after Alexander's sudden death. The prize was both easy and rich.[24] Egypt had its own Macedonian garrisons and a well-stocked treasury. Most significantly, it was not under the command of any Macedonian rival but rather a corrupt administrator, Cleomenes from Naucratis, a

Greek colony in the Delta. Cleomenes proved easy to remove. He was venal, self-serving and had been formally warned by Alexander in the year before the Great Conqueror's death to put his house in order. According to all the sources available, Ptolemy took over Egypt, he was welcomed ecstatically, removed Cleomenes and faced no opposition within the kingdom of the Two Lands.[25] Egypt was also of tremendous strategic importance in the Macedonian Empire. According to Arrian, who must have based his account on Ptolemy, just before Alexander attacked the city of Tyre, Alexander called an important council meeting in which he described how important it was to conquer Palestine and so move into Egypt. He concluded his speech by pointing out that once Egypt was in their hands it would diminish any real threat from across the sea, particularly Greece. Ptolemy must have recalled these words as would other commanders such as Perdiccas, so it adds even more intrigue to the question, how did Ptolemy acquire such a powerful prize so quickly and so easily?[26] The only answer must be that Ptolemy was directly supported by the other great power in the Macedonian Empire, Antipater, regent of Macedon, virtual ruler of the homeland, whose ambassador, his own son Cassander, was present at Alexander's death and the deliberations which followed. One of the constant, political, strategic facts which dominated that long and bloody struggle between Alexander's successors was the friendship between Cassander and Ptolemy and between the new Egyptian ruler and the house of Antipater.[27]

I suggest that this alliance was forged shortly after Alexander emerged from the Gedrosian Desert and began his purge both at home and abroad. Ptolemy became fearful, as did Antipater, and they conspired together to bring about the Great Conqueror's death. This was the only choice open to them where they had so much to gain and, if they failed to take action, so much to lose. The first seeds of the conspiracy must have been sown in India where the army had reached well beyond the limits of exhaustion. Diodorus seems to be drawing from a close primary source when he describes the Macedonians as they became locked in confrontation with Alexander. They appear like a defeated army, and this is before they experienced the horrors of the Gedrosian Desert.

They had spent almost eight years among toils and dangers . . .
There had been many losses among the soldiers, and no relief
from fighting was in sight. The hooves of the horses had been
worn thin by steady marching. The arms and armour were
wearing out, and Greek clothing was quite gone. They had to
clothe themselves in foreign materials, re-cutting the garments of
the Indians. This was the season also, as luck would have it, of the
heavy rains. These had been going on for seventy days, to the
accompaniment of continuous thunder and lightning.[28]

Such an experience must have seriously affected Ptolemy,
deepened by the exhausting march back and the near fatal wound
he sustained. By the time he reached the western provinces of Persia
in 325 BC, Ptolemy had been campaigning for almost nine years. He
had experienced searing hardship and danger, forced to march to
the edge of the world because of Alexander's *pothos* – his belief he
was *aniketos*, invincible! Such an attitude had cost Alexander a greater
part of his army whilst Ptolemy had nearly lost his life. In that two-
year period following the retreat from India other fears would
surface. When would Alexander stop? Ptolemy and the rest had
achieved the vision so loudly proclaimed by the great thinkers of
Greece – the total destruction of the Persian Empire.

Nevertheless, by 323 BC, Alexander was again experiencing *pothos*
– a desire to continue – either north-east against the Scythians or
west to attack the powerful city states of North Africa. What had
Ptolemy achieved from all this? Promotion in an army which went
hand-in-hand with summary trial and execution. A cartful of treasure
which Alexander could seize or burn whenever he wished, and a
Persian wife he didn't want and soon discarded after Alexander's
death. There is no hint of Alexander about to bestow on Ptolemy
some great lasting prize, such as a province or satrapy. Ptolemy was
now in his early forties and had become nothing more than a glorified mercenary. Other more sinister issues had to be addressed.
Blood, sweat and tears, not to mention loyalty, appeared to mean
little to Alexander. Men who had stood in the battle line but had
the temerity to oppose Alexander soon disappeared, whatever the

pretext, and the list was getting longer. The king's increasingly psychotic rages were not limited to the rank-and-file but to his Companions, Polyperchon or Cassander, not to mention Persian satraps, one of whom Alexander executed by his own hand. And the future? More campaigning, more hard knocks. During the mutiny at Opis, Alexander had screamed at the Macedonians and jumped down to execute the ring of leaders himself. He decimated the troops of disgraced governors whilst brigading Persian fighters with Macedonians. Alexander was increasingly ruthless, and Ptolemy realized that his own profound silence and unspoken opposition at the Beas River in India would never be forgotten. Now Alexander was determined on more wars, more expeditions, he was also turning on the House of Antipater – determined to bring it down.

Cassander had hardly received a loving reception when he arrived in Babylon. Whilst Antipater, already fearful and secretly plotting, had been summoned to court, only to prevaricate. Curtius reports that General Craterus, leading the 10,000 veterans back to Macedon, carried secret orders not only to depose Antipater but to kill him.[29] Craterus' attitude to such orders is not just a matter of speculation. Craterus had proved to be a leading figure in the anti-Persian faction in Alexander's court. True, he had to attend to certain duties in Cilicia before he reached Macedon and he must have welcomed any delay in the coming confrontation with Antipater. When Alexander died, Craterus was still only halfway home; it is significant that he received no governorship or portion of the empire and, when Antipater moved to demonstrate he was still the rightful ruler of Macedon, Craterus had no choice but to submit and put his forces at Antipater's disposal.[30] Antipater's removal would have constituted a real threat to Ptolemy. If Antipater fell, Alexander, through Craterus, would control the Macedonian homeland, its supplies and resources as well as the different clans of the kingdom. Alexander would also be able to strengthen his grasp over Greece. If matters turned sour, Ptolemy would have nowhere to go; the fate of Harpalus had proved this. In view of their close mutual support later on, Antipater and Ptolemy were in secret alliance over what they must have regarded as their 'mutual problem' by early summer 323 BC. Alexander had to be removed before Craterus reached home or Alexander struck, be it at Cassander or even Ptolemy. Once Craterus left, the opportunity presented itself. Alexander was now devoid of one close friend and loyal senior commander, which left Hephaestion recently promoted to even further glory and status.

In Arrian's account, Alexander's love of Hephaestion is made very clear. Ptolemy could not deny it, yet here, as usual, Ptolemy is also silent. He doesn't say anything bad about the royal favourite but doesn't say anything good, whilst Hephaestion's death is dismissed in a few lines, as it is in the other sources. There is every possibility that Hephaestion was also murdered. In any plot against a ruler, the guards have to be weakened or removed. Antipater and Cassander must have realized this, which explains their alliance with Ptolemy. If Craterus was gone and Ptolemy the bodyguard was on their side, Hephaestion would be their only real obstacle.

By 324 BC, Hephaestion, apparently a handsome, healthy but very arrogant man, had virtually become Alexander's lieutenant. His death in the summer of 324 was extremely swift and unexpected. The first symptoms of his illness seem very similar to those of Alexander: a raging fever and terrible thirst. Nevertheless, Hephaestion seems to have been about to recover; Alexander was so confident that he decided to watch some athletics whilst Hephaestion's physician, Glaucas, went to the theatre. Hephaestion left his sick bed and declared that he was feeling better. He ate a whole boiled chicken, drank a deep draught of chilled wine and immediately suffered what was described as a quick and fatal relapse. Alexander was hastily summoned back but Hephaestion's decline was so rapid, his favourite was dead before he reached the sick room. Now, the evidence is meagre: very high fever, raging thirst, followed by an amelioration of the symptoms, unsuitable food and drink, then an abrupt fatal relapse. Alexander may have suspected poison; he certainly blamed the hapless physician Glaucas and had him crucified. In my view, bearing in mind that Hephaestion died only after Craterus left, as well as the abrupt suddenness of Hephaestion's decline, the favourite could have been poisoned and Ptolemy had a hand in it.

A.S. Taylor in his book *On Poisons* talks of a great thirst being a common symptom of arsenic poisoning. Hephaestion suffered from this yet he appears to have recovered, probably purging his system by vomiting, but the relapse was so swift that what was mixed with this chicken and white wine does provoke suspicion. This suspicion is deepened when viewed against the circumstances. Hephaestion had improved so much that both Alexander and the physician had left the sick room. When Alexander tended Ptolemy, he'd moved his bed into the room – he would have surely done the same for Hephaestion the beloved. Nevertheless, Alexander left, fully confident all was well – a feeling shared by the luckless Glaucas. Hephaestion shared their optimism enough to order a very substantial meal. Ptolemy was the royal steward, responsible for Alexander's meals; he was certainly well placed to influence whatever Hephaestion ate or drank.[31]

Ptolemy may have also recommended the selection of Craterus to lead the veterans home, secretly assuring himself and the allies in the House of Antipater that by the time Craterus reached Pella the situation would have radically changed. If Hephaestion, or even Craterus, had been in Babylon when Alexander died, the political situation would have been much more volatile. Hephaestion, whom Alexander valued as precious as 'life itself', would have certainly been appointed regent or viceroy. He would have been a fervent supporter of Roxane and Alexander's posthumous child. The same can be said of Craterus – there is every possibility that Alexander, whilst dying, did not leave his empire to the strongest (Kratisto) but to Craterus. The absent general, in view of Hephaestion's death the previous year, would have been Alexander's natural choice. However, by June 323, the man Alexander described as 'Alexander's friend' was dead and Craterus whom Alexander described as the 'King's friend' were removed from any source of real power. There is no record of any friendship between Ptolemy and Hephaestion. Certainly, if the favourite had survived it would have proved more difficult to remove Alexander and, even if Alexander did die, Hephaestion would have been a major obstacle. He would have emerged as regent, or viceroy, and, in such circumstances, I doubt whether Ptolemy could have seized power in Egypt.

By the time Cassander arrived in Alexander's court, Hephaestion was dead and the secret and serious negotiations between his family and Ptolemy would have continued in earnest. The timing of Medius' banquet was also appropriate. No evidence exists about Alexander's immediate plans but the next expedition was certainly under way. Nearchus was on the point of leaving and taking the fleet with him. Alexander's frustrations against the House of Antipater were mounting; Craterus was drawing nearer Macedon and the Lords of the Purple would also receive their different tasks. If Alexander died, Ptolemy would need ships for Egypt because the land route from Babylon to the Delta was long and arduous: Ptolemy's brigade would require transport whilst both he and Antipater would regard it as essential that senior commanders such as Nearchus be present when decisions had to be made regarding Alexander's death. The events following the king's confrontation with the Macedonian assembly at Opis would have added fresh urgency for Ptolemy. True, Alexander and his men exchanged the kiss of peace at a truly royal banquet but Alexander still continued with his plans. He not only pensioned off the rank-and-file but also senior commanders such as Cleitus the White, Gorgias, Polydamas and the rest.

Alexander then moved on to the next part of his plan. Diodorus talks of Persian units 'now capable of serving as a counterbalance to the Macedonian phalanx'.[32] Quintus Curtius adds that it was more than just counterbalance: the Macedonians were being infiltrated at every level by Persians. It was only to be a matter of time before dinner parties to which Medius invited Alexander, where he would feast with Macedonians and/or Greeks, might become a rarity. Ptolemy would have felt increasingly vulnerable. In some accounts of the mutiny at Opis, the impression given is that Alexander and his personal command executed mutineers. Curtius presents a different picture – the so-called mutineers, which also included veteran officers, were handed over to Persians and, because of Alexander's fury, were not even given an honourable death but loaded with chains and drowned in the river. Quintus Curtius describes the scene.

Alexander distributed to Persian nobles the principal military commands . . . distinguished particular bodies of Persian infantry and cavalry by the appellation 'royal' . . . selected from them an armed retinue, and committed to Persians the guard of his body. As Barbarian officers were leading to execution several Macedonians who had kindled the sedition, one of the latter, distinguished by rank and seniority, is reported thus to have addressed the king. 'How long sir, will you gratify your anger, by executions conducted in a foreign manner? Your own soldiers, your fellow citizens are hauled to punishment by their captives, without being allowed to plead. If you deem us to merit death, at least change our executioners.' Alexander had received the friendly remonstrance, could he have borne the truth: but his rage had developed into madness. Therefore, he ordered those who had charge of the prisoners, because they had paused a moment, to plunge them into the river, chained as they were.[33]

Such developments must have deeply concerned Ptolemy. The Macedonian element of the army was being weakened, what remained was being infiltrated, whilst Persians were being given high-ranking posts and important tasks in the enforcement of security of the royal person, Ptolemy's particular responsibility. The reconciliation at Opis did not hinder this process.

Meanwhile, Alexander, at once repairing the waste of the army, and assimilating the manners of his subjects, adopted into the Macedonian ranks the best of the Persian soldiers: to a superior thousand, separated from the excellent, he gave the intimate station of bodyguards: another, a band of not less than 10,000 spearmen, he appointed to watch round his pavilion.[34]

The reference to Persian bodyguards does not mean Ptolemy was removed but that Alexander was setting up a parallel system as he was at every level of civic and military life.

The timing of Medius' banquet also coincided with the arrival of envoys from different states and nations who hurried to pay their respects to Alexander. In the main they all received little satisfaction. Alexander's plans would continue, and he issued two decrees – the return of the exiles and the granting of divine honours to himself. All this would only increase agitation amongst the Greek states and cause serious unrest in cities such as Athens. Alexander's death at a time of such disquiet might take the passion out of such opposition. The arrival of these envoys would certainly be the most appropriate occasion to announce his death as well as what decrees had been issued by the subsequent Council of Regency. The management of these envoys was, despite Alexander's death and the immediate chaos which ensued, seen as a high priority. Quintus Curtius remarks that 'the ambassadors of the nations continued to present themselves' illustrates how important Alexander's generals regarded them as a means of informing the world about the abrupt change in power at its centre.[35]

Finally, the timing of Medius' banquet coincided with Alexander's plans (and Ptolemy's secret plots) regarding future campaigns. From Arrian's account it would appear that Alexander was not only commissioning Nearchus but had decided to go with him (Arrian refers to those sailing with Alexander). Others were to march by land, leaving a day earlier.[36] Now, if Alexander was going by sea, there is every chance that Ptolemy would be in charge of land forces – perhaps second-in-command to Perdiccas. The opportunity of being so close to the king at such a time might not be available for weeks, months, if ever and, all the time, Craterus was drawing closer to Pella, Alexander's anger against Antipater was deepening and the process of Persianization continued apace. Just as important, if Arabia and North Africa were, according to Alexander's plans, to become theatres of war, Egypt, Ptolemy's prize, would be turned into an armed camp and not be so easy to seize and hold.

The timing of Alexander's death in Babylon was crucial but it had to be set in a fitting context of 'auguries' and signs. Nothing hides human-designed cunning more successfully than ascribing the cause of events to 'Fickle Fortune' or, even better, the will of the Gods. Such a context was deliberately created around Alexander's death in 323 BC. The omens which greeted Alexander in and around Babylon should not be dismissed as the mere phenomena read by hindsight into the death of a great man. Such supernatural phenomena are quite common in accounts of the births, deaths and achievements of world figures. If omens and spiritual phenomena can be viewed in hindsight and turned into prophecies, well-planned omens can also help to condition the mind of the intended victim as well as the attitude of those around him. They can be used as preparation for the hand of God, the act of some vengeful deity as well as be a cloak to conceal more human, sinister designs. Plutarch relates how the omens which confronted Alexander after he had entered Babylon deeply agitated him. They certainly prepared the ground for his death. The king also lacked the spiritual comfort or moral support Hephaestion or Craterus might have offered. The death of Hephaestion undoubtedly sharpened Alexander's anxiety, deepened his depression and heightened his tension, which he sublimated by his swift, murderous attack upon the Cossean tribesmen. Of course military activity might placate his soul but such omens and auguries would influence Alexander to drink long and deep on uncut wine. The prospect of a drinking bout at a privately arranged party would be most attractive to him, something to dull the senses and prepare the mind for sleep.

The circumstances surrounding Alexander's death do appear to be permeated with a deliberate theatre, full of drama of events being arranged by a stage manager and, who better fills that role than Ptolemy, the Companion entrusted with 'guarding the door to the royal chamber'. Certain events were the result of mere chance such as the king's hat being blown off during a boating trip along the Euphrates. Others, however, can be more deliberate. Chaldaean soothsayers can be bribed, crows can be gathered then drugged so that, when released, they fall to the ground. Apollodorus' sacrifice where the victim's liver had no lobe could be arranged to recall another sacrifice performed in Euripides' play where such an augury was the harbinger of ill fortune. Apollodorus' sacrifices were analysed by his brother Peithagoras who later prophesied the death of Perdiccas, Ptolemy's great rival who died only a few years later, assassinated by his own men along the Nile. Peithagoras also made similar prophecies about another of Ptolemy's enemies, the ancient and one-eyed Antigonus, who was killed during the bloody scramble for empire in the decades following Alexander's death in Babylon. Apollodorus informed the king what had happened, so a procedure had to be followed. Apollodorus would first have to approach the person responsible for the king's security, Ptolemy of Lagus, who was also directly responsible for the building of the funeral pyre for Calanus, the Indian holy man who committed self-annihilation but prophesied, before he died, that he would later meet Alexander in Babylon. There is no evidence that such prophecies were the work of Ptolemy. Only that he was a constant factor in them as he was in the most surprising omen, the prisoner who escaped, wandered into the royal quarters and sat down at the king's throne.[37]

Alexander was deeply disturbed by this affair. According to Arrian, he feared it was some sort of plot against him. In fact Alexander was not far from the truth. He had the prisoner closely interrogated and later executed. Now this man's wandering was a breach of royal security, Ptolemy's responsibility, but he could always pass the blame to someone else, especially as he was now sharing security of the king's person with hated Persians.

Plutarch's version of the story is even more interesting. He claims that the man who wandered on to the throne gave his name as Dionysius, the same as the God whom Alexander regarded as so hostile to him because of his destruction of Thebes and whose malign influence was blamed for the king's brutal murder of Cleitus. Plutarch's version contains further fascinating additions. The prisoner told Alexander he'd escaped and had a vision from the God Serapis who had told him what to do. Once again this Graeco-Egyptian God plays a role in the events surrounding Alexander's death. Given that the cult of Serapis was introduced by Ptolemy some time after 301 BC, the obvious conclusion is that Plutarch took this story from some of the sheaves of propaganda which originated in Ptolemy's Egypt. It does seem more than a coincidence that the story of a prisoner escaping and sitting on the royal throne was closely connected with the religious cult introduced by the man who later occupied Alexander's Egyptian throne yet who was also responsible for the king's security at the time.[38] Who this unfortunate 'Dionysius' was is a matter of speculation, but the simplicity with which he answers

Alexander's questions indicates, that he must have been weak-minded, a man easily managed who would be immediately handed over to Ptolemy for questioning. He would not be the first 'catspaw' used in any conspiracy, ancient or modern, be it the murder of Philip of Macedon or any leading politician of our own era. It could also be argued that this 'Dionysius' was really a Messenger from the Gods to warn Alexander. After all, when Cleitus was murdered, Alexander had been quick to accept the conclusion of Aristander, that it was all the work of a malicious God. If the divine could be blamed for Cleitus' death – why not Alexander's?

Quintus Curtius' account deepens the mystery of this 'omen' because it contains a parallel story which occurred during one of Alexander's campaigns. The king and his army were in night quarters high on a freezing mountainside, when a weary Macedonian soldier, part of the army's rear guard, stumbled into the camp, freezing cold, desperate for warmth. Quintus Curtius provides the details.

> A private soldier, at length gained the camp. The king, who was warming himself at a fire, on perceiving him, sprang from his seat, and having assisted the soldier, stricken with frost, and nearly insensible, to take off his armour, desired him to sit down in his place. This man, for some time, knew neither where he was, nor by whom entertained. At length his vital heat was restored, he saw the royal chair and the king, and rose up in affright. Alexander, observing this, said 'Are you ignorant, fellow-soldier, how much happier the Macedonians live under their king than the Persians? To these it were death to sit in the king's seat yet it has preserved your life.'[39]

The contrast between the two stories is too obvious to miss, as is its obvious moral. On campaign Alexander is the true Macedonian leader: ritual and status mean nothing to him compared to the health of one of his men. In Babylon, however, Alexander has been seduced by Persia and its ways, so a man who stumbles on to his throne is brutally tortured and executed. Someone in Babylon, in the months before Alexander's death, was playing with Alexander's mind, deepening his anxiety, sharpening the tension, a wily plotter, encouraging the king to drink so as to forget. The person responsible was devious; stage-managing scenes to remind Alexander about how much he had changed, like a killer who plays with his victim before he strikes. Ptolemy fits this description: the references to Serapis, the fact that he was responsible for guarding the king whilst he would certainly be close enough to Alexander, in those campaigning days before a campfire, to recall such an incident.

It is interesting that Arrian never cites Ptolemy, the bluff soldier, the loyal commander, as a source for such uncanny happenings. Arrian's source for the story of Apollodorus, and Calanus as well as the man who occupied Alexander's throne, is that irrepressible gossip, Aristobulus who, as we have noted, later became secretary to Cassander at the House of Antipater, the close friend of Ptolemy, ruler of Egypt.[40]

The murder of Alexander is suffused with even more dramatic flourishes, allusions to past events and references to Alexander's favourite poet Euripides. Ptolemy was not only intent on murder but enjoyed the plotting, using those last days as a mirror to recall what had happened before. For a start it is remarkable how the circumstances surrounding Alexander's death reflected those surrounding Philip's, some thirteen years earlier. In 336 BC, before he was assassinated, Philip was on the verge of new conquests; so was Alexander in 323 BC. Philip was receiving the plaudits and honours of Greece at the height of his power; as was Alexander. In 336 BC, Philip had taken a new wife who was expecting a child; so was Alexander thirteen years later. Philip died in the presence of Perdiccas, Leonnatus and Attalus; so did Alexander. Two of Philip's closest friends, Parmenio and Attalus, were absent at his death; Alexander, in 323 BC, lacked the protection of Hephaestion and Craterus. Philip was about to receive divine honours, and so was Alexander. Philip never suspected the danger was so close, and nor did Alexander. Philip's death was cloaked in mystery and so was Alexander's. The Great Conqueror's death had other dramatic flourishes. During the great crises of Alexander's life, lines from the poet Euripides had been quoted, such as Alexander's enigmatic remark just before the death of Philip and those of his newly wed wife and child. During his confrontation with the king, Cleitus quoted lines from Euripides' *Andromache*, as did Callisthenes shortly before he fell from power. When he entered Babylon Alexander heard of the sacrificial victim which had no lobe in its liver; this is reflected in a scene from one of Euripides' plays. Alexander died, according to one source, toasting Dionysius the God who persecuted him; moreover he did so drinking cup by cup with Proteas, the nephew of Cleitus whom he had so cruelly killed, whilst quoting from Euripides' *Andromache* – the same play Cleitus echoed just before his death. The overall conclusion is that Ptolemy, Alexander's murderer, was someone who enjoyed plotting his king's death, who deemed it necessary, and evoked symbols and memories from the past about Alexander's own conduct. Ptolemy, that student of Aristotle, who had the deviousness, the means and the motive to carry out the act. The Spanish proverb, 'Revenge is a dish best served cold' certainly fits what Ptolemy intended and successfully carried through.

The careful and elaborate preparations by Ptolemy in his murder of Alexander, for example, the quoting from Euripides' *Andromache* and the other psychological touches, beg the question: was there personal animosity between the Great Conqueror and his able lieutenant? If Ptolemy was the illegitimate son of Philip (or even suspected of being), he must have been trained in the art of dissimulation and deceit to survive the murderous jealousy of Olympias as well as Alexander's deeply suspicious nature. Ptolemy must have assured Alexander that he posed no threat and was only there to serve. Nevertheless, Ptolemy's blood ties to Philip could explain why he seems to have been given no independent command until about 330 BC. Only then does Ptolemy, even by Arrian's admission, emerge on to the political military scene to act the loyal subordinate, highly valued by Alexander for his skill in dealing with the Macedonian rank-and-file.

Ptolemy had been a member of Alexander's entourage in the Groves of Mieza. He was exiled by Philip, along with other of Alexander's Companions and recalled shortly after Philip's assassination. No record or evidence exists as to how Ptolemy regarded Philip except that he appears to have had close ties with the likes of Cleitus, whose admiration of Philip cost him his life, whilst he hated Perdiccas who may have been in the plot against the old king. There seems every likelihood that Ptolemy would have had his own reservations about Philip's murder and Alexander's involvement. It may have rankled but, there again, Ptolemy was too much of a pragmatist and a survivor to implement an open blood feud or provoke a confrontation.

Other more personal, pressing issues surfaced to prompt Ptolemy to act. The historian Pausanias describes Ptolemy 'as a great lover of women'. We know that he later married Eurydice, sister of Cassander, by whom he had four children and then, following the polygamous fashion of Macedon and Egypt, fell in love and married Berenice, Eurydice's lady-in-waiting.[41] However, Ptolemy's first wife was the Athenian courtesan Thaïs and she may have played a prominent role in Ptolemy's decision to plot against Alexander. Thaïs appears to be a mysterious personality yet the few references we have about her depict a tough, strong-willed woman. Plutarch mentions her involvement in the burning of Persepolis. Apparently, at that banquet the women 'arrived in masquerade to seek their lovers'. Thaïs was one of these. She is described as a 'native of Attica and mistress of Ptolemy'. At the Persepolis banquet, Thaïs gained Alexander's attention by her flattery and good humour and delivered a speech in which she admits that she has endured the rigours of Alexander's campaigns. Thaïs demands that 'the proud courts of the Persian kings be burnt as Xerxes burnt Athens' – her speech was received with rapturous applause and Alexander promptly led his guests into that great act of arson.[42] With this Plutarch gives the impression that Thaïs was Ptolemy's mistress. Apparently, she and others joined the Macedonian court after Alexander's visit to Athens following the Great Victory at Chaeronea in 336 BC. Now Athenaeus reports:

> And did not Alexander the Great keep with him Thaïs, the Athenian prostitute? Cleitarchus speaks of her as having occasioned the burning of the Palace at Persepolis. This Thaïs, after Alexander's death was married to Ptolemy, the first King of Egypt and bore him Leontiscus and Lagus, also a daughter.[43]

The impression given here is that Thaïs was not Ptolemy's mistress, but Alexander's, and only began her relationship with Ptolemy after Alexander's death. Is it possible that Ptolemy plotted against Alexander and desired his death because he was infatuated by this famous Athenian courtesan whom he later took as his wife? Such a possibility could exist but, there again, Alexander's court was kept under such close scrutiny, any affair or relationship would have been soon discovered. It's more probable that Thaïs was first Alexander's mistress and was then discarded by him when he met Barsine and later married Roxane as well as the two daughters of the previous kings of Persia. In 308/307 BC, Ptolemy visited Athens, his eldest son Lagus accompanied him and took part in a chariot race; this would seem highly unlikely if Lagus was born even just after Alexander's death, e.g. 322 BC, which would make him fourteen years of age and certainly not mature or strong enough to be a charioteer and take part in a public race.[44] There is every likelihood, therefore, that Lagus was born before the Great Conqueror's death. This gives rise to two further possibilities. First, by 323 BC, Ptolemy himself was approaching his mid-forties with a child, and possibly another one, yet he was still nothing more than a glorified mercenary. If anything happened to him there would be little left for Thaïs and his two sons. Fatherhood, and the obligations which go with it would be a powerful deterrent to further campaigning on the Great Conqueror's behalf. A family also made Ptolemy vulnerable. Alexander had proved, when he struck at Parmenio (or Olympias at Eurydice), that kinship to someone who was disgraced could be the source of grave danger, even for the innocent. During his attack on Parmenio's family, Alexander had used as his messenger a high-ranking Macedonian officer, Polydamas. He was sent to Ecbatana with orders for Parmenio's execution and warned that his family would be held as hostage until the task was done. Ptolemy would reflect how in the case of Amyntas, the Lyncestian and Cleander, Alexander was always prepared to strike at his victim's kin in order to carry out his vengeance.

Thaïs, too, would have an interest in Alexander's death. The old cliché 'Hell hath no fury like a woman scorned' certainly applies to Thaïs. If Athenaeus is to be believed, Thaïs left the comfort of Athens and followed Alexander. She was still with the king, exercising

considerable influence over him by 330 when Alexander burnt
Persepolis. Later on, Thaïs was supplanted in Alexander's affections,
first by Barsine then by Roxane, followed by two further Persian
princesses. Like used goods she was then handed over to Ptolemy.
Now Thaïs, by Plutarch's account, does not come across as some
passive, obedient, Persian princess, but a woman of independent
mind, physically and morally tough enough to endure military
campaigns, the hardship of army life, the rigours and dangers of
battlefield as well as possibility of capture and, in her case, hideous
humiliation and death. She also comes across as an Athenian with
a deep hatred for the Persian Empire. She believes the Persian
palaces should be razed to the ground and has the strength of
character to persuade Alexander to achieve this. Consequently, it is
not fanciful to conclude that Thaïs would not have taken too kindly
to being supplanted by at least four Persian women.

Quintus Curtius, in describing Alexander's marriage to Roxane,
concludes by summarizing the Macedonian's attitude to such a
marriage. 'Thus the king of Asia and Europe married a lady, introduced at an entertainment, designing, by offspring from a captive, to
furnish the victors with a sovereign. His friends felt inward shame, that
he should, amid the blandishments of the table, choose a father-in-law
among his vassals.'[45] Quintus Curtius could be describing the attitude
of Ptolemy and his mistress Thaïs. Little wonder that on the day after
Alexander's death, Ptolemy, amongst all the generals, utterly rejects
bending the knee to any son of Alexander born of a Persian princess.
Behind every great man is a great woman. Ptolemy is simply enunci-
ating what Thaïs herself felt – an attitude Ptolemy continued for the
rest of his political career; never once, in any shape or form, did he
offer any sustenance or comfort to Roxane or to her baby son. They
are as brutally ignored, as was Ptolemy's Persian wife who, as soon as
the Great Conqueror died, disappears from history. Thaïs emerges as
a very strong-willed woman who wielded considerable influence over
successful generals and politicians such as Alexander and Ptolemy.
Being rejected by the Great Conqueror in favour of four Persian
princesses, Thaïs would not have taken too kindly to Ptolemy being
forced married to a Persian princess at the great wedding ceremony at

Susa in 324 BC. She would certainly have nourished great resentment against Alexander. The fact that Athenaeus claims that she and Ptolemy only married after Alexander's death hints at the possibility that the Great Conqueror might have vetoed such a marriage between one of his leading generals and an Athenian courtesan. Thaïs had a great deal to settle, and to profit, from Alexander's murder, as did her future husband, Ptolemy.

Of course, this begs the question if Ptolemy, and possibly Thaïs, wanted Alexander to die and plotted his death, they ran the risk of discovery by Alexander, a born street-fighter already paranoid about possible conspiracies and threats about his life. The answer to this is quite simple. According to Aelian, Alexander considered Ptolemy 'devious' or 'cunning'. Ptolemy was a true politician, a Machiavellian figure who acted the part, a man totally underestimated by Alexander and the rest of the panthers. Quintus Curtius describes Alexander's Companions' attitude: 'Liberty of speech having been taken away since Cleitus' death, their faces smiled assent. It is in dressing the face that the service of a despot chiefly lies,' a fitting description of Ptolemy.[46]

No better proof exists of this underestimation of Egypt's future ruler than the actions and attitude of Perdiccas following Alexander's death. Perdiccas had served with Ptolemy for at least thirteen years. At Babylon, due to the support given to Ptolemy by the House of Antipater, Perdiccas was forced to concede the satrapy of Egypt to Ptolemy. However, according to the sources, Perdiccas fully intended to take Egypt back, thinking his ally Cleomenes would hold the ground till he acted. Perdiccas also hoped that Alexander's decree against recruiting mercenaries would hamper Ptolemy, who would not take hated Persians to Egypt, whilst the Macedonian army, seriously weakened by the Gedrosian débâcle, was further depleted by Craterus' departure, as well as Perdiccas' control of the central command.

Perdiccas never intended Ptolemy to hold Egypt for long. Diodorus mentions this, as does Pausanias who writes, 'really, he [Perdiccas] was plotting to take the kingdom of Egypt from Ptolemy'.[47] Ptolemy himself realized this. 'After the death of Alexander . . . Ptolemy crossed over to

Egypt in person and killed Cleomenes whom Alexander had appointed satrap of that country, considering him a friend of Perdiccas and, therefore, not faithful to himself.'[48] The Byzantine historian Photius, in his summary of a now lost work by Arrian, describing events after Alexander's death, claims that Perdiccas, when he invaded Egypt, published 'many charges against Ptolemy'.[49] What these were is not clear but in the end Perdiccas totally underestimated Ptolemy who seized Egypt, executed Perdiccas' friend, plundered the treasury and, contrary to Alexander's edict of 324 BC, immediately began to hire mercenaries, including the famous adventurer Ophellas.[50] Ptolemy then bribed high-ranking Macedonians to hand over Alexander's corpse, he circumvented Perdiccas' ally Polemon and successfully brought the Great Conqueror's corpse back to Memphis in Egypt.[51]

Ptolemy showed similar negotiating skills in dealing with Perdiccas' invasion of Egypt, which proved to be a complete disaster. Ptolemy lured Perdiccas and his army into the marshy, treacherous land around the Nile whilst conducting a secret but very successful attempt to suborn and bribe Perdiccas' leading officers. As a result Perdiccas was assassinated and his entire power base collapsed.[52] Ptolemy emerges on to the pages of history as a cunning politician, who hid his own secret designs and powerful ambitions behind a smiling face. If a man like Perdiccas could be misled, then the same applies to Alexander and others of the panthers. Ptolemy was the Iago of Alexander's court, a true reflection of Machiavelli's Prince.

Finally, there is the question of Ptolemy's guilt. If he did murder his half-brother, the Great Conqueror, this must have been a decision, an act which would have a lasting effect upon him for the rest of his life. Of course, Ptolemy could appeal to the sheer necessity of kill or be killed. If he reflected upon Aristotle's *Politics*, Ptolemy could even invoke the concept of tyrannicide, that slaying a despot was, indeed, an intrinsically pious act. Such ideas would have all played their part in Ptolemy's mind, but he may have articulated his innocence in a more sinister way.

Reference has already been made to how the Egyptian God Serapis is mentioned in two very important incidents surrounding

Alexander's death. Now Serapis was a new god, the direct product of Ptolemy's fertile imagination. The idea of the Man-God, the Healer, was developed in Egypt: Ptolemy either imported it from the town of Sinope on the Black Sea or took over and encouraged a private cult he discovered in Memphis.[53] Whatever its origin, the devotion to Serapis was Ptolemy's personal contribution to religious development in the Ancient World. The references to Serapis in the Royal Diaries, as well as in the story about the prisoner who escaped from his bonds and sat on Alexander's throne in Babylon, may not just be anachronisms, the slip of some inattentive scribe or priest. They could be quite deliberate. When Alexander murdered Cleitus, Aristander the seer was quick to point out that Cleitus' death was the work of the God Dionysius. Aristander was trotting out a clichéed excuse often used by rulers who cited the Gods to explain their actions. There is every likelihood that Ptolemy followed a similar vein of argument which would explain the references to Serapis in the above-mentioned incidents. In the Royal Diaries, Serapis the God is asked if Alexander should be brought into the God's temple for healing? The reply, given by the Oracle, that it would be 'better' if Alexander stayed where he was, is the God's verdict that he could not, or would not, do anything for the sick king: his fate was sealed. The warning involving the intruder on to the royal throne also has its origins in Serapis. Alexander's death may have been a political necessity but it was also the work of Ptolemy's tutelary god: a deed which had its true origin, not in Ptolemy's will, but the inscrutable mind of the Divine.

Ptolemy must, therefore, have played a major role in that fateful banquet of 29 May 323 BC. The sources are quite explicit. Alexander had gone to an official banquet. He was about to retire when Medius invited him to a *comus*, a 'drinking carouse'. Plutarch reports:

> One day after he had given Nearchus a sumptuous treat he went, according to custom, to refresh himself in the bath in order to retire to rest. In the meantime, however, Medius came and invited him to take part in a carousal and he could not deny him.

Diodorus claims Alexander was 'called away by Medius the Thessalian, one of his friends to take part in a comus'. Arrian reports substantially the same. The impression given by all the texts and emphasized by 'The Pamphlet' in the *Alexander Romance* is that the second party was a surprise one given by his Companions, an invitation Alexander couldn't refuse with his unsettled state of mind and love of wine. However, given the king's paranoia, his suspicions, superstitions and fears, he would be very wary of anything untoward. The banquet must be seen against the background of the omens and Alexander's fears, his constant sacrifices to placate the gods. He would certainly be most vigilant regarding the likes of his purported cupbearer Iolaus whose father was under suspicion and whose brother Cassander Alexander had so recently violently assaulted. Ptolemy was different, the loyal commander, the steward and the taster, who'd secretly decided to strike before Alexander turned on him. More importantly, Medius would never have arranged such a banquet without the full approval of the king's steward and taster, General Ptolemy, who had the direct responsibility for Alexander's security. The party may well have been Ptolemy's idea, the time was certainly ripe and matters had to go forward as quickly as possible. Ptolemy had added a few dramatic twists of his own, ensuring that Proteas the drinker, Cleitus' nephew, was present whilst it is only a matter of speculation how the conversation turned to include that ominous play, Euripides' *Andromache*.

Ptolemy the steward and taster must have been close by, though he never makes any reference to this in his own account. Indeed, judging by the so-called Royal Diaries, the impression created is that when the king fell ill and died, Ptolemy was nowhere in sight. In view of Ptolemy's role and status, this is impossible to accept. In fact, Justin talks about Alexander and a 'companion' or 'attendant' being invited to Medius' party. If the king was paranoid about security, if Ptolemy was his personal bodyguard and 'taster', then this mysterious attendant or 'companion' must have been Ptolemy of Lagus who would, of course, recommend acceptance. Everyone else was ready and the plot was going to plan. Proteas was a heavy drinker, the cups were filled and re-filled and Ptolemy used his position of trust, his closeness to the

king to mix the fatal poison, arsenic. Arsenic must have been the
poison used, it was well known to the ancients and quite common in
the eastern provinces of the Persian Empire as well as in the Punjab,
an area recently occupied by Alexander's army where it was regarded
as an aphrodisiac. In fact, Strabo in his fifteenth book, quoting
Onescritus, says that in Carmania, the eastern province to which
Alexander returned after his Indian expedition, were two mountains,
one consisting of salt and the other of arsenic.[54]

The symptoms of arsenic are violent pain, shock, severe discomfort,
raging thirst and skin problems. Violent pain can occur within about
an hour, a true shock to the system. Diodorus Siculus specifically
describes these symptoms as those of Alexander at Medius' banquet:

> filling a great cup he downed it in one gulp. Instantly, he
> screamed aloud, as if smitten by a piercing pain [in my view, the
> result of arsenic taken before] and was conducted by his friends,
> who led him by the hand back to his apartment.

Plutarch mentions the same symptoms, only to reject them. Arrian
is more circumspect, he actually mentions the reaction, as if quoting
from an unknown source, possibly the same as Diodorus': 'he felt a
sharp pain after draining the cup and left the party because of it'.
Acute arsenic poisoning will cause death within hours. One of the
prescribed methods of dealing with arsenic is vomiting or the stomach
being purged. Drinking vast amounts of water will also help the
kidneys expel the poison but, in most cases, arsenic will bring about
death. Alexander's wine drinking and subsequent vomiting ['the great
discomfort'] may have given him some immediate relief to reduce the
'acute' symptoms to what physicians term the 'subacute'. Blyth, in his
very detailed study of poisons, lists the symptoms of arsenic: 'the
tongue is thickly coated, there is great thirst . . . nearly always pain is
felt . . . spreading all over the abdomen'. Blyth continues to describe
how a single dose of arsenic may not bring immediate death but in the
first instance cause a prolonged and fatal illness.

A single dose of arsenious acid may cause a prolonged and fatal

illness, one of the best-known examples being that of the suicide of
the Duc de Praslin, who took with suicidal intent, on Wednesday
August 18 1847, a dose of arsenious acid. The exact time of the act
could not be ascertained, but the first effects appeared at 10 p.m.;
there were the usual signs of vomiting, followed on the next day by
diarrhoea, fainting, and extreme feebleness of the pulse. On Friday
there was a remission of the symptoms, but great coldness of the
limbs, intermittency and feebleness of the heart's action, and
depression. On Saturday there was a slight fever, but no pain or
tenderness in the abdomen, vomiting, or diarrhoea; on this day no
urine was passed. On the Sunday he complained of a severe
constriction of the throat, and deglutition was extremely painful;
thirst was extreme, the tongue intensely red, as well as the mucous
membrane of the mouth and pharynx, and the patient had a
sensation of burning from the mouth to the anus. The abdomen
was painful and distended, the heat of the skin was pronounced, the
pulse frequent and irregular – sometimes strong, at other times
feeble – the bowels had to be relieved by injections, the urine was in
very small quantity; during the night there was no sleep. The duke
died at 4.35 a.m. on Tuesday 24th, the sixth day; intelligence was
retained to the last. As the end approached, the respiration became
embarrassed, the body extremely cold, and the pulse very
frequent.[55]

Most of these symptoms are very similar to those of Alexander and
the duke did not die immediately – his illness lasted six days,
Alexander's a little longer. Of course the Great Conqueror's splendid
physique, the vomiting and the wine may have delayed the onset of
death, but the damage was done.

Arsenic comes in many forms and strengths. Vomiting could purge
it, which might explain the Royal Diaries' account of Alexander
rallying – as Hephaestion did. However, the Royal Diaries, suspect as
they are, mention the king taking more food – as Hephaestion did –
and growing worse. Ptolemy, as steward and taster, would be responsible for such food. The presence of arsenic in Alexander's untimely
death is verified by even stronger evidence.

Up until the late nineteenth century, arsenic was the assassins' most skilful tool. Unlike Hellebore which has an extremely bitter taste and quickly affects the heart, arsenic can be cleverly disguised and the symptoms can replicate those of malaria or cholera. Alexander's thirst, his desire to be bathed are further indications. However, arsenic possesses one great weakness and this led to many exhumations in the late nineteenth and early twentieth centuries, namely the decomposition of the corpse is greatly retarded. Two sources, Plutarch and Quintus Curtius, specifically mention that this happened to Alexander's corpse, despite the intense heat of a Babylonian summer. As Blyth reports:

> A remarkable preservation of the body is commonly observed. When it does occur it may have great significance, particularly when the body is placed under conditions in which it might be expected to decompose rapidly. In the celebrated Continental case of the apothecary Speichert (1876), the body of Speichert's wife was exhumed eleven months after death. The coffin stood partly in water, the corpse was mummified. The organs contained arsenic, the churchyard earth no arsenic. R. Koch [the defendant's lawyer] was unable to explain the preservation of the body, under these conditions, in any other way than from the effect of arsenic; and this circumstance, with others, was an important element which led to the conviction of Speichert.[56]

Ptolemy was not only able to poison the Great Conqueror but also control the aftermath – as he was guardian of the king's chamber and his official taster and steward. During his final illness Alexander would have bouts of lucidity when he could make arrangements for the succession, such as nominating Perdiccas and handing him his ring of office. Nevertheless, virtually every source indicates that during the king's final illness, a strict watch was kept over the royal chamber and most people were shut out. The physicians were summoned but they were confused by the symptoms. This is not remarkable: until the end of the nineteenth century, as in the notorious Maybrick arsenic case of the 1880s, physicians were commonly misled by the true cause of a victim's illness after she or he had been secretly poisoned with arsenic.[57] Matters would not have been helped by the fate of poor Glaucas the physician, crucified after the swift and unexpected death of Alexander's favourite Hephaestion, only a year before. The physicians would be reluctant to act for fear of worsening Alexander's state and laying themselves open to accusation.

Ptolemy controlled the game; it was only towards the end that the news was given to the rank-and-file and they were allowed into the death chamber, but by then it was too late. It is interesting to note that Justin reports how the rank-and-file suspected 'a conspiracy', whilst all sources describe agitation in the army. This could explain the support given to a rabble-rouser such as Meleager once Alexander was dead.[58] Ptolemy, like Iago, would continue to be the loyal commander. The faithful subordinate who like Hamlet's *Claudius* 'may smile, and smile, and be a villain'. His actions echo those of the sixteenth-century Harington's definition of treason: 'Treason doth never prosper, what's the reason? For if it prospers, none dare call it treason.'[59]

Ptolemy's own silence during this most important period of his life, not to mention that of his master, is extremely telling. In the end, Ptolemy would have been more concerned about what was to happen afterwards. No evidence exists that Alexander, whilst dying, believed that he was the victim of a plot, although his much debated words that he left his empire 'to the strongest' or 'to the most fitting', as well as his remark that 'his generals would stage the most magnificent funeral games', could be taken as a sardonic reference to Alexander predicting that the question of the succession would end in bloodshed.

Part Eight

The Aftermath

'πως ὀυν, ταδ' ὡς ἐιποι τις ἐξημαρτανες'

'How then did you come to commit such serious sins – as others
might call them?'
Euripides, *Andromache*
(line 929)

Alexander died 9/10 June 323 BC. The only real source of what
happened afterwards is Quintus Curtius. He describes the feeling of
shock which spread through the city.

In the first fit of grief, the whole palace resounded with lamenta-
tions and with smiting of the breast: anon all things lay, as in a
desert, couched in dreary silence; anguish diverted to the
contemplation of what was to follow. The young nobles accustomed to guard his person, with ungoverned distress, passed out
of the palace and, wandering like maniacs, filled the city with
sorrow and complaint; nor omitted any extravagance which
mournful emotions could prompt. The guards, who had stood
without the palace, as well Barbarians or Macedonians, in

consequence rushed in; nor, in the common distraction, could the vanquished be distinguished from the victors.

Quintus Curtius then goes on to describe a night of silent terror as the news spread across the city and beyond the walls.

As they were revolving these apprehensions, night surprised them, and increased their terror: the troops watched under arms: the Babylonians stood, some on the walls, others on the tops of the houses, inquisitively looking, as expecting decisive things. None dared to employ lights; and as vision was suspended, the ear, devoted to the din, analysed every sound. Great numbers, roving panic-struck, encountered in alleyways; borne along, mutually suspected and anxious.

The Persians, their heads, according to their manner, shaven, habited in mourning, with their wives and children, forgetting how recently the conqueror had been an enemy, bewailed him, with true affection, as their lawful king. Accustomed to live under a monarch, they confessed that they had never had a ruler worthier to be remembered. Nor was their grief circumscribed by the city-walls: with the report of its calamitous cause, it spread to the adjoining country, and afterwards pervaded that large section of Asia on this side of the Euphrates.

Darius' mother was so stricken that she refused food and pined away with grief. According to Quintus Curtius, Alexander's generals were made of harder stuff. The morning following his death they immediately convened an assembly. Quintus Curtius calls the prime movers of this meeting 'the Lords of the Purple' or 'the Nine': Perdiccas, Leonnatus, Aristonus, Ptolemy, Lysimachus, Pithon, Seleucus, Eumenes, Nearchus. Another title given is the 'Guards of the Presence' – whatever they wished to call themselves, these men had apparently met during the king's final illness and the hours following his death. They had decided to call an assembly which they hoped to control but, in the final resort, were unable to do so.[1]

The consequent lack of unity amongst the high command, as well as the division between these Lords of the Purple and other sections of the army, indicate the bitter rivalries seething beneath the surface. It strengthens the case that Alexander's murder was not the clever work of his general staff but that of a devious mind ready to exploit the chaos and confusion which followed. Perdiccas, no fool, also sensed this and he immediately surrendered the signet ring and the office bestowed upon him by Alexander and invited the assembly to debate what might happen next.

In their discussion the principal speakers advocated contrasting if not conflicting strategies. Perdiccas, Nearchus and Aristonus stand in stark contrast to Ptolemy. Here is Alexander's bodyguard, personal friend, possible half-brother yet, within hours of his master's death, he is totally rejecting his king, the idea of Alexander's unborn son by Roxane eventually succeeding, or even accepting Perdiccas as viceroy. Ptolemy is quite insistent – no Persian should rule over them and vice-regal powers should be vested in a Council of Regency. Of course, both he and Cassander would support this. Such an attitude is a logical consequence of the conspiracy between Ptolemy and the House of Antipater to remove Alexander and divide the empire. Ptolemy and Antipater wanted no more kings, particularly one with Persian blood in his veins. Nor did they want Perdiccas to be given a position of supremacy, and the consequent power, to impede their progress. Curtius' account shows that there was little love between Ptolemy and the rest. In the end, however, Perdiccas won the day and Ptolemy may have well conceded this in return for concessions he would demand later.

The assembly was swayed by a speech from Aristonus who recommended that Perdiccas resume his power as viceroy. What happened next was probably unexpected and certainly unplanned. The rank-and-file under Brigadier Meleager declared Perdiccas unsuitable. There is no evidence of a deep-rooted conspiracy but a sharp division between the cavalry under the command of the Lords of the Purple and the phalanx, the veteran foot soldiers, the backbone of the Macedonian army. Meleager has been mentioned before – he was the officer who objected to Alexander's lavish rewards for the Indian prince Taxiles – only to receive the king's stinging rebuke that an envious man was his own worst enemy. Meleager's objections to Perdiccas, as described by Quintus Curtius, may be correct. He was inspired by greed, fearful that Perdiccas might 'pillage the treasuries'. Meleager was also voicing the conservative attitude of the Macedonian rank-and-file, as well as searching for a substitute for Perdiccas.

Meleager argued that they didn't need a regent, a viceroy or to wait for a Persian queen to give birth to a boy. They already had a Macedonian prince, Philip's half-witted son Arridhaeus, who was brought forward and given the additional name of Philip. The Lords of the Purple objected, countering with their proposal that Perdiccas be regent and guardian of Roxane's unborn son. Meleager led a mutiny. At one point there was violence in the very chamber where Alexander's corpse lay. Meleager tried to have Perdiccas arrested but this cunning Lord of the Purple withdrew from the palace and, using the cavalry, he blockaded all entrances into Babylon and prevented any food supplies reaching Meleager's troops. Perdiccas and his companions then engaged in a widespread campaign of bribery to suborn Meleager's position. Philip Arridhaeus was only a figurehead and eventually the mutiny was quelled and a reconciliation effected.

Perdiccas then planned his own revenge. He decided the entire army needed purifying in accordance with the ancient Macedonian tradition.

> The kings of Macedon were accustomed thus to purify the troops. At the extremities of the fields into which the army was to be led, the innards of a bitch, cut in two, were deposited by each party. In the intermediate space ranged all the forces, the cavalry on one side, the phalanx on the other.[2]

Perdiccas, however, used the occasion not only to purify the army but unify it by removing all dissident elements. Leading mutineers were singled out, arrested, then thrown to the elephants to be crushed underfoot. The mutiny was quelled by terror. Meleager tried to seek refuge in a temple but was hunted down and killed.

Ptolemy's role in these dramatic affairs was apparently limited to his forthright speech against both a possible half-Persian king or, indeed, Perdiccas becoming viceroy. There's a passing reference to how Ptolemy joined Perdiccas in battling against Meleager but, there again, Ptolemy had little choice. To have sided with the phalanx would have been abdicating his responsibilities as a senior commander.

Either during, or just after these stirring days, the Lords of the Purple turned to the vexed question of dividing the empire. There is no evidence that these individual lords intended to turn the territories they had seized into independent fiefs, although, with Ptolemy at least, this idea might have been secretly nourished from the start. Alexander had gone – there was no apparent heir and Ptolemy was clearly unwilling to accept a successor. He immediately repudiated his Persian wife and could now claim Thaïs as his own. More importantly, he could withdraw from ceaseless war, he was free of threat and had the power and personality to act on his own, to rest on his laurels and enjoy the spoils of victory. However, no evidence exists as to why Ptolemy, a senior general, but a relative outsider, and hostile to Perdiccas, should have been given Egypt, the richest and most strategically placed sovereign kingdom, annexed by Alexander.

By 323 BC, Egypt was a kingdom with a history dating back at least 2,000 years, possessing natural and human resources with well-defined borders; it was the most supportive of those territories conquered by Alexander in his war against Persia. It is obvious that Perdiccas neither trusted nor liked Ptolemy and fully intended to take Egypt back. Ptolemy could not claim that Egypt was a gift of Alexander. Curtius refers to a will left by the Great Conqueror only to reject the notion. In Chapter 83, of his twentieth book, Diodorus Siculus also mentions a will drawn up by Alexander and deposited for safe keeping on the island of Rhodes. However, if such a will existed, it promptly disappeared, and little or no reference is made to it by the *diadochoi*, the Successors, the Lords of the Purple.[3]

In my view, Ptolemy was given Egypt as a reward, a direct result of his secret alliance with the House of Antipater in removing Alexander and ensuring that both their interests were well served. In 323 BC, after Alexander's death, Antipater was the strongest and most powerful ruler. Perdiccas could be given titles but Antipater had been regent of Macedon for eleven years. He had suppressed rebellion, won an outstanding victory against the Spartans, seen off the redoubtable Olympias and had been left virtually as a ruler in his own right. He was master of the homeland with all its resources as well as the status and power such a title provided. Perdiccas and the others had no choice but to recognize this when they confirmed Antipater as 'Master of Europe' with the rather vague phrase that he should share such power with Craterus. Ptolemy would have argued for this, as would Cassander, still present in Babylon. In view of the fact that the hapless Craterus was only halfway home with his 10,000 veterans, this supposed partnership with Antipater would be most difficult to enforce, a fact recognized by Craterus who soon put himself and his troops at the disposal of Antipater. Antipater therefore had a secure power base whilst his son Cassander could act as his official envoy in Babylon. Cassander would insist, as would Antipater from behind the scenes, that Ptolemy be given Egypt, a gift by them to their secret ally who had done so much to advance and defend their cause. Perdiccas would be given no choice, even though he might secretly resolve that, in the future, Ptolemy would be removed.

When Ptolemy became master of Egypt four factors characterized his foreign policy: his friendship and alliance with both Antipater and Cassander, a refusal to give up Egypt to anyone, a firm reluctance to be drawn into the governance of the rest of the Macedonian Empire, and an implacable hatred of Perdiccas. Ptolemy's own standing with the troops would have served him well. He could depict himself as a son of the great Philip, brother to Alexander, a senior general and an accomplished strategist, a member of the Lords of the Purple, and a Macedonian who wanted no truck with Persian ritual or custom.[4] In many ways Ptolemy is so reminiscent of Philip, with his good humour and lavish hospitality. In the *Moralia*, Plutarch makes a passing reference to Ptolemy's open-handed but rather idiosyncratic generosity.

Ptolemy, the son of Lagus, frequently supped with his friends and lay at their houses; and if at any time he invited them to supper, he made use of their furniture, sending for vessels, carpets, and tables; for he himself had only things that were of constant use about him, saying it was more becoming a king to make others rich than to be rich himself.[5]

Diodorus also praises Ptolemy for his courage and honest treatment of friends. Ptolemy seems to have gone out of his way to attract to his standard any Macedonian disaffected with their own leader. This included generals such as Seleucus, because 'word had spread abroad of Ptolemy's kindness and of his hospitality and friendship shown to those who fled to him for protection.'[6] Now free of Alexander's shadow, Ptolemy was to justify his master's judgment of him that he was devious. Ptolemy proved to be an excellent negotiator and a skilled suborner of men. He was reluctant to fight but always prepared to reward, flatter and bribe, actions so reminiscent of Philip of Macedon.

At Babylon, the Lords of the Purple decided upon two further important issues: Alexander's burial and the shelving of the Great Conqueror's future plans. The former will be discussed later, the latter was soon dispensed with. Perdiccas took Alexander's plans before the now quiescent Macedonian army who, in view of what had happened and what was being planned, rejected the list outright. The rank-and-file had had enough of war and glory, whilst the leaders were eager to assume power over their respective territories. The die was now cast. Perdiccas was technically in control, but the Lords of the Purple must have known that it was only a matter of time before real differences surfaced and they went to war.

Ptolemy was determined to hold what he had won. He must have left Babylon in the late summer of 323 BC and moved his treasure, his household, his troops, and whoever wished to follow him, to Memphis, the old capital of Ancient Egypt, 'the White Walled City', the home of the man-god Ptah. The new city in the Delta, founded by Alexander and bearing his name (Alexandria), was still not yet completed and vulnerable to attack both from the sea or from along the Horus Road which stretched across Sinai into Canaan. Ptolemy found it easy to take over the kingdom. Alexander had left garrisons in Egypt who welcomed this Macedonian hero whilst the Egyptians would regard him as Alexander's heir to their kingdom, a welcome relief from the corrupt and venal administrator Alexander had left in charge, the Greek mercenary, Cleomenes of Naucratis. Cleomenes, just before Alexander's death, had been accused of serious corruption and maladministration. He was a Greek, highly unpopular with the Macedonian soldiers and the civilian population. Ptolemy promptly had Cleomenes executed and seized the treasury containing 8,000 talents as well as winning the allegiance of the Macedonian garrisons. To the Egyptians, Ptolemy proved to be a *soter* – a Saviour.[7]

The new satrap was under no illusion that time was scarce, and he must prepare for whatever onslaught was launched against him. Diodorus emphasizes the important strands of the new satrap's policy: seizing treasure, placating the civilian population, hiring mercenaries, inviting others to join him, and working in close cooperation with the House of Antipater. Ptolemy was aided by the growing confusion following the outbreak of hostilities in both Greece and Asia. For eighteen months Ptolemy enjoyed an uneasy peace as the different Lords of the Purple manoeuvred into position and the power blocs and alliances became more defined. Antipater had to face serious revolt in Greece as well as the growing opposition of the Perdiccan party.[8]

Antipater, supported by Craterus, carried on secret negotiations with Ptolemy. It was probably during this period that the first propaganda about Alexander's death began to surface, what Robin Lane Fox calls, 'The Pamphlet' in the *Alexander Romance* describing the murder of the Great Conqueror by the House of Antipater. The Perdiccan party were probably responsible for this, eager to besmirch the House of Antipater, who could do little in reply except punish individuals found guilty of spreading such stories, as they did with the hapless Hyperides of Athens. Ptolemy would look on. Such stories could not hurt him; if the House of Antipater was blamed, that was their problem. Cassander and his father were in no position to refute the story and any attempt to spread the blame would only incriminate them further. Ptolemy, the former bodyguard and trusted confidant of the king, remained silent. He was more concerned with building up his forces, extending his power across North Africa and bringing about the final part of his conspiracy, the seizure of Alexander's corpse.

During the disturbances following Alexander's death, his corpse had been left unattended, whilst fierce fighting took place near the chamber where the body lay. Ptolemy must have been concerned at the way the corpse did not decompose. Plutarch comments on this phenomenon as did those who, according to Quintus Curtius, eventually arrived to embalm the body.[9] The preservative effects of arsenic were not known, the wholesome nature of the corpse being ascribed to Alexander's greatness.

Once the Lords of the Purple had settled matters with the phalanx, they implemented plans for the corpse to be brought home in great glory. By 'home' they intended the royal necropolis at Vergine, in Macedon, where Philip and his forebears had their graves. A high-ranking officer, Arridhaeus (not the mentally defective half-brother of Alexander), was ordered to supervise the burial arrangements. Naturally Alexander's corpse was regarded as a sacred relic, and whoever owned it could bask in some form of glory. The Roman writer Aelian records a rather strange story, which not only emphasizes the fact that Alexander's corpse did not decompose, but also the glory and aura which surrounded the corpse.

Alexander, son of Philip and Olympias, lay dead in Babylon – the man who said he was the son of Zeus. While his followers argued about the succession, he lay waiting for burial, which even the very poor achieve, since the nature common to all mankind requires a funeral for those no longer living. But he was left unburied for thirty days, until Aristander of Telemesus, whether by divine inspiration or for some other reason, entered the Macedonian assembly and said that of all kings in recorded history Alexander was the most fortunate, both in his life and in his death; the Gods had told him that the land which received his body, the earlier habitation of his soul, would enjoy the greatest good fortune and be unconquered through the ages.

On hearing this they began to quarrel seriously, each man

wishing to carry off the prize to his own kingdom, so as to have a relic guaranteeing safety and permanence for his realm. But Ptolemy, if we are to believe the story, stole the body and hurriedly made off with it to Alexandria in Egypt. [Aelian, wrongly, gives the impression that this all happened in a matter of weeks, if not days.] The other Macedonians did nothing, whereas Perdiccas tried to give chase. He was not so much interested in consideration for Alexander and due respect for his body as fired and incited by Aristander's prediction. When he caught up with Ptolemy there was quite a violent struggle over the corpse, in some way akin to the one over the 'Phantom' at Troy, which Homer [*Iliad* 5.449] celebrates in his tale, where Apollo puts it down among the heroes to protect Aeneas. Ptolemy checked Perdiccas' attack. He made a likeness of Alexander, clad in royal robes and a shroud of enviable quality. Then he laid it on one of the Persian carriages, and arranged the bier sumptuously with silver, gold and ivory. Alexander's real body was sent ahead without fuss and formality by a secret and little used route. Perdiccas found the imitation corpse with the elaborate carriage, and halted his advance, thinking he had laid hands on the prize. Too late he realized he had been deceived; it was not possible to go in pursuit.[10]

Diodorus' account is more measured and infinitely more accurate: it reveals the glory of the funeral cortège as well as singing the praises of the arch-conspirator Ptolemy who ambushed and captured it.

'In this year Arridhaeus, who had been placed in charge of conveying home the body of Alexander and having completed the vehicle on which the royal body was to be transported, made preparations for the journey. Since the finished structure was worthy of the glory of Alexander, it surpassed all others in cost. It had been constructed at the expense of many talents and was famous for the excellence of its craftsmanship. Accordingly, I believe it is appropriate to describe it. First they prepared a coffin of an appropriate size for the body out of hammered gold, whilst the space about the corpse was filled with costly spices which made it sweet-smelling and incorruptible. Upon this chest there had been placed a cover of gold, matching precisely, and fitting about its upper rim. Over this was laid a magnificent purple robe edged with gold, beside which they placed the arms of the deceased, wanting the entire design to be in harmony with Alexander's achievements. They set this up next to the covered carriage which was to carry it. At the top of the carriage was built a vault of gold, eight cubits wide and twelve long, covered with over-lapping scales studded with precious stones. Beneath the roof, all along the work, was a rectangular cornice of gold, from which heads of goat-stags projected in high relief. Gold rings, two hands broad, were suspended from these, and through the rings a gloriously decorated festive garland of every colour was looped. At the ends, it had tassels of network from which hung large bells, so that any who approached it heard the sound from a great distance. On each corner of the vault, on either side, stood a golden Statue of Victory holding a trophy. The colonnade supporting this vault was of gold with Ionic capitals. Within the colonnade was a golden net, fashioned out of cords the thickness of a finger, this displayed four long painted tablets, their ends adjoining, each equal in length to a side of the colonnade.

'On the first of these tablets was a chariot decorated with relief work, and sitting in it was a figure of Alexander holding a truly glorious sceptre in his hands. About the king were cohorts of armed attendants, one group of Macedonians, another of Persians, with the bodyguard, and armed soldiers in front of them. The second tablet depicted the elephants arrayed for war following the bodyguard: these carried Indian mahouts in front with Macedonians fully dressed in their battle armour behind them. The third tablet showed troops of cavalry in battle formation. The fourth, ships prepared for naval combat. Beside the entrance to the chamber crouched golden lions with eyes turned towards those who would enter. A golden acanthus curled, little by little, up the centre of each column to the capital. Above the chamber, in the middle of the top, under the open sky was a purple banner emblazoned with a huge golden olive wreath; when this caught the sun's rays, it emitted a bright and vibrant gleam so, from a great distance, it seemed like a flash of lightning.

'The body of the chariot beneath the covered chamber rested on two axles upon which turned four Persian wheels, the naves and spokes of which were gilded, but the rim which touched the ground was of iron. The projecting parts of the axle were made of gold in the form of lion heads, each holding a spear in its jaws. Along the middle of these axles was an ingenious bearing fitted just beneath the chamber, because of this device the chamber would remain cushioned against jolts along rough terrain. There were four poles and, to each of them, were fastened four teams with four mules harnessed in each team, in all sixty-four mules, selected for their strength and size. Each of these was crowned with a gilded crown, each had a golden bell hanging by either cheek, and about their necks were collars of precious stones.

'In this way the carriage was constructed and ornamented. Indeed it appeared more magnificent when seen than described. Because of its widespread fame it attracted many spectators. In every city it visited, the whole population came out, to meet it to escort it on its way, not just becoming satisfied with the pleasure of beholding it. To correspond to this magnificence, it was accompanied by a crowd of road-menders and mechanics, as well as soldiers sent to escort it.

'When Arridhaeus had spent nearly two years finishing this work, he brought the body of the king from Babylon to Egypt. Ptolemy, however, eager to do honour to Alexander, went to meet it with his army as far as Syria, and, receiving the body, judged it worthy of the greatest respect. He decided for the present not to send it to Ammon [Ammun of Siwah], but to entomb it in the city which had been founded by Alexander himself: this lacked little in being the most famous of the cities of the inhabited earth. There Ptolemy prepared a mausoleum worthy of the glory of Alexander in both size and construction. Entombing him in this and honouring him with sacrifices, such as are paid to the demigods, as well as magnificent games, Ptolemy won grateful thanks not only from men but also from the Gods. For men, because of Ptolemy's graciousness and nobility of heart, flocked eagerly from all sides to Alexandria, and gladly enrolled in the campaign against Perdiccas. Even though the risks were both obvious and great, yet all of them gladly volunteered, at personal risk, for the preservation of Ptolemy's safety. The Gods also miraculously saved him from the greatest dangers on account of his fortitude as well as the honest treatment of all his friends.'[11]

Although the sources are confused, it is apparent that Ptolemy secured Alexander's corpse by force as well as wholesale bribery and trickery. Perdiccas tried to prevent this but he was totally out-manoeuvred. Ptolemy certainly didn't take Alexander's corpse immediately to Alexandria – it was still too vulnerable to attack – but to Memphis. As Quintus Curtius narrates:

> Intercepting the funeral procession travelling, after a delay of two years, from Babylon to Ammon, Ptolemy, to whom Egypt had devolved, conveyed Alexander's body to Memphis, and thence, subsequently to Alexandria, where was erected to the founder of the city, a magnificent temple, surrounded by a grove for the celebration of military games and sacrifices, and where all heroic honour is continued to his memory and name.[12]

All these reports illustrate the deviousness of Ptolemy's character. He emerges as a shrewd politician, a superb negotiator who could bribe and suborn high-ranking officers, a dashing commander, a ruler quite prepared to accept the consequences of what he had done. Ptolemy's theft of Alexander's corpse was a brilliant coup, a subtle piece of propaganda as well as a display of Ptolemy's standing amongst the Macedonians. Ptolemy, in one incredible stroke, snubbed Perdiccas and seized Alexander's corpse to use as a standard to draw Macedonians to his side. The theft might be explained as an attempt by Ptolemy to depict himself as Alexander's successor, but Ptolemy never entertained any ideas about empire. He positively rejected such a notion at subsequent peace negotiations. Only when his interests were threatened, would he go to war with any Lords of the Purple. Ptolemy's seizure of Alexander's corpse was a mixture of the pragmatic and the political. He wanted, first, custody of the corpse of the man he had murdered, possibly to avoid further investigation into Alexander's death and so conceal his own guilt. Secondly, Ptolemy wasn't concerned about empire but about Egypt, where the duty of any Pharaoh was to supervise the burial of his predecessor. In fact, such a sacred act was part of the ritual of succession in Pharaonic Egypt. There are many examples of this, the most famous being that of Ay, Pharaoh of the Eighteenth Dynasty who, garbed in the full regalia as king of the Two Lands, is depicted as supervising the burial of his now famous predecessor Tutankhamun.[13]

Whatever Ptolemy's motivation, he had to face the consequences. Perdiccas was determined to answer the snub as well as regain the important province of Alexander's empire which circumstances had forced him to concede in that stifling hot summer at Babylon some two years earlier. Perdiccas had hoped Cleomenes would contain Ptolemy, but Perdiccas had hopelessly misjudged his opponent. The battle lines were soon drawn, Perdiccas was determined to crush Antipater in Europe and Ptolemy in Egypt. Perdiccas' ally Eumenes would check Antipater at the Hellespont while Perdiccas took his army to Egypt. In the end his invasion of Egypt was a disaster. Perdiccas was repulsed by Ptolemy and his army suffered a hideous setback trying to cross a crocodile-infested part of the Nile.

Ptolemy was also busy bribing Perdiccas' commanders and, one night, shortly after the disastrous river crossing, Perdiccas was murdered by a coterie of officers led by Pithon (321 BC). Ptolemy was immediately invited into the camp of his enemy where he promptly rewarded the ringleaders, Arridhaeus and Pithon, by making them temporary regents. Whenever possible, Ptolemy followed this policy for the rest of his reign; he tried to stay out of the savage Wars of the Successors, more determined to regain those territories which, by tradition, were part of Egypt's sphere of influence: the islands of the Mediterranean, Libya and the city-states of North Africa as well as Phoenicia and Syria in ancient Canaan. He continued his alliance with the House of Antipater and married Cassander's sister, the princess Eurydice by whom he had four children. When Antipater died in his bed, Ptolemy and Cassander continued their friendship and close alliance against the common threat of Antigonus the One-eyed, another general of Alexander, who managed to survive the crash of empire.[14]

Like the other Lords of the Purple, Ptolemy eventually assumed the title of King, founding a dynasty which would last until the time of Augustus. Ptolemy defended his external interests ruthlessly, but he also worked to be accepted by his new subjects who gave him the title of Saviour. He founded a famous museum and library and attracted scholars to enjoy his patronage. Alexandria became one of the glories of the Ancient World; it not only boasted Schools of Life and Academies but also wonderful shrines to the Great Conqueror which dominated the grand crossroads of Alexandria where the Canopic Way crossed the Street of the Soma. This became the burial site for later rulers of the Ptolemaic dynasty, as well as a place for pilgrimage. Alexander's marble mausoleum was finally completed by Ptolemy's successor and survived until the reign of Aurelian late in the third century of the Christian era.

Ptolemy proved to be a formidable ruler, the founder of a great dynasty who watched as the other Lords of the Purple fought to the death. Cassander, Seleucus and Antigonus were survivors, but Eumenes, Craterus, Polyperchon, Leonnatus, Pithon and the rest, who had lived by the sword, died by the sword. Ptolemy was a spectator to the savage extermination of Alexander's own family. Olympias fought to the very end; besieged by the hate-filled Cassander, she was reduced to feeding sawdust to her elephants. She was forced to surrender but was later murdered whilst the same fate befell both Roxane and the Great Conqueror's teenage son.[15]

Ptolemy died in 282 BC, surviving many of his contemporaries. According to legend, shortly before his death, Ptolemy abdicated in favour of his son and, once again, resumed the duties of a common guardsman.[16] If this is true, the venerable old man of eighty was going back in time. Perhaps that is why he wrote his history to depict himself as the loyal subordinate, the bluff Macedonian, trekking faithfully in the footsteps of the Great Conqueror. Ptolemy wanted to put the record straight – at least in his own eyes. During those long, balmy nights in his Egyptian palace, Ptolemy must have taken a cup of wine and gone down to the mausoleum to stare at Alexander's corpse. He must have sat and recalled that fateful banquet, on that hot summer's evening so many years ago in Babylon, when the Great Conqueror raised his poisoned-filled cup, quoted Euripides and, across its winking rim, toasted Ptolemy, his loyal taster, for the final time. Perhaps Ptolemy Soter toasted him back even as he'd quote these sombre lines of the chorus which ends Euripides' play *Andromache*:

'τολλαι μορφαι των δαιμονιων' . . .

'Divinity has many forms whilst the Gods achieve many things against our expectations. What man expects might not happen but a God will find the way to achieve the unexpected. Such was the outcome of this our story.'

Sources and References

Principal Sources

I have deliberately concentrated on the primary sources. I read copiously and surveyed all the accounts of historians but I tried to keep free of the propaganda which forms the 'ideal Alexander' and let the 'Voices of the Time' speak for themselves. I also wanted to focus fully on Alexander's murder and the motives behind it. I have, in the footnotes, referred to appropriate secondary sources such as Bosworth and Fox. The principal primary sources are as follows:

Aelian He lived about AD 200. A Roman writer, Aelian is a born gossip. His *Historical Miscellany* or *Varia Historia* are really a collection of tittle-tattle and chatter collected from a variety of sources. There is sometimes little organization or method to what he collects, but he is a rich source of anecdotal evidence. The best translation of Aelian is the Loeb edition by N.G. Wilson (1997).

Aristotle A contemporary of Alexander, and his tutor. Philosopher and scientist, a student of Plato, Aristotle's most famous works are the *Politics* and *Ethics* edited by H. Rackham in the Loeb edition (1932–5).

Arrian, Flavius   He flourished about AD 134, a civil servant and soldier under the Roman Emperor Hadrian. Arrian's history of Alexander is based on the writings of Ptolemy and Aristobulus of which only fragments remain outside Arrian's work. Arrian was once regarded as the prime source for Alexander. Historians now tend to regard him a little more warily. Arrian's adulation for the Great Conqueror is unmistakable, hence he can be rather selective in choosing his evidence. A second work, the *Indica*, depends a great deal upon Alexander's admiral, Nearchus, a man much given to his own advancement. The best edition of both Arrian's works, *The History and the Indica*, are E.I. Robson, Volumes I–II, in the Loeb edition (1929–33). Robson's translation is sometimes highly erratic and often interpretative. Nevertheless, he does try to capture the flavour of Arrian's writing.

Athenaeus of Naucratis   A Greek from the Hellene colony of Naucratis in Egypt. His one claim to fame is his *The Deipnosophists* edited by C.B. Gulick in seven volumes in the Loeb edition (1927–41). Athenaeus is a gossip columnist who collected scraps of information about the great, the good and the notorious in the Classical World. He literally lurches from one topic or theme to another, be it the great courtesans of Athens or the sayings of statesmen and soldiers. Nevertheless, many of the fragments he collected are very valuable and often supplement other pieces of evidence.

Claudius Claudianus   Considered to be the last classical poet of Rome. He lived about 400 AD. His poems are published in two volumes in the Loeb edition. Volume I is edited by M. Platenaur (London 1963).

Demosthenes   A contemporary of Alexander – an Athenian, orator and demagogue, bitterly opposed to Macedonian power, he fought at Chaeronea and remained a constant thorn in the side of the House of Macedon. His speeches, edited by J.H. & C.A. Vince, are available in the Loeb edition (1926–30).

Diodorus Siculus   He lived about 45 BC, a Sicilian who wrote *A Universal History* in forty books. In my view Diodorus is probably the most trustworthy of historians for Alexander's reign. He devotes the entire Book XVII to the period 336–323 whilst Book XVIII is an invaluable source for the infighting which took place after Alexander's death. Understandably, Diodorus can be careless with dates and chronology but, in my view, he is unbiased and was drawing directly on primary sources, some of which only exist in fragments, e.g. the writings of Hieronymus of Cardia who definitely fought in the Wars of Succession. The translation in the Loeb edition can be interpretative, but both Book XVII and XVIII are very dramatic accounts of the rise and fall of Macedon. I find them much more enjoyable than Arrian's history. Books XVII and XVIII edited by C.B. Wells and R.M. Geer (Volumes VIII–IX) are available in the Loeb translation (1947).

Euripides   Lived in the fifth century BC. Alexander's favourite playwright: author of plays such as *Andromache*.

Herodotus   He lived about 450 BC – a valuable source of information in matters of geography and history. The finest edition of his work, *The Histories*, is that of A. de Selincourt (Penguin Classics, London 1954).

Homer   Greek poet, author of the heroic sagas the *Iliad* and the *Odyssey* – published by Loeb.

Isocrates   A contemporary of Philip of Macedon, orator and pamphleteer, a fierce opponent of the Persian Empire. His collected works are edited in the Loeb edition (London 1928–45), edited by G. Norlin, and La Rue Van Hook.

Justin   A Roman historian who lived in the third century AD. He made a detailed summary of an earlier work, Trogus Pompeius' *Historiae Philippicae*, written some 200 years earlier, during the reign of Augustus. Justin used to be derided by historians but a great deal of what he writes can be verified by other sources, particularly Diodorus Siculus. I found the best translation of his work is that of John Selby Watson (London 1875).

Pausanias A Greek who lived in the second century AD, a traveller and an inveterate gossip. Pausanias' *Description of Greece* provides some very important fragments. The Loeb edition (Volume I by W.H.S. Jones) includes the first two books of Pausanias (London 1918).

Photius Byzantine historian of the Christian era who wrote a *Digest of the Great Works of Historians and Philosophers*. He provides a summary of Arrian who wrote a *History of Events* following Alexander's death. Photius is particularly useful for the beginning of Ptolemy's reign in Egypt. I found J.H. Freeses' *The Library of Photius* (Volume I, Macmillan, New York 1920, pages 157 *et seq.*) to be particularly useful.

Plutarch of Chaeronea He lived about AD 100. A contemporary of Arrian, Plutarch was also a civil servant, as well as a priest, during the reign of the Emperor Hadrian. Plutarch's *Life of Alexander* tends to follow the same mood and tone of that of Arrian, although, towards the end, as well as in other works, Plutarch's doubts about Alexander begin to surface, particularly the Great Conqueror's drinking and savage temper. Plutarch also provided an invaluable source in his *Life of Eumenes*, Chief of the Secretariat of Alexander's army. Plutarch's other works particularly the 'Moralia' are a source of valuable information. I was weaned on Langhorne's translation of Plutarch's *Lives* which I still believe is the best. The source I used for Alexander/Eumenes is contained in John and William Langhorne's translation, Volume 4 (London 1801). For the *Moralia*, the edition favoured is that by W.W. Goodwin, Volumes I–V (Little Brown and Co., Boston 1870).

Pseudo-Callisthenes The name given to the unknown author of what is now called the *Alexander Romance*. This can be found in many versions. It originated in the late second century AD, although a section of it relating to Alexander's death, what Robin Lane Fox calls 'The

Pamphlet' (*Alexander the Great*, Futura 1975, page 462 *et seq.*) originated probably shortly after Alexander's death and was used by the different rivals as part of the propaganda campaign in the Wars of Succession. I have studied two versions, the Ethiopian edited by E.A. Wallis Budge (Oxford 1933) and the Armenian translated by A.M. Wolohojian (Columbia University Press 1969). I have cited the Armenian version.

Quintus Curtius   Roman writer of the first century AD: his *History of Alexander* (certain portions of it are missing) was often derided by historians as being too vivid and not accurate enough. He has recently undergone a rehabilitation. True, Curtius does write his history with an eye on political developments in Rome during his own lifetime. Nevertheless, Quintus Curtius provides a vast corpus of evidence for Alexander's reign, especially the events following the Great Conqueror's death. The most vivid and accurate translation of the Latin, which manages to catch that slightly excited breathlessness of Quintus Curtius, is that of Peter Pratt, Volumes I and II (London 1809–12).

Strabo   A Greek who lived at the time of Christ: author of the *Geography* (edited by H. Jones in eight volumes: Loeb, London 1917–32), a rich source of evidence about people and places.

Tacitus   Lived in the first century AD: prolific historian. *The Histories*, a recent translation by K. Wellesley (Penguin 1975) is a valuable source.

Xenophon   Soldier, historian who lived in the fourth century BC. Author of a dramatic account of a celebrated incident in the Persian Wars as well as the *Cyropaedia* – Volumes I and II, edited by W. Miller (Loeb 1979–83).

The Fragments   One of the great problems of studying the reign of Alexander the Great is that we have no real, true, contemporaneous account. In my view, there was a period of censorship following Alexander's death as his generals divided his empire and fought for power. As I have demonstrated in the text, after 323 BC, Alexander did not lack biographers, historians, commentators, eye-witness accounts, etc. However, after 323 BC, there does appear to be a general cautiousness about publishing narrative accounts of his reign, and especially of his death. Many of Alexander's contemporaries, such as Aristobulus, did not start writing until long after the deaths of many of the Great Conqueror's successors. Most of their accounts now only exist in fragment form and can be found, with translation, in C.A. Robinson, *The History of Alexander the Great*, Volume 1 (Providence Rhode Island 1953). An excellent companion to Robinson's volume is L. Pearson's *The Lost Histories of Alexander the Great* (Blackwell, Oxford 1957). Pearson gives a detailed description of those valuable sources which only exist in either fragments or in the works of others such as Arrian. They are as follows:

Aristobulus –architect and engineer in Alexander's army. It would appear that he was writing his account during Alexander's life, but he never actually published it until as late as 285 BC, some thirty-eight years after Alexander's death.

Callisthenes of Olynthus – Aristotle's nephew and Alexander's official historian, later executed by Alexander on alleged charges of treason.

Chares of Mitylene – Chamberlain to Alexander, a veritable source of gossip used by the likes of Plutarch.

Ephippus of Olynthus – a member of Alexander's entourage, slightly hostile to Alexander and Macedon, his works only exist in fragment form.

Medius of Larissa – a high-ranking officer in Alexander's navy, who later fought in the Wars of Succession, a man who could tell us so much. According to all the sources, Medius was the person, the flatterer, who invited Alexander to that fateful banquet in Babylon at the end of May 323.

Nearchus of Crete – Alexander's admiral, famous for his exploration of the northern rim of the Indian Ocean. He, too, left an account used by different historians.

Onescritus – a high-ranking officer in Alexander's navy, whose account of his travels exists only in fragments.

References

Abbreviations

These refer to the editions of the primary sources cited above: e.g.,
Plut. 4 (*op. cit.*) Alex: Langhorne's edition of Plutarch's *Lives* volume 4:
Life of Alexander. The same volume includes the *Life of Eumenes*. The
references to Aelian, Pausanias, Diodorus Siculus, Arrian, Justin, etc.
are to the editions cited above.

J.H.S. = *The Journal of Hellenic Studies*
C.Q. = *The Classical Quarterly*

Prologue: Babylon – 29 May 323 BC

1. Book of Daniel, V
2. The primary source accounts for Alexander's death are as
   follows:
   Plut. 4 (*op. cit.*) Alex pp. 321–4
   Diod. Sic. VIII (*op. cit.*) XVII pp. 465–9
   Quin. Curt. Vol. II (*op. cit.*) X: V pp. 406–10

Justin (*op. cit.*) pp. 118–120

Arrian Vol. II (*op. cit.*) VII: 21 pp. 280–95

Alex. Rom. (Armenian Version: *op. cit.*) pp. 150–9

The most modern scholarly analysis can be found in A.B. Bosworth's 'The Death of Alexander the Great: Rumour and Propaganda' C.Q. 21 (1971) pp. 112–36

3. Plut. 4 (*op. cit.*) *Alex.* pp. 231–2

4. Plut. 4 *Ibid. Alex.* p. 254

5. Plut. 4 *Ibid.* pp. 222–33

    Diod. Sic. (*op. cit.*) XVII: 1 p. 121

6. Homer *Iliad* (*op. cit.*) I 146

    Homer *Odyssey* (*op. cit.*), II 488–91

7. Homer *Iliad* (*op. cit.*) 19: 409 and 13: 667

Part One: The God

1. A good study of Philip is G.L. Cawkwell's *Philip of Macedon* (London 1979)

2. A good general study is N.G.L. Hammond's *A History of Greece* (2nd edition, Oxford 1967)

3. A.H.M. Jones *The Greek Army from Alexander to Constantine* (Oxford 1940) is one of the best studies

4. G.L. Cawkwell., *ibid.*

5. Plut., (*op. cit.*) *Moralia* Vol. I pp. 194 *et seq.*

6. *Ibid.*

7. Athenaeus VI (*op. cit.*) (quoting Satyrus' *Life of Philip*) XIII: 557 pp. 13–15

8. Plut. 4 (*op. cit.*) *Alex.* p. 224

9. Justin (*op. cit.*) p. 87

10. Quin. Curt. II (*op. cit.*) X: IX pp. 430–1

11. The usual spelling is Pella but Pelle is also used

12. Athenaeus II (*op. cit.*) III: 120, p. 61 quotes Ephippus' remark

    Plut. 4 (*op. cit.*), *Alex* p. 312

13. Athenaeus II (*op. cit.*) IV: Most of this book is a discourse on wine and food
14. Athenaeus II (*op. cit.*) IV: 155 p. 207
15. Athen. II (*op. cit.*) IV: 166 pp. 257–9
16. Demosthenes (*op. cit.*) *Olynthus* 1.13
17. Plut. (*op. cit.*) *Moralia* Vol. I p. 194 *et seq.*
18. *Ibid.*
19. Justin (*op. cit.*) p. 78
20. Athenaeus II (*op. cit.*) IV: 166 pp. 257–9
21. Isocrates (*op. cit.*) 'The Panegyricus' pp. 140–3: *Address to Philip*, pp. 99–120
22. Macedon is the main theme of Demosthenes' printed speeches and Philip his main target
23. Diod. Sic. VIII (*op. cit.*) XVI pp. 44–50
24. Plut. 4 (*op. cit.*) *Alex.* p. 226
25. *Ibid.* pp. 224, 225
26. Plut. (*op. cit.*) *Moralia* II p. 494 and Athen. V (*op. cit.*) XIII p. 13
27. W.W. Tarn *Alexander the Great*, Vol. II p. 326 (Oxford 1948)
28. Hyperides
29. Plut. 4 (*op. cit.*) *Alex.* pp. 279–80
30. *Ibid.* p. 243
31. Quin. Curt. II (*op. cit.*) 9.6. p. 343
32. Justin (*op. cit.*) pp. 136–7
33. Plut. 4 (*op. cit.*) *Alex.* p. 224
34. *Ibid.*
35. *Ibid.* p. 225
36. *Ibid.* p. 225; Robinson *The History of Alexander I* p. 165 no. 15
37. Plut. 4 (*op. cit.*) *Alex.* p. 225
38. *Ibid.* pp. 225–6
39. *Ibid.* p. 252
40. *Ibid.* p. 228
41. *Ibid.* p. 324
42. Justin (*op. cit.*) p.136
43. E.N. Borza *In the Shadow of Olympus: the Emergence of Macedon* (Princeton 1990) p. 165, n. 15

44. Such insults pervade Demosthenes' speeches: e.g. Demosthenes' *Philippics* (ed. J.H. Vince) p. 69 *et seq.*

45. J.L. Ackrill's *Aristotle the Philosopher* (Oxford 1981) and W. Jaeger's *Aristotle* (trans. R. Robertson, Oxford 1962) are two of the best studies

46. Plut. 4 (*op. cit.*) *Alex.* pp. 230–1

47. *Ibid.* p. 235

48. Herodotus (*op. cit.*) 8.138 p. 495

49. Plut. 4 (*op. cit.*) *Alex.* pp. 232–3

50. Strabo VII (*op. cit.*) XV. 2. pp. 3–5

51. Quin. Curt. II (*op. cit.*) Bk V: II pp. 15–16

52. *Alex. Rom* (Armenian): (*op. cit.*) p. 33

53. Plut. 4 (*op. cit.*) *Alex* p. 226
    Quin. Curt. I (*op. cit.*) I: II pp. 12–15

54. Plut. 4 (*op. cit.*) *Alex.* pp. 231–2

55. *Ibid.* p. 232

56. *Ibid.* p. 235

57. Athen. V. (*op. cit.*) XII p. 429 *et seq.*
    Euripides *Hell.* (lines 1151–4)

58. Jaeger *Aristotle* (*op. cit.*) pp. 119–20

59. *Ibid.* p. 253 *et seq.*
    Aristotle *Politics* (*op. cit.*) 1256b: 25

60. Jaeger (*op. cit.*) pp. 117–19. Where Aristotle expounds on 'Arete' as exemplified by his heroic father-in-law Hermeias

61. Quin. Curt. II (*op. cit.*) VIII: XIV p. 297

62. Plut. 4 (*op. cit.*) *Alex.* p. 230

63. Quin. Curt. I (*op. cit.*) I: III p. 28

64. *Ibid.* p. 19

65. Quin. Curt. I (*op. cit.*) I: IX pp. 98–9

66. Plut. 4 (*op. cit.*) *Alex.* p. 232

67. Plut. 4 (*op. cit.*) *Alex.* p. 228
    Arrian II (*op. cit.*) 7.2.2. p. 209

68. Plut. (*op. cit.*) *Moralia* I: Philip's 'Apopthegms': pp. 194 *et seq.*

69. Plut. 4 (*op. cit.*) *Alex.* p. 227

70. *Ibid.* p. 231

71. Athenaeus IV (*op. cit.*) X p. 47

72. Plut. 4 (*op. cit.*) *Alex*. p. 252
73. *Ibid*. pp. 232–3
    Quint. Curt. I (*op. cit.*) IV p. 38
74. *Ibid*. p. 41
75. Demosthenes' constant theme. Demos I (*op. cit.*) p. 27
76. Plut. 4 (*op. cit.*) *Alex*. p. 233
77. Quin. Curt. I (*op. cit.*) I: VIII p. 92
78. *Ibid*. pp. 92–3
79. Quin. Curt. II (*op. cit.*) VIII: I p. 216
80. Quin. Curt. I (*op. cit.*) I: IX p. 98 *et seq.*
81. *Ibid*. pp. 38 and 99
    Justin (*op. cit.*) p.100
82. Pausanias II (*op. cit.*) V: 20 p. 85
83. Arrian I (*op. cit.*) 3.6.5 p. 241
    Plut. 4 (*op. cit.*) *Alex*. p. 233
84. Athen. VI (*op. cit.*) XIII: 557 p. 15
85. Arrian I (*op. cit.*) 3.6.5 p. 241
86. Athen. VI (*op. cit.*) XIII: 557 pp. 15–16
    Plut. 4 (*op. cit.*) p. 233
87. *Ibid*. p. 234
88. *Ibid*. p. 234
89. *Ibid*. pp. 234–5
90. Diod. Sic. VIII (*op. cit.*) XVI: 92 p. 89
91. Athen. VI (*op. cit.*) XIII: 557 p. 15
    Justin (*op. cit.*) p. 86
92. Diod. Sic. VIII (*op. cit.*) XVI: 91 p. 89
93. Plut. 4 (*op. cit.*) *Alex*. p. 235: Plutarch's account is suspiciously very brief – bearing in mind the praise he had written earlier in his *Life of Alexander* as well as the flattery contained in Plutarch's *Moralia* I (*op. cit.*) p. 491 *et seq.* Arrian is even briefer and more superficial: e.g. Arrian I (*op. cit.*) 3.6.5. p. 241
    Diod. Sic. VIII (*op. cit.*) XVI: 91–5 pp. 90–103
    Quin. Curt. I (*op. cit.*) I: IX–X pp. 105–20
    (This also includes Alexander's allegation against Persian involvement in his father's murder *ibid*. p. 120)
    Justin (*op. cit.*) pp. 85–8

Aristotle (*op. cit.*) *Politics* 1311

94. M. Andronicas 'The Royal Tomb of Philip II'
    Archaeology 31: p. 33 *et seq.* (1978b)
    and M. Andronicas *Vergina: the Royal Tombs and the Ancient City* (Athens 1984)
    Diod. Sic. IX (*op. cit.*) XVIII: 4. 2–6 pp. 22–3

95. The sources all provide details of this famous pilgrimage and what happened there
    Arrian I (*op. cit.*) 3.3: 1–4 p. 229 *et seq.*
    Quin. Curt. I (*op. cit.*) IV: VII pp. 392–9
    Diod. Sic. VIII (*op. cit.*) XVII: 49–51 pp. 259–67
    Justin (*op. cit.*) XI:11 2–11 pp. 100–101

96. Plut. 4 (*op. cit.*) *Alex.* p. 225

97. Arrian II (*op. cit.*) VII: 8 pp. 225–33
    Homer *Iliad* (*op. cit.*) 6.479

98. Plut. 4 (*op. cit.*) *Alex.* p. 283
    Arrian II (*op. cit.*) VII 2 p. 209 and VII: 28 p. 297

99. Plut. 4 (*op. cit.*) *Alex.* pp. 238–9

100. Diod. Sic. VIII (*op. cit.*) XVII: 2 p. 121
     Quin. Curt. II (*op. cit.*) VII: I p. 138

101. Plut. 4 (*op. cit.*) *Alex.* p. 235
     Justin (*op. cit.*) p. 91. Justin claims the baby Caranus was killed on Alexander's orders

102. This alliance could have gone back to 338/337: Antipater joined Alexander in the embassy to Athens after Chaeronea. Justin (*op. cit.*) p. 84

103. Diod. Sic. VIII (*op. cit.*) XVII: 2 p. 123

104. *Ibid.* p. 121 Justin (*op. cit.*) p. 91

105. *Ibid.*
     Plut. 4 (*op. cit.*) *Alex.* pp. 235–6

106. Demosthenes' contempt is evident in his alleged speech 'On the Treaty with Alexander'. Demos. I (*op. cit.*) p. 465 *et seq.* and Plut. (*op. cit.*) *Moralia* Vol. V p. 55

107. Plut. 4 (*op. cit.*) *Alex.* p. 236

108. *Ibid.*
     Justin (*op. cit.*) pp. 90–3

109. Plut. 4 (*op. cit.*) *Alex.* p. 239

110. *Ibid.* p. 236. Justin (*op. cit.*) p. 92
Diod. Sic. VIII (*op. cit.*) XVII: 8 pp. 139–41

111. Plut. 4 (*op. cit.*) *Alex.* pp. 236–8
Diod. Sic. VIII (*op. cit.*) XVIII: 9–16 pp. 141–61 Diodorus'
account covers this campaign and the effects of Alexander's
campaign of terror

112. *Ibid.* pp. 137–9
Quin. Cur. I (*op. cit.*) II: I pp. 168–9

113. J. Warry *Alexander 334–43 BC. Conquest of the Persian Empire* (Osprey
1991)

114. Diod. Sic. VIII (*op. cit.*) XVII: 16 pp. 163–5
Justin (*op. cit.*) pp. 94–5

115. A recent comprehensive summary of Alexander's campaigns can
be found in A.B. Bosworth's *Conquest and Empire: The Reign of
Alexander the Great* (Cambridge 1988) pp. 35–158

Part Two: Warnings at Babylon

1. Quin. Curt. II (*op. cit.*) V: I p. 6 *et seq.*

2. Plut. 4 (*op. cit.*) *Alex.* p. 312

3. Strabo VII (*op. cit.*) 16: V p. 197 *et seq.*

4. Philostratus, *Life of Apollonius of Tyna* (Loeb edition, 1953): a very
garrulous account of a tourist visiting ancient places in Babylon

5. Plut. 4 (*op. cit.*) *Alex.* p. 24

6. Justin (*op. cit.*) p. 94

7. Quin. Curt. I (*op. cit.*) IV: II pp. 353 *et seq.* and pp. 374–5
Plut. 4 (*op. cit.*) *Alex.* p. 255

8. Quin. Curt. I (*op. cit.*) IV: VI pp. 384–91

9. Plut. 4 (*op. cit.*) *Alex.* p. 267

10. Quin. Curt. I (*op. cit.*) III: I p. 276

11. *Ibid.* IX: V p. 330

12. Plut. 4 (*op. cit.*) *Alex.* p. 300

13. Plut. 4 (*op. cit.*) *Alex.* pp. 315–16
    Strabo VII (*op. cit.*) pp. 119–21
    Diod. Sic. VIII (*op. cit.*) XVII: 114 p. 457
    Quin. Curt. II (*op. cit.*) X: IV p. 405
14. Plut 4 (*op. cit.*) *Alex.* p. 319
    Arrian II (*op. cit.*) VII: 16 p. 259
15. Diod. Sic. VIII (*op. cit.*) XVII: III p. 449 *et seq.*
16. Arrian II (*op. cit.*) VII: 18 pp. 263–4
17. Diod. Sic. VIII (*op. cit.*) XVII: 116 p. 463 *et seq.*
18. Arrian II (*op. cit.*) VII pp. 281–2
19. Plut. 4 (*op. cit.*) *Alex.* p. 321
20. *Claudian* I (*op. cit.*) ed. M. Platnauer (Heinemann 1973) p. 37
21. Quin. Curt. II (*op. cit.*) VII: VII pp. 187–9
22. *Ibid.* p.249 'Who guarded the chamber door [of the king]'

Part Three: The Death of a God

1. Quin. Curt. II (*op. cit.*) X: IV p. 405
2. Diod. Sic. VIII (*op. cit.*) XVII: 117 pp. 465–7
3. Arrian II (*op. cit.*) VII: XXV pp. 289–95
4. Plut. 4 (*op. cit.*) *Alex.* pp. 322–4
5. Justin (*op. cit.*) pp. 118–20
6. Aelian (*op. cit.*) 3: 23 pp. 157–8
7. Athen. IV (*op. cit.*) X pp. 467–9
8. A.B. Bosworth's *From Arrian to Alexander* (Oxford 1988) p. 173 *et seq.* provides a thorough and clear analysis
9. Robinson (*op. cit.*) Vol. 1 p. 93

Part Four: Alexander, the Drunken Libertine?

1. Plut. 4 (*op. cit.*) *Alex.* pp. 252–3
   Plut. (*op. cit.*) *Moralia* I pp. 500 and 505
   Quin. Curt. II (*op. cit.*) V: VII pp.40–2
   Arrian I (*op. cit.*) IV: 8 p. 365
   Justin (*op. cit.*) p. 88
2. Athen. VI (*op. cit.*) XIII: 576 p. 113
3. Plut. 4 (*op. cit.*) *Alex.* pp. 241–2
4. Athenaeus V (*op. cit.*) XII p. 429
5. Arrian II (*op. cit.*) V: I p. 5
6. Diod. Sic. VIII (*op. cit.*) XVII: 113 pp. 455–6
   Quin. Curt. I (*op. cit.*) III: XII p. 331 and Quin. Curt. II: X: IV
   p. 396
7. Quin. Curt. II (*op. cit.*) X: 1 p. 378
8. Diod. Sic. VIII (*op. cit.*) XVII: 16 p. 161
9. Plut 4 (*op. cit.*) *Alex.* pp. 250–1, 288
   Quin. Curt. II (*op. cit.*) VIII: IV pp. 237–8
   Diod. Sic. VIII (*op. cit.*) XVII: 107 p. 433
10. *Ibid.* XVII: 77 p. 343
11. Plut. 4 (*op. cit.*) *Alex.* pp. 251–2
12. *Ibid.* pp. 255–6
13. *Ibid.* pp. 268–9
14. Diod. Sic. VIII (*op. cit.*) XVII: 99 pp. 403–4
15. Plut. 4 (*op. cit.*) *Alex.* p. 296
    Athen. IV (*op. cit.*) X pp. 467–9
16. Arrian II (*op. cit.*) V: 2 pp. 9–10
17. Strabo VII (*op. cit.*) XV: 2 p. 153
    Diod. Sic. VIII (*op. cit.*) XVII: 105 p. 427
18. Plut. 4 (*op. cit.*) *Alex.* p. 313
19. Arrian I (*op. cit.*) III: 18 p. 285
    Diod. Sic. VIII (*op. cit.*) XVII: 72 pp. 325–6
    Plut. 4 (*op. cit.*) *Alex.* pp. 276–7
20. Quin. Curt. II (*op. cit.*) V: VII p. 40 *et seq.*
21. *The Romance of Alexander* (*op. cit.*) p. 150

22. This is implicit from Plutarch's account. Plut 4 (*op. cit.*) *Alex.* pp. 318–19

    Arrian is more explicit. Arrian II (*op. cit.*) VII. 14 pp. 249–51

23. A.B. Bosworth *Conquest and Empire: the Reign of Alexander the Great* (Cambridge 1988) p. 173

    Robin Lane Fox. *Alexander the Great* (Futura 1975) p. 461 *et seq.*

24. Plut. 4 (*op. cit.*) *Alex.* p.288

25. Athenaeus V (*op. cit.*) XII p. 537: the actual Greek verb can be translated 'to act the part' not just 'to recite'

26. Plut. 4 (*op. cit.*) *Alex.* p. 287. For the article: *Sunday Times Magazine*, 12 Oct. 2003, and Channel 5, 22 Oct. 2003

27. Plut. 4 (*op. cit.*) *Alex.* p.324 Quin. Curt II (*op. cit.*) X: X pp. 434–5

28 *Ibid.* pp. 435–6

29. Diod. Sic. VIII (*op. cit.*) XVII: 117 p. 469

30. Arrian II (*op. cit.*) VII: 26 p. 295

31. Plut. 4 (*op. cit.*) *Alex.* pp. 323–4

32. *Alex. Rom.* (*op. cit.*) pp. 150–1 Robin Lane Fox *Alexander* (*op. cit.*) p. 462 *et seq.*

33. *Alex. Rom.* (*op. cit.*) pp. 150–9

34. Plut. 4 (*op. cit.*) *Alex.* p. 325

    Diod. Sic. VIII (*op. cit.*) XVII: 117–18 pp. 467–9

    Arrian II (*op. cit.*) VII: XXVII pp. 295–7

35. Robinson I *The History of Alexander* p 165. fragment 37

36. Plut. (*op. cit.*) *Moralia* V pp. 25 and 55–6

37. Diodorus IX (*op. cit.*) XIX: 11 p. 259 – under the year 319 BC

38. A. Pearson *The Lost Histories of Alexander the Great* (Blackwell 1960) p. 150 *et seq.*

39. Plut. 4 (*op. cit.*) *Alex.* p. 287

40. The references and passages to these sources have already been given

41. A clear example of the confusion these diaries causes is A.B. Bosworth's *From Arrian to Alexander* (Oxford 1988) p. 157 *et seq.*

42. Athenaeus IV (*op. cit.*) X: 434 p. 467

43. Plut. 4 (*op. cit.*) *Life of Eumenes* pp. 35–7

44. *Ibid. The Life of Eumenes* pp. 37 *et seq.*

45. Tacitus (*op. cit.*) *Histories* 4: 83–4 pp. 264–5

Plut. 'Isis and Osiris' in Vol. IV of the *Moralia* (*op. cit.*) pp. 361–2

46. Plut. 4 (*op. cit.*) *Alex.* p. 282
47. Pearson (*op. cit.*) *The Lost Histories of Alexander* pp. 68 and 117
48. Robin Lane Fox (*op. cit.*) *Alexander* p. 468
49. *Alex. Rom.* (*op. cit.*) pp.151–2

Part Five: The Motive

1. The intense opposition from Athens is obvious. Alexander died in June 323 – before the year ended, Athens was at war
   Diod. Sic. IX (*op. cit.*) XVIII: 8 p. 33. But see 'Alexander and the Greeks' in *Alexander the Great: A Reader* ed. I Worthington (Routledge 2003) p. 65 *et seq.*
2. Plut 4 (*op. cit.*). *Alex.* pp. 237–8
3. Diod. Sic. VIII (*op. cit.*) XVII: 13 p.155
4. *Ibid.* XVII: 35 pp. 217–18
5. Plut. 4 (*op. cit.*) p. 278
6. Plut. 4 (*op. cit.*) *Alex.* p. 305: a description of the death of this elephant
7. Plut. 4 (*op. cit.*) *Alex.* p. 304: Diod. Sic. VIII (*op. cit.*) XVII: VI p. 158
8. Plut. 4 (*op. cit.*) *Alex.* p. 257
9. *Ibid.* p. 234
10. For the entire Philotas affair: Quin. Curt. II (*op. cit.*) VI: VII p. 102 *et seq.*
    Plut. 4 (*op. cit.*) *Alex.* p. 289 *et seq.*
    Arrian I (*op. cit.*) III: 27 p. 313 *et seq.*
    Diod. Sic. VIII (*op. cit.*) XVII: 79 p. 345 *et seq.*
11. Quin Curt. II (*op. cit.*): Nicanor 'by sudden death' VI: VI p. 99: 'Hector of a boating accident.' (Quin Curt I: IV: VIII p. 402) Alexander grieved – but, there again, he did the same for Cleitus
12. Plut. (*op. cit.*) *Moralia* I pp. 205–6
13. Quin Curt. II (*op. cit.*) vii: ii pp. 152–3
14. For the account of the entire Cleitus incident: see p. 200 *et seq.*

15. Plut. 4 (*op. cit,*) *Alex.* p. 286

16. *Ibid.* p. 261

17. Xenophon (*op. cit.*) *Cyropaedia* Vols. I–II
     Strabo (*op. cit.*) *The Geography* XI: II. He calls Alexander an
     'admirer of Cyrus'

18. Quin. Curt. II (*op. cit.*) VIII: pp. 244–5 for the Pages' conspiracy

19. On Callisthenes conspiracy Quin. Curt. II (*op. cit.*) VIII: VI
     p. 245 *et seq.*
     Arrian I (*op. cit.*) IV: X p. 371 *et seq.*
     Plut 4 (*op. cit.*) *Alex.* pp. 296–9

20. Quin. Curt. II, (*op. cit.*) VIII: VII p. 257 *et seq.*

21. Plut. 4 (*op. cit.*) *Alex.* p. 299

22. Arrian II (*op. cit.*) V: 27 p. 91 *et seq.*
     Quin. Curt. II (*op. cit.*) IX: III p. 321

23. Strabo *Geography* VII (*op. cit.*) 15: 2 p. 135 *et seq.*
     Strabo also provides an excellent summary of the horrors of the
     march

24. Diod. Sic. (*op. cit.*) XVII: 103 pp. 415–17
     Arrian II (*op. cit.*) VI: 23 p. 177 *et seq.*
     Arrian's description is one of the most vivid about the retreat: his
     assessment of the losses can be found in the *Indica*. Arrian II (*op.
     cit.*) *Indica* 26:1 p. 383. See also Bosworth's *Conquest and Empire* (*op.
     cit.*) p. 142 *et seq.*

25. Diod. Sic. VIII (*op. cit.*) XVII: 108 pp. 433–5
     E.J. Badian *Cambridge History of Iran* pp. 476–81
     Quin. Curt. II. (*op. cit.*) X: I p. 383

26. *Ibid.* IX: p. 371 and X: I pp. 373–4
     Arrian II (*op. cit.*) VI: XXVII pp. 187 and 189
     Plut 4 (*op. cit.*) *Alex.* p. 314

27. Arrian II (*op. cit.*) VII: 4 p. 215 *et seq.*

28. *Ibid.* VII: 6 pp. 219–21

29. *Ibid.* VII: 5 pp. 217–19

30. Bosworth *Conquest and Empire* (*op. cit.*) 148 *et seq.* and p.165 *et seq.*

31. Arrian II (*op. cit.*) VII: 19 & 20 pp. 267–81
     Plut. 4 (*op. cit.*) *Alex.* p. 314
     Quin. Curt. II (*op. cit.*) X: I pp. 376–7

32. Quin. Curt. II (*op. cit.*) X: II–IV pp. 384–96
     Diod. Sic VIII (*op. cit.*) XVII: 108 p. 439 *et seq.*
     Arrian II (*op. cit.*) VIII pp. 225–43
33. Plut. 4 (*op. cit.*) *Alex.* pp. 280–1
34. Quin. Curt. II (*op. cit.*) VIII: XIII p. 285
35. Plut 4 (*op. cit.*) *Alex.* p. 320
36. Arrian II (*op. cit.*) *Indica* 20 p. 365
37. Aelian (*op. cit.*) 12: 16 p. 367
     desioi (cunning: devious)
38. Quin. Curt. II (*op. cit.*) VIII: V pp. 344–5
     Plut. 4 (*op. cit.*) *Eumenes* p. 36 and *Alex.* p. 300
39. Quin. Curt. II (*op. cit.*) X: IV pp. 398–9
     Plut 4 (*op. cit.*) *Alex.* p. 288
     Athen. V. (*op. cit.*) XII p. 431
40. Plut. 4 (*op. cit.*) Eumenes p. 37
     Quin. Curt. II (*op. cit.*) X: IV p. 401
41. On Antipater: Quin. Curt. II (*op. cit.*) V: I pp. 70–4 and X: IV
     pp. 395–7
     Plut. 4 (*op. cit.*) *Alex.* p. 299
42. *Ibid.* pp. 320–1

Part Six: The Conspirators?

1. Arrian II (*op. cit.*) *Indica* 35 p. 411
    Plut. 4 (*op. cit.*) *Eumenes* p. 34
    Quin. Curt. II (*op. cit.*) X: X p. 432
2. Plut. 4 (*op. cit.*) *Eumenes* p. 43
3. Plut. 4 (*op. cit.*) *Alex.* pp. 281–6
4. Quin. Curt. II (*op. cit.*) VI: VIII p. 109 *et seq.*
5. Plut. 4 (*op. cit.*) *Eumenes* pp. 43–4 and p. 60
    Diod. Sic. IX (*op. cit.*) XVIII: 36 p. 115
6. Quin. Curt. II (*op. cit.*) X: V p. 407
7. Justin (*op. cit.*) p.122

8. *Ibid.* p. 137 and p. 139
9. Plut. (*op. cit.*) *Moralia* I p. 200

Part Seven: Ptolemy the Assassin?

1. Quin. Curt. II (*op. cit.*) IX: VIII p. 354
    Pausanias *Description of Greece* I (*op. cit.*) VI p. 29
2. N. Davis and C.M. Kraay *The Hellenistic Kingdoms: Portrait Coins and History* (Thames & Hudson 1973)
3. N. Davis and C.M. Kraay *Ibid.*
4. Plut. (*op. cit.*) *Moralia* p. 45
5. J.R. Ellis *Philip II and Macedonian Imperialism* (London 1976) pp. 161–2
6. Quin. Curt. I (*op. cit.*) I: IX pp. 104–5
7. Arrian I (*op. cit.*) III p. 241
8. *Ibid.* III p. 327
9. *Ibid.* IV p. 389
10. Quin. Curt. II (*op. cit.*) IX: VIII pp. 354–5
11. Arrian II (*op. cit.*) VII: 2 p. 211 and VII: 15 p. 255
12. Diod. Sic. VIII (*op. cit.*) XVII: 103 pp. 417–19
13. He guarded the door to the king's tent. Quin. Curt. II (*op. cit.*) VIII: VI p. 249
    Arrian describing the Pages Conspiracy: the informant goes to the king's tent and Ptolemy: Arrian I (*op. cit.*) IV p. 383
14. Athen. II (*op. cit.*) IV: 171 pp. 277–9
15. Diod. Sic. IX (*op. cit.*) XVIII: 32 p. 105
16. Plut 4 (*op. cit.*) *Alex.* p. 293 makes reference to this: Arrian recalls Aristobulus for the specific details: Arrian I (*op. cit.*) IV p. 365
17. Arrian I (*op. cit.*) III p. 287
18. On these courtesans: Athen. VI (*op. cit.*) XIII: 576 p. 113
    Diod. Sic. VIII (*op. cit.*) XVII: 108 p. 437
19. Arrian II (*op. cit.*) V: 27 pp. 91–5

20. Quin. Curt. II (*op. cit.*) XVI pp. 414–19

21. Pausanias I (*op. cit.*): VI p. 29

22. Diod. Sic. IX (*op. cit.*) XVIII: 3 4. p. 109 talks of the 'surpassing rivalry' between Ptolemy and Perdiccas and *Ibid.* XVIII: 13 p. 109 shows how Ptolemy knew Perdiccas was going to try and wrest Egypt from him

23. *Alex Rom* (*op. cit.*) p. 156

24. Diodorus Siculus remarks 'Ptolemy took over the rule of Egypt without any difficulty.' Diod. Sic. IX (*op. cit.*) XVIII: 13 p. 51. Compare this with the difficulties the other successors had to face. The best and most thorough analysis of the first part of the Wars of Succession is R.M. Errington's 'From Babylon to Triparadeisos' *J.H.S.* 1970 Vol. 90 pp. 49–77

25. Diod. Sic IX. (*op. cit.*) XVIII: 13 p. 51
    Pausanias I (*op. cit.*) VI p. 29 On Cleomenes' evil regime – Arrian II (*op. cit.*) VII: 23 pp. 285–7

26. Alexander's analysis of the importance of Egypt in the great scheme of things is in Arrian I (*op. cit.*) II pp. 187–9

27. For example: Pausanias I (*op. cit.*) pp. 33–5
    Diodorus claims Ptolemy was 'utterly hostile to Perdiccas but *friendly* to the House of Antipater': Diod. Sic. IX (*op. cit.*) XVIII: 25 p. 85

28. *Ibid.* VIII (*op. cit.*) XVII: 93 p. 391

29. Quin. Curt. II (*op. cit.*) X: X p. 436

30. On this, see Errington 'From Babylon to Tripardeisos' (*op. cit.*)

31. On Hephaestion's death: Quin. Curt. II (*op. cit.*) X: IV p. 400
    Diod. Sic. VIII (*op. cit.*) XVII: 110 p. 445
    Arrian II (*op. cit.*) VII: 14 pp. 249–51
    Plut. 4 (*op. cit.*) *Alex.* p. 318
    On the effects of arsenic: the two most thorough accounts are A.S. Taylor *On Poisons* (London 1848): Ch. XXIII p. 308 *et seq.* And what I regard as even more analytical: A.W. Blyth *Poisons: their effects and detection* (London 1920). Although both works are 'dated', they still cannot be equalled. Blyth's description of arsenic and its symptoms is most thorough and thought-provoking: Blyth (*op. cit.*) Part IX p. 554 *et seq.*

32. Diod. Sic. VIII (*op. cit.*) XVII: 108 p. 435 and 109 p. 439
    Quin. Curt. II (*op. cit.*) X: IV pp. 393–8 this provides a detailed analysis

33. Quin. Curt. II (*op. cit.*) X: III and IV pp. 392–3

34. *Ibid.* pp. 397–8

35. *Ibid.* X: VIII p. 426

36. Arrian II (*op. cit.*) VII: 25 p. 291

37. For these auguries and omens see above p. 90 *et seq.*

38. Plut. 4 (*op. cit.*) *Alex.* p. 320

39. Quin. Curt. II (*op. cit.*) VIII: IV pp. 235–6

40. The evidence cited in this summation has been given earlier

41. Pausanias I (*op. cit.*) VI p. 33

42. Plut. 4 (*op. cit.*) *Alex.* pp. 276–7

43. Athen. VI (*op. cit.*) XIII: 576 p.113

44. J.R. Hamilton *Plutarch's Alexander* (Oxford 1969) p. 100

45. Quin. Curt. II (*op. cit.*) VIII: IV p. 238

46. *Ibid.*

47. Diod. Sic. IX (*op. cit.*) XVIII: 28 p. 95
    Pausanias I (*op. cit.*) VI p. 29

48. *Ibid.*

49. Photius (*op. cit.*) Arrian p. 163

50. Pausanias I (*op. cit.*) VI p. 29
    Diod. Sic. IX (*op. cit.*) XVIII: 21 p. 75

51. *Ibid.* 28 p. 95

52. *Ibid.*

53. Tacitus *Histories* (*op. cit.*) 4: 83–4
    Plut. (*op. cit.*) *Isis and Osiris*

54. Strabo VII (*op. cit.*) 15: 2 p. 153

55. Taylor (*op. cit.*) p. 313 *et seq.*
    Blyth (*op. cit.*) (references to the Punjab) p. 569; Duc de Praslin p. 575

56. Blyth (*op. cit.*) p. 581

57. *Ibid.* pp. 577–8

58. Justin (*op. cit.*) pp. 119–20
    Quin. Curt. II (*op. cit.*) X: V p. 408 *et seq.*

59. Shakespeare *Hamlet*: I:V. 108

Sir John Harington *Epigrams* IV. 5
'Of Treasons'

Part Eight: The Aftermath

1. Quin. Curt. II. (*op. cit.*) bk X chaps V–X pp. 406–36 provide a vivid account of the aftermath of Alexander's death
2. *Ibid.*
3. *Ibid.* chap. X p. 434 (and footnote)
4. R.M. Errington *From Babylon to Triparadeisos* (*op. cit.*)
5. Plut. (*op. cit.*) *Moralia* I p. 202
6. Diod. Sic. IX (*op. cit.*) XVIII 13 p. 51
   Ptolemy's support: *Ibid.* XVIII 32 p. 105
   Seleucus takes refuge:*Ibid.* XIX 55 p. 385
7. Diod. Sic. IX (*op. cit.*) XVII: 32 p. 105
   Pausanias I (*op. cit.*) VI p. 29
8. R.M. Errington *From Babylon to Triparadeisos* (*op. cit.*)
9. Plut 4 (*op. cit.*) *Alex.* p. 324
   Quin. Curt. II (*op. cit.*) X: X pp. 434–5
10. Aelian (*op. cit.*) 12: 64 pp. 404–7
11. Diod. Sic. IX (*op. cit.*) 26 p. 89 *et seq.*
12. Quin. Curt. II (*op. cit.*) X: X p. 436
13. P.C. Doherty *Tutankhamun* (Constable 2003) pp. 3–24
14. R.M. Errington (*op. cit.*)
15. Justin (*op. cit.*) provides a vivid summation of events p. 131 *et seq.*
16. Justin *Ibid.* XV: 2 p. 145

Index of People and Places

All dates are BC unless specified, *c.* if approximate. Years given may be those of life (356–323), death (*d.* 336), reign (*r.* 342–331) or activity (*fl.* AD 400)

Index